Christian de Chergé

CISTERCIAN STUDIES SERIES: NUMBER TWO HUNDRED FORTY-SEVEN

Christian de Chergé

A Theology of Hope

By

Christian Salenson

Translated by

Nada Conic

Foreword by

Jean-Marc Aveline

α

Cistercian Publications
www.cistercianpublications.org

LITURGICAL PRESS
Collegeville, Minnesota
www.litpress.org

A Cistercian Publications title published by Liturgical Press

Cistercian Publications
Editorial Offices
Abbey of Gethsemani
3642 Monks Road
Trappist, Kentucky 40051
www.cistercianpublications.org

4   5   6   7   8   9

Library of Congress Cataloging-in-Publication Data

Salenson, Christian.
    [Christian de Chergé. English]
    Christian de Chergé : a theology of hope / by Christian Salenson ; translated by Nada Conic.
        p.   cm. — (Cistercian studies series ; no. 247)
    Includes bibliographical references (p.   ).
    ISBN 978-0-87907-247-6 — ISBN 978-0-87907-745-7
    1. Chergé, Christian de, 1937–1996.   2. Christianity and other religions—Islam.   3. Islam—Relations—Christianity.   4. Theology of religions (Christian theology)   I. Title.

BX4705.C463585S25   2012
261.2'7—dc23   2012017761

Contents

Foreword

This book is offered as a modest essay. It proceeds from the author's spiritual and intellectual experience and leads the reader in a way that is at once demanding and accessible into the same experience. Christian Salenson, director of the Institute for Sciences and Theology of Religions in Marseille, was brought to this experience when, "by a combination of circumstances," he began to study the writings of Christian de Chergé and to let himself be touched by the thought and spirituality of the prior of Tibhirine and his community. "Few meetings are the result of chance."

In a small book that is now a standard reference, Christian Salenson has already explored the spiritual richness of the texts of Christian de Chergé.[1] In that volume he demonstrates how this man could be considered a pioneer given by God to our time to help the Church discern the way on which the Spirit of Jesus wants to lead it. What is this way? It is, in a word, a new openness to the foundational evangelical experience of what de Chergé calls "Visitation."

The cultural and religious diversity that marks our era inevitably leads believers of all religions to confront the temptation of relativism. The evangelical witness of Visitation—the very experience of encountering the other—is offered as a way to transform this temptation into a promise. The mystery of encounter, which is at the heart of the apostolic life, is a sign of the Church's essential

---

1. Christian Salenson, *Prier 15 jours avec Christian de Chergé, prieur des moines de Tibhirine* (Paris: Nouvelle cité, 2006).

vocation: the God whom it professes is revealed in the encounters that this same God instigates.

Christian de Chergé understood this mystery and this vocation the day when a Muslim village policeman, a father of ten and a wise man, gave his life to save de Chergé's, then a young seminarian confronted, along with the rest of his generation, with the hard realities of the Algerian war. This friendship sealed in blood determined de Chergé's vocation and the spiritual direction of his life. "Few meetings are the result of chance."

The question Christian Salenson now invites us to ask is the following: can de Chergé's spiritual intuitions, emerging out of long experience of monastic life in a Muslim context, ripened in personal and community prayer, and nourished by the most ordinary, everyday things—work in the fields and the welcoming of guests—be theologically fruitful for the work of "faith seeking understanding"? Christian Salenson wrote this new book because he was convinced that the answer to this question is affirmative. And we owe him our thanks.

Briefly, this is the book's argument: while the theme of the Visitation defines the spiritual posture of Christian de Chergé, it is the theme of *hope* that distills his theological reflection. Indeed, just as the story of the Visitation (Luke 1:39-56) offers an evangelical interpretative key for living out as promise the sometimes disconcerting experience of existential encounter with brothers and sisters of other religions, so the category of hope is the resolutely eschatological center of gravity on which to build a contemporary theology of religious encounter.

Christian Salenson leads the reader patiently and surely through Christian de Chergé's writings, often luminous in their conciseness. On questions as difficult as the place of Islam in the plan of God, Christology, ecclesiology, and especially eschatology, Salenson, with only the briefest, but pertinent, comments of his own, lets us appreciate the theological richness of de Chergé's texts, texts that are far more monastic than academic. By introducing into the contemporary debate on the theology of religions a voice formed within the setting of monastic life, Salenson has done a great service. This particular monastic voice, arising from the deep waters of contemplation and daily fraternal life, is bold, sometimes even dazzling.

This is not the first time in the history of theology that new routes have been opened by the monasteries and not by the universities. I say this not to disqualify academic work but rather to highlight the fact that there are other ways of arriving at theological knowledge. By introducing us to the theological richness of de Chergé's writings, Christian Salenson, alert to what the Spirit is saying to the Churches through the experience of a tiny monastery lost in the foothills of the Atlas Mountains in Algeria, makes a major contribution to the debates of contemporary theology, a contribution, moreover, that is much broader than the sole question of interreligious dialogue.

I would like to end these few opening lines with a more personal note. As a result of a "combination of circumstances" that is doubtless not "the result of chance," I have been working with the author for more than fifteen years now. I know his desire to contribute, with courage and modesty, to the debates shaking society, the Church, and theology. He contributes from a stance in real life, taking into account pastoral questions on the existential terrain of spiritual experience. I know his determination to accompany theologically the local Churches, convinced as he is of the necessary link between theological work at the university and the concrete life of these Churches, their pastoral questionings, their experiences of precariousness, their search for paths faithful to the Lord's call.

With this book, conceived after a long personal maturation, based on solid teamwork within the framework of the Institute of Sciences and Theology of Religions of Marseille, and refined in the practice of teaching, Christian Salenson allows us not only to appreciate the theological relevance of the writings of Christian de Chergé but also to taste the joy and fruitfulness of an ecclesial and fraternal work of understanding of the faith. He deserves our profound appreciation.

Jean-Marc Aveline
Director of the Institut Catholique de la Mediterranée

Introduction

When, by a combination of circumstances, I was led to study the writings of Christian de Chergé, I had no idea what sort of personal adventure I was going to find myself embarked upon. Through my years of involvement with the Institut de Sciences et de Théologie des Religions of Marseille (ISTR), I had already been sensitized to religious diversity and its relevance to an understanding of theology as a whole. In de Chergé I found a witness and a pioneer capable of leading me on this path both by his thought and by his spirituality. After I published some of de Chergé's texts and meditations[1] I realized that my interest in Christian de Chergé was widely shared by others. The conviction that his theological reflections could connect with an even greater number of Christians and that his theology ought to be presented and made accessible led me to produce the present book.

This modest work was born out of a conjunction of several realities. On the one hand, there was the unavoidable recognition of the fact that our societies are irreversibly pluralistic, both religiously and culturally. On the other hand, there was the foundational experience in my personal life that the encounter with the other, in the most diverse forms, is the privileged locus of God's self-revelation. The journeys of numerous people whom I accompanied in my ministry gave me the opportunity to verify this experience.

---

1. Christian Salenson, *Prier 15 jours avec Christian de Chergé, prieur des moines de Tibhirine*, Praying 15 Days Series (Paris: Nouvelle Cité, 2006).

Finally, this book was born of a faith conviction—namely, because the master of history is no stranger to this cultural and religious plurality, we can receive plurality as an opportunity offered to our societies and to the Church, an opportunity bearing a promise for each individual and for humankind as a whole.

God does not abandon God's Church; on the contrary, I believe God gives to each era the pioneers it needs. In our own era, God has given Christian de Chergé and the brothers of Tibhirine. For my part, I would like simply to contribute one small building block to the project by introducing the thought of Christian de Chergé. For me this is more a joy to be shared than a duty to be fulfilled, despite the hours when writing becomes laborious.

The context of the book's gestation was the growth and development of the Institut de Sciences et de Théologie des Religions of Marseille and of the Institut Catholique de la Mediterranée.[2] The climate of research and of mutual questioning, the interface with civil society through the many organizational bodies maintained by the Institute, the effective collaboration with the pastoral services of the local Churches of the region all furthered this work. I have enjoyed for years the fraternal atmosphere of a team rich in diverse competencies, animated by a serene confidence in the tradition of the Church, desirous of serving local Churches, and alert to the latest research. In short, I have benefited from a university and Church microclimate that is more than favorable.

Finally, this book is born from my relationship with the Cistercian Abbey of Our Lady of Aiguebelle, the motherhouse of Tibhirine. After the dramatic events of 1996, the archives and the writings of the monks were brought back to Aiguebelle. A working group was founded at the ISTR that, in conjunction with the Abbey of Aiguebelle, had the double objective of publishing the writings of the monks and of working on the thought of Christian de Chergé. I have benefited from the work and research of this

---

2. The Institute of Sciences and Theology of Religions (ISTR) of Marseille was founded in 1992 at the instigation of Cardinal Coffy and under the direction of Jean-Marc Aveline. Today, it is part of the Catholic Institute of the Mediterranean (ICM).

group as much from the fraternal support of those who participated in it: Françoise Durand, André Barbeau, Anne-Noëlle Clément, Roger Michel, and Christophe Purgu. Fraternal bonds unite
us to the monastic community of Our Lady of Atlas at Midelt in
Morocco. We cannot fail to see, given the presence there of the
two brothers, Amédée and Jean-Pierre who survived the dramatic
events of the murder of seven monks of the community in 1996,
that in that place the experience of Tibhirine lives on.

This book is intended as an introduction to Christian de Chergé's
theology of religious encounter. How to describe his theology?
I prefer the term "theology of encounter" because Christian de
Chergé develops not simply a theology of religions but a theology
of the *encounter* of religions, particularly the encounter between
Christianity and Islam. By theology of encounter, I want to indicate that it is a matter not solely of considering Islam from the
point of view of Christian faith but also of how this encounter
allows Christian faith to be deepened. The more appropriate term
is, therefore, "theology of encounter." One could just as well say,
"theology of encounter with Islam." I use the term "theology
of religious encounter" because what de Chergé experienced in
his encounter with Islam is broadly valid for a theology of the
encounter of the religions in general.

I have arranged this introduction to de Chergé's theology
of religious encounter in three parts. In the first part, I present
Christian de Chergé and sketch his theological and political context. In the second part, which will take up the major portion of
this work, I show how the engagement of de Chergé with dialogue
with Islam led him to develop a way of thinking theologically
about the place of Islam in the plan of God and in interreligious
dialogue, and about Christ and the Church. Finally, I show how
de Chergé's thought builds to an understanding of eschatology.
In the third part, I highlight, with regard to certain selected topics, the impact a theology of religious encounter can have on our
way of living and understanding Christian life and ecclesial life.

Chapter 1

The Context

Christian de Chergé was the prior of the community of the monks of Tibhirine, a Cistercian monastery in the Atlas Mountains of Algeria.[1] In 1996, during the years of the Algerian troubles, seven of the Atlas community were abducted, officially by the GIA,[2] and held prisoner for two months[3] before coming to a tragic

1. This monastery, founded in 1938, was the successor of the monastery of Staouéli, founded in 1843 and closed in 1904 at the time of the antireligious laws. [The Third Republic enforced *laïcité* (secularism) by formally separating Church and state in 1905, taking over religious buildings and properties, and ending state funding of religious bodies. Education had been removed from Church control in the 1880s. – Tr.] Tibhirine became an abbey in 1947 and was later reduced again to the status of priory.

2. *Groupe Islamiste Armé* [Armed Islamist Group].The extent of responsibility for the monks' death of the GIA and of the French and Algerian governments has not been established to date. A "complaint against a person or persons unknown" was lodged at the Superior Court of Paris in the names of Dom Armand Veilleux, OCSO, the abbot of Scourmont, Belgium, and of the family members of Fr. Christophe Lebreton, with no outcome as yet. [An article in the British Jesuit journal *The Tablet* by Alain Woodrow (December 4, 2010, pp. 10–11) reports Dom Armand's conclusions from his own investigation: The Algerian military used Djamel Zitouni, a double agent, and an infiltrated GIA cell to capture the monks. The idea was then to "liberate" them and force them to leave the country for their own safety. But the plan backfired when another terrorist cell stole the monks from their original captors. The monks probably died as "collateral damage" when the army strafed the second group from helicopters with bullets and napalm in a botched rescue attempt. Only the monks' severed heads were recovered and put in coffins to make it look like a terrorist execution: the bodies would have borne the marks of military weaponry. – Tr.]

3. They were abducted the night of March 26–27. On April 26, communiqué no. 43 of the GIA, dated April 18, signed by the Emir Abu Abdel Rahman

1

end. Two brothers, Amédée and Jean-Pierre, survived.[4] Thanks
to them, Our Lady of Atlas continues, no longer in Algeria but in
Morocco, at the monastery of Midelt.

Christian de Chergé entered Our Lady of Atlas in 1971.[5] He
had been ordained a priest for the Diocese of Paris and, after
five years of ministry, entered the Cistercian abbey of Our Lady
of Aiguebelle[6] in 1969. Soon after, he joined the community at
Tibhirine and thereby answered the call to live in Algeria as "one
who prays among others who pray."

De Chergé entered the monastery with a solid theological formation acquired at the Institut Catholique de Paris.[7] He went on to
study two years in Rome at PISAI,[8] an institute run by the White
Fathers. There, he studied under Robert Caspar and Maurice
Boormans, with whom he established lasting friendships despite
their divergent views. He lived as a monk in the community of
Tibhirine for twenty-five years, and he spent the final twelve years

---

Amin, alias Djamel Zitouni, and published in the London daily *Al Hayat*,
gave "theological" reasons for the abduction. On April 30, a certain Abdul-
lah delivered an audiocassette to the French embassy in Algiers on which
the voices of the seven monks had been recorded the night of April 20. They
were executed the morning of May 21. On May 23, communiqué 44 of the
GIA announced their death. On June 2, their funeral was celebrated in the
basilica of Our Lady of Africa, at the same time as that of Cardinal Duval.
They were buried at Tibhirine on June 4.

4. [Tr. note: Amédée died in July 2008 at the age of 87.]

5. He was ordained a priest on March 21, 1964, at the Church of Saint-
Sulpice in Paris. For his biography, see especially Marie-Christine Ray, *Chris-
tian de Chergé, prieur de Tibhirine* [*Christian de Chergé: Prior of Tibhirine*] (Paris:
Bayard/Centurion, 1998); and John Kiser, *The Monks of Tibhirine* (New York:
St. Martin's Griffin, 2002); *Passion pour l'Algérie, les moines de Tibhirine* [*A Pas-
sion for Algeria: The Monks of Tibhirine*], trans. Henry Quinson (Paris: Nouvelle
Cité, 2006).

6. [Tr. note: A French monastery of the Cistercians of the Strict Observance
(= Trappists), and mother house of Our Lady of Atlas in Tibhirine.]

7. De Chergé was a student at the Catholic Institute of Paris from October
1956 to June 1964.

8. He was a student at PISAI, Pontificio Istituto di Studi Arabi et Islamis-
tica, from August 1972 to the summer of 1974. The aim of this institute is
to promote interreligious dialogue. It was founded in 1926 in Tunis and
transferred to Rome in 1964.

as prior.[9] We possess a certain number of his writings, mostly homilies,[10] chapter talks given during the twelve years he was prior, and a few lectures[11] or retreats[12] that he delivered. We are convinced that Christian de Chergé's theology of religious encounter is sufficiently original and rich so as to be a valuable contribution to current theological reflection and to the lives of Christians and communities in a context of religious diversity. This conviction has guided our efforts, and this work is intended to share the results of our research with all those who, for whatever reasons, are interested in religious encounter.[13]

The Engagement of the Church

The theology of religious encounter is still in its infancy. We believe, however, that this admission is not simply an elegant manner of laying down one's cards and saying that the sides

9. From 1984 to 1996.

10. In the context of the research laboratory at the Institut de Sciences et de Théologie des Religions of Marseille, in cooperation with the Abbey of Our Lady of Aiguebelle, and thanks to the work of Dom André Barbeau, a certain number of the writings of Christian de Chergé have been published. To date: Christian de Chergé, *Dieu pour tout jour, chapitres du père Christian de Chergé à la communauté de Tibhirine (1985–1996)* [*God for Each Day* (or "All Time"— cf. *toujours*, "always"): *Chapter Talks of Fr. Christian de Chergé to the Community of Tibhirine*], 2nd ed., Les cahiers de Tibhirine (Montjoyer: Abbé d'Aiguebelle, 2006); Christian de Chergé, *L'autre que nous attendons, homélies du père Christian de Chergé (1970–1996)* [*The Other Whom We Await: Homilies of Fr. Christian de Chergé*], Les cahiers de Tibhirine (Montjoyer: Abbé d'Aiguebelle, 2006); the article Christian de Chergé, "Prier en Église à l'écoute de l'islam" ["Praying as Church While Listening to Islam"], *Chemins de dialogue* 27 (2006).

11. Some of these have been published by Bruno Chenu in *L'invincible espérance* [*Hope Unconquerable*] (Paris: Bayard, 1996); and in *Sept vies pour Dieu et l'Algérie* [*Seven Lives for God and Algeria*] (Paris: Bayard, 1996).

12. Forthcoming.

13. The research laboratory at the ISTR of Marseille has published a collection of studies on Christian de Chergé: "Relecture de l'expérience of Tibhirine" ["A Rereading of the Experience of Tibhirine"], *Chemins de dialogue* 24 (2004), with contributions from Anne-Noëlle Clément, Françoise Durand, Roger Michel, Christophe Purgu, and Christian Salenson. Also of interest is *Chemins de dialogue* 27 (2006), on the theme "L'Écho de Tibhirine."

have been heard and the case is closed. Rather, it should serve as a stimulus for research. The same clear-eyed view prompts us to affirm that in the course of a few years, thanks especially to Pope John Paul II and certain prophetic acts of his ministry[14] and, though less visible, to the work accomplished within the Church (in particular, within the Church of France, to which the ISTR has made a significant contribution), Christian communities have steadily increased their awareness of the situation of religious diversity to the point that it can rightly be said that religious diversity is the new reality of Christian existence. Though there is no lack of difficulties, in view of the remarkable progress that has been made and of the changes that have taken place in this area in a relatively short period of time, difficulties should not discourage us. There is every reason to marvel, despite our legitimate frustrations, at the fact that an institution as massive as the Catholic Church has managed, in the space of a few years, to reconsider its relationship to Judaism, Islam, and the other world religions, despite the weight of centuries. The field lies open.

The International Situation

These changes are all the more remarkable in view of the fact that the present context is not promising. The international situation has become increasingly tense over the last several years, especially since September 11, 2001. The "clash of civilizations,"[15] dreaded by the most lucid minds, is welcomed by others, and not solely by al-Qaeda networks. We were filled with admiration at the political clear-sightedness and commitment to peace displayed by John Paul II during the events of September 11, not only in his choosing not

14. To which must be added the acts of the ministry of Benedict XVI, in particular his prayer in the Blue Mosque of Istanbul: "Pausing for a few minutes of recollection in that place of prayer, I addressed the One Lord" (General Audience, December 6, 2006. [Tr. note: An official English version is available at the Vatican web site: http://www.vatican.va/holy_father/benedict_xvi/audiences/2006/documents/hf_ben-xvi_aud_20061206_en.html]).

15. Samuel P. Huntington, *The Clash of Civilizations and the Remaking of World Order* (New York: Simon & Schuster, 1996).

to align himself with the Machiavellian ideology implied by the identification of a so-called axis of evil, but also in his calling upon Catholics to fast on the last day of Ramadan[16] and his invitation to leaders of the world to convene at Assisi on January 24, 2002.[17] These gestures did not have all the impact they should have had, neither inside the Church (fasting one day of Ramadan seemed so incredible that many people could not even understand the pope's request) nor in society (because the media, so often at the service of the dominant thinking, were unable to let an initiative that failed to correspond to the ideology of the moment be heard).

It is into this context that a theology of religious encounter inserts itself. The political dimension of religious diversity—where what is at stake is nothing less than peace—is sufficient to explain this theology's importance, urgency, and originality. Establishing a just relationship with other believers, one that is rooted in Christian revelation, is both a necessity and an excellent means of working, independent from passing trends, for a durable peace.

Working for a just peace is a sufficient motive for legitimizing a theology of religious encounter, but it is not the principal one. In fact, it behooves us to ensure that the political stakes remain secondary with respect to the theological stakes. Politics have not hesitated to make a tool of religion, and today there is no shortage of political leaders who highlight the role that religions can play in our present social context. Our vigilance should be all the greater because history teaches us that representatives of religions are not good at resisting the siren song of power. They love to have the front row seat and to believe themselves influential in current affairs, and so they quickly forget that religion's worth lies elsewhere. Many times over the course of the centuries, religious leaders have not shrunk from obtaining a certain kind of notoriety from their alignment with power. This is happening today with American Protestant Evangelicals and with the political exploitation of Islam.

16. December 14, 2001.

17. The invitation was made during the *Angelus*, on Sunday, November 18, 2001. On January 24, the religious leaders joined in signing a charter of peace that was sent to all governments. It was published in *Chemins de dialogue* 20 (2002): 195.

Aim of Religious Encounter

A theology of religious encounter does not have political issues as its primary aim, however important these may be. On the
contrary, the meaning of political issues is revealed only when
they are resituated within the authentic vocation of world religions. The meeting at Assisi on October 27, 1986, an emblematic
and symbolic act of a theology of encounter, set the tone. To be
sure, this meeting took place as a response to the International
Year of Peace, a year decreed by the United Nations, but the response proper to the religions was to celebrate a day of prayer.
Some observers of the encounter at Assisi might have asked if
there were not more urgent and effective things to do than pray.
Ought not the participants rather to have given priority to action
plans, organized international colloquia, and stepped up the fight
against injustice? The fact is, they had tried all of this at previous meetings[18] without striking the right chord; they succeeded
only in turning the religions into facsimiles of nongovernmental
organizations.

The genius of Assisi, which gave birth to what has since been
called the "spirit of Assisi,"[19] was, among other things, to give
religions their rightful place and allow them to respond to their
common vocation.[20] Once assembled, the religions affirmed their
common vocation: to open humanity to transcendence. The aim
of interreligious dialogue is not peace in a sociopolitical sense
of the word. To be sure, religions have an original contribution

18. For instance, at the international meeting at Kyoto in 1970.
19. "[The meeting at Assisi] was a prophetic intuition and a moment of
grace. . . . The 'spirit of Assisi,' which has continued to spread throughout
the world since that event." (Benedict XVI, Pastoral Visit to Assisi, Homily at
the Eucharistic Concelebration, June 17, 2007. Official English version available at Vatican web site, http://www.vatican.va/holy_father/benedict_xvi/
homilies/2007/documents/hf_ben-xvi_hom_20070617_assisi_en.html.)
20. John Paul II, Address to the Cardinals and Members of the Roman
Curia, December 2, 1986. To the Roman Curia at the Exchange of Christmas
Wishes, December 22, 1986. [Tr. note: The official version is only in Italian
on the Vatican web site (but see the English edition of *L'Osservatore Romano*
for January 5, 1987): http://www.vatican.va/holy_father/john_paul_ii/
speeches/1986/december/index.htm.]

to make, so that peace is unimaginable without dialogue among them. Nevertheless, it would be reductionist to assign this aim to interreligious dialogue. The goal of interreligious dialogue is theological. The proper aim of interreligious dialogue is to call all sides to turn more resolutely to the One, the Ineffable, the Ultimate.

Trends change quickly. Within the Church interreligious dialogue has been, for some, one trend among others: to talk about it, to write an article on it. It was the thing to do before moving on to other things. In the meantime, in spite of trends and independent of them, the real work of religious dialogue goes. Religious diversity is always with us. If interreligious encounter had not provoked at the very heart of the Christian faith theological reflection upon questions about the vocation of the religions in the world and their place in the plan of God, we would have missed the opportunity that our sensitivity to the questions offers us today; we would have deprived ourselves of knowing what "the Spirit is saying to the Churches"[21] in and through this unprecedented situation of religious diversity. Thus, it is important to continue the work of dialogue in order to give a Christian account of religious diversity and its theological consequences that both is faithful to the Church's living tradition and avoids relativizing it.

A Christian theology of religious encounter takes into account that it is not only from the point of view of the Christian faith that the theological questions raised by the fact of diversity, some of them delicate, are addressed. All parties of the encounter should be open to questions, to going deeper into their own traditions, and to new and unexpected developments that the encounter itself might give rise to. In other words, the confrontation with other religions has the potential to be theologically fruitful for all.

The encounter can even be considered a veritable *kairos*[22] for the Churches. In any case, I concur with the opinion of Paul Tillich: "[A] Christian theology which is not able to enter into a creative dialogue with the theological thought of other religions misses

---

21. [Tr. note: Compare Rev 2:7–3:22.]
22. The word *kairos* can be translated as "favorable time" [as in 2 Cor 6:2 – Tr.]. It is the moment of the in-breaking of revelation.

a world-historical occasion and remains provincial."[23] This judgment is accompanied by a promise: a theology that takes up this challenge is a theology that can hope to enter more deeply into the mystery of the covenant between God and humanity.

Interreligious Dialogue

It suffices for now to mention in this regard the dialogue between Jews and Christians since the Second Vatican Council. The determination of both John XXIII and Paul VI is well known, as is the remarkable work of Augustine Cardinal Béa in managing to produce the text of *Nostra Aetate*[24]—originally intended as a friendly gesture directed to the Jews.[25] Centuries of resistance had to be overcome in order for the great majority of the council fathers, little by little, to glimpse the importance of Jewish-Christian relations. Today, several decades later, even though there is still much ground to cover before arriving at a more accurate approach toward Judaism, the Catholic Church truly has been engaged in a positive consideration of Judaism, something many see as a veritable Copernican revolution. The results of this conversion have been beneficial on many levels beyond the Church's relations with the Jewish world and thought: for instance, the Church's

---

23. Paul Tillich, *Systematic Theology*, vol. 3 (Chicago: University of Chicago Press, 1963), 6. On Paul Tillich and the theology of religions, we cannot recommend highly enough the noteworthy thesis of Jean-Marc Aveline, *L'enjeu christologique en théologie des religions* [*What Is at Stake for Christology in the Theology of Religions*] Cogitatio Fidei Series 227 (Paris: Cerf, 2003). Also, Jean-Marc Aveline, *Paul Tillich* (Marseille: Publications Chemin de dialogue, 2007), in which the author refers to the famous lecture of Paul Tillich at Tübingen in 1963 on "Christianity's Claim to Absoluteness and the World Religions."

24. *Nostra Aetate* (Declaration on the Relation of the Church to Non-Christian Religions), October 28, 1965.

25. On the history of the elaboration of the text and the numerous debates it occasioned, see G.-M. Cottier, "Historique de la declaration" ["A Review of the Declaration"], in *Les relations de l'Église avec les religions non-chrétiennes: Nostra Aeìate; texte latin et traduction française* [*The Relations of the Church with Non-Christian Religions:* Nostra Aetate; *Latin Text and French Translation*], Unam Sanctam Series 61 (Paris: Cerf, 1966).

relationship to and understanding of its own Scriptures, its sacramental rites, and its mission; its knowledge of Jesus; and even its own ecclesial identity. There is much yet to be done in order to construct a true Christian theology of Judaism,[26] and vigilance is still necessary, but it is reasonable to suppose that the work that has been undertaken will be continued.

Interreligious dialogue cannot be limited to Jewish-Christian dialogue. It is urgent for the Church to establish a solid foundation for dialogue with other religious traditions, whether Islam or the great religions of Southeast Asia, as well as the traditional religions of Africa and the Americas. The Church must avoid the temptation to reduce interreligious dialogue to the single dialogue between Jews and Christians, whose foundations have begun to be established, and to consider the relationship with other religions exclusively on the basis of social welfare by affirming certain ethical convergences concerning justice or respect for life. To be sure, the relationship with Judaism is decisive for Christian revelation and, from this standpoint, it is unique. But if we were to reduce interreligious dialogue to Jewish-Christian dialogue, we would turn our back on a promise made to both Jews and Christians, and, frankly, we would distort the very relationship between Jews and Christians, for we exist together only by virtue of a relationship with others, with "the nations." Jewish-Christian dialogue is validated by its capacity to consider other religions and to enter into relationship with them. That is why an all-embracing interreligious dialogue is important to Christians and why everything that has up to the present contributed to moving it forward merits admiration. The Church's history of dialogue is influenced by its pioneers in eras when hardly anyone gave it any thought. Christians are learning to reread their history. Not all its moments were glorious, and though it behooves us to avoid making anachronistic judgments on the past from our contemporary viewpoint, it is also important to be clear-sighted and face our history squarely in order to accept it in its totality.

---

26. Clémens Thoma, *A Christian Theology of Judaism: Studies in Judaism and Christianity*, trans. Helga B. Croner (Mahwah, NJ: Paulist Press, 1980).

Only by rejecting nothing and weighing the value of everything do Christians show their love for the Church.

Precursors

This history has a pedigree and ancestors. They are like gifts God has given to the Church and to humanity. On the one hand, they opened a way forward, traced out a path, set off a chain of thought. Sometimes the significance of their actions did not become apparent until much later.[27] We are the happy beneficiaries of all that. The ancestors of Christian interreligious dialogue are many and diverse. They include vowed religious like Francis of Assisi; monks like Peter the Venerable, Henri Le Saux, and Thomas Merton; popes like Gregory VII and John Paul II; as well as the long list of those who experienced the full brunt of another culture and were transformed by it: Charles de Foucauld, Louis Massignon, Jules Monchanin, among others. Above all, there are those whose names are unknown but who with trust and in faith put themselves at risk in the encounter, drawing from the Gospel the boldness to confront the prejudices of their time.

It is against the backdrop of this great cloud of witnesses that the life and thought of Christian de Chergé is situated. None of these witnesses could have claimed to have understood everything they experienced and were asked to do. Some were precursors without even knowing it, simply by being faithful to their own vocation, by trying to respond day by day to what life offered and asked of them. Others, like Christian de Chergé, brought their experience to the level of thought and language. What they experienced did not belong exclusively to them. Christian could not have said and written what he did if he had not been embedded in a monastic community, within a local Church, and with Muslim friends and neighbors.

---

27. Gwénolé Jeusset, "François d'Assise et les musulmans" ["Francis of Assisi and the Muslims"], *Chemins de dialogue* 18 (2001): 89–103. Francis's meeting with the sultan Al Malik al-Kamil was not understood by his contemporaries.

In this context, too briefly described, I would like to introduce the reader to a few determinative elements in de Chergé's thought in the hopes that his witness may profit all those who, in the Church or elsewhere, whatever their position and function, their charism and state of life, sense that there is something important at stake here and wish to try, despite hindrances, to take some steps along this path of encounter with the Other.

Today's social and ecclesial contexts are changing rapidly. The future of theology is open to question and its role in the Church and the world is developing. No one knows what form the Catholic Church will take in the coming years. Now and in the future, an understanding of faith in relation to culture will always be necessary. The thought of Christian de Chergé is original. It was born, nurtured, and purified in the crucible of a profound human experience, a spiritual experience. His thought cannot be grasped without understanding and constantly revisiting his context and that grounding experience. Thus, I would like to begin by tracing the conditions that made de Chergé's theology possible and to eliminate at the same time some *a priori* assumptions.

Chapter 2

The Conditions of Christian de Chergé's Theology

The originality of Christian de Chergé's thought is due in part to the rootedness of his theology in a powerful spiritual experience and in part to the cultural and social contexts in which this theology was elaborated.

A Monk

Christian de Chergé was a Cistercian monk, and his theology was elaborated through the observances of monastic life. De Chergé did not write any theological treatises. As we said in the previous chapter, he did *theology in action* in the framework of monastic liturgical life, through homilies, and, in his position as prior, giving chapter talks to the brothers of the community three times a week for twelve years. He gave a few retreats and a few formal lectures, but these were relatively rare. So we are in the presence of a *theology in action*, a theology that is tested against the measure of the reality that provided the conditions for its elaboration.

Christian de Chergé gives not so much a theoretical exposition of the nature of dialogue, dissecting its foundations and its anthropological and theological conditions. Rather, he lives dialogue in terms of his own situation as a Christian monk in a Muslim culture. Nevertheless, we must not yield to the easy and too common opposition between concrete experience and theoretical reflection that would disqualify an experience on the pretext that it is too personal, and then turn around and disqualify theoretical reflection on the pretext that it is removed from reality. There is no opposition between theory and practice in the area of dialogue. Christian de Chergé was sufficiently aware of the necessity of thought always to submit his experience to lengthy, enlightened reflection and, conversely, to test his own reflection against concrete reality. For de Chergé, monastic life in a community of brothers came first, but it was inseparable from Islam, in continuous, friendly, and existential relation with Muslim friends and neighbors. His reflection was always presented *in situ* but, as we shall see later, its apparent simplicity is nourished by abundant documentation, numerous references, and a thought-in-gestation that only gradually reveals itself. It is clear that the prior of Tibhirine is not a professional theologian. He is a monk at every point of his thought; that is his way of being a theologian.

He is not the only monk to have made a mark in the history of interreligious dialogue. Monastic interreligious dialogue began a long time ago. As mentioned just above, Peter the Venerable and Abelard come to mind, even if apologetic motives dominated their work. In our own era, monks are far from the last to hear the call to open themselves to religious diversity. Along with Thomas Merton and Henri Le Saux we can mention Francis Archaya and Bede Griffiths. People like Thomas Merton have given decisive thrusts to the movement; others have humbly but tenaciously worked at opening up monastic life to this dimension. Homage must be paid to the tireless architects, past and present, of Monastic Interreligious Dialogue. Now there are Christian de Chergé and the monks of Tibhirine.[1]

---

1. Christian Salenson, "De *Nostra Aetate* à Assise, contribution de la vie monastique" ["From *Nostra Aetate* to Assisi, the Contribution of Monastic Life"], *Chemins de dialogue* 28 (2006). Jean Leclercq, *Nouvelle page d'histoire monastique, histoire de l'AIM, 1960–1985* [*A New Page of Monastic History: The History of the AIM*] (Belmont-Tramonet, 1986).

There is a great affinity between monastic life and interreligious dialogue. The particular vocation of monks at once opens up and grounds dialogue, prevents it from drifting toward political shoals, and recalls its foundation in the plan of the Father. Christian de Chergé was an architect of dialogue because he was a monk to his core, and he became a monk to his core because he opened himself up to the influence of religious diversity and the Church's involvement in interreligious dialogue. The monastic life with its observances had a significant impact on the very content of his thought; it nourished it and gave shape to its expression.

Conversely, the irreducible otherness of the Muslim believer carved out in de Chergé's soul what he called "a most avid curiosity" that ceaselessly opened him up to the magnitude of the Father's love.

In Algeria

Another context of de Chergé's theology pertains to the particular social situation in which he, along with his brother monks, found himself: Algeria, a country traumatized by colonization. The colonization of Algeria between 1830 and 1849 spawned a genocide: seven hundred thousand dead out of a little more than three million inhabitants. The Algerian war of independence (1954–62) was the cause of two hundred thousand deaths, though it was denied the name "war"; instead, it was euphemistically termed "the events in Algeria." Christian de Chergé's father was in a garrison in Algeria. Christian himself was a soldier in the war of independence and was profoundly affected by the experience. As he would later say, "I do not have the innocence of childhood." The violence that broke out in Algeria in the 1990s was the legacy of the violence perpetrated during the war of independence.[2]

Many of de Chergé's brother monks had known the monastery during the colonial era. Luc arrived in 1946. An amateur film of

2. Sadik Sellam, *La France et ses musulmans, un siècle de politique musulmane, 1895–2005* [*France and Its Muslims: A Century of Muslim Policy, 1895–2005*] (Paris: Éditions Fayard, 2006). Pascal Blanchard, Nicolas Bancel, and Sandrine Lemaire, *La fracture colonial* [*The Colonial Fracture*] (Paris: Éditions La Découverte, 2005).

the period (shot in Super 8) shows a procession of the Blessed Sacrament in the streets of Medea on the occasion of the profession of Brother Amédée. The monks knew the history of independence and the numerous difficulties in Algeria since that time. But times had changed, and in the 1980s and 1990s, Christian de Chergé and his brothers were in a minority position: they were the rare Christians among Muslims in an Algeria that had undergone dreadful convulsions under the regime of the generals and that, in 1989, with the blessing of the Western democracies, saw the interruption of the democratic process. Heirs of the colonial era, the monks were now welcomed in this country as guests,[3] and their position as guests in a wounded country, in this culture, and in this religious environment, contributed to the originality of de Chergé's thought. The monks did not try to reciprocate with some specific social activity the hospitality they enjoyed. They made the choice not to offer charitable help to the population, and rather than hiring workers and thus establishing a hierarchical relationship with the inhabitants of Tibhirine, the brothers preferred instead to work in a cooperative arrangement with their neighbors. As a condition for dialogue, the position of stranger is different from that of being in the majority. The conditions for theology are not the same when one is a member of a massive institution enjoying high social visibility, as when one is in the minority in a society and dependent on its welcome.

In a Precarious Situation

The brothers lived quite precariously. Politically, they were in a strange situation. They had made a vow of stability, but most of them did not have Algerian citizenship, so they had to renew their residence cards periodically.[4] Ecclesiastically, the situation was almost equally precarious. As early as 1963, the Cistercian abbot

3. Hospitality is another name for dialogue. Of interest are the remarks on this subject by Pierre de Béthune in *L'Hospitalité sacrée entre les religions* [*Sacred Hospitality between Religions*] (Paris: Albin Michel, 2007).

4. On the vow of stability, the reader is referred to the correspondence of de Chergé with Vincent Desprez, a monk of Ligugé: "Père Christian de

general at the time, Gabriel Sortais, had decided, soon after Algerian independence, to close down the monastery. Léon-Etienne (later Cardinal) Duval, archbishop of Algiers, remonstrated with him vehemently one day during a break in a session of the Second Vatican Council, which both men attended. The following night the father general died, and the decision to close the monastery was never carried out.

Their precariousness did not stop the monks from founding a small priory in Morocco at the request of the bishop of Rabat at the time, Hubert Michon. To be sure, they had some solid support. Christian told of the dream of Dom Bernardo Olivera, abbot general from 1990 to 2008, during his visit to Our Lady of Tibhirine:

> A brother of the Order grabbed a brother of Atlas by the throat and said: "First, you're wasting your life, up against this Muslim world that wants nothing from you and laughs at you, when there is so much to do elsewhere, so many peoples waiting only for your witness in order to embrace the contemplative life and come to increase your community. . . . Secondly, you poor man: our Order has no use for a foundation like yours: what a dead weight!" In the dream Dom Bernardo answered with a defense of the foundation. When he awoke, he took the trouble to write down his answer.[5]

However uncomfortable it might have been, its precarious situation was also fruitful for this small community. It is worth remembering that "precarious" and "prayer" have the same etymology. This fragile monastery, lost in the Atlas Mountains of Algeria, had, in fact, a radiance that grew year by year. Precariousness also had an effect on the development of the theological discourse of Christian de Chergé. Today, European Christianity is in a precarious situation. What is the future of our Christian

---

Chergé, lettres à un ami moine" ["Father Christian de Chergé, Letters to a Monk Friend"], *Collectanea cistercensia* 60 (1998): 193–215.

5. "Conférence du frère Christian au chapitre général de Poyo en Espagne 1993" ["Brother Christian's Talk to the Chapter General of Poyo, Spain, 1993"], in Christian de Chergé, *Sept vies pour Dieu et l'Algérie* [*Seven Lives for God and Algeria*], ed. Bruno Chenu (Paris: Bayard, 1996), 83.

communities in old Europe? Where will an articulation of an understanding of faith for our time come from? The precarious situation of the Churches is not necessarily an obstacle to a meaningful discussion of the faith.

In a Local Church

A new theological horizon opened by the Second Vatican Council was the understanding of the local Church as a theological actor. De Chergé and his brother monks lived in this horizon. Our Lady of Atlas was very closely tied to the local Church. It is seldom that relations between a diocese and a monastery are so deep. Our Lady of Atlas was considered, in the words of Cardinal Duval, as "the lung of the diocese." The underlying reason for this, according to de Chergé, was that "our vocation keeps us close to Algerian Christians who must bring the hidden life and the Gospel together while remaining in the thick of things."[6] Thus, the theology that was worked out at Our Lady of Atlas was not the theology of one single man, or of one community. It was the theology of a local Church. This caused Abbot General Bernardo Olivera to say, after the death of the monks, that the Church of Algeria is "a true guardian of the memory of the Atlas monks. She has received a heritage which is too big for us."[7]

A Theologian

Deeper acquaintance with de Chergé's writings has convinced me beyond what I had first thought of his theological competencies. It is true, de Chergé wrote no book on theology, and even in

6. "Questionnaire sur la preparation du synode 1994 sur la vie consacrée" ["Questionnaire on the Preparation of the 1994 Synod on Consecrated Life"], in de Chergé, *Seven Lives.*

7. Dom Bernardo Olivera, "Tibhirine Today (Circular Letter to the Members of the Order on the Tenth Anniversary of the Passage of Our Brothers of Our Lady of Atlas)," May 21, 2006, http://www.ocso.org/index .php?option=com_docman&task=doc_download&gid=279&Itemid=147& lang=en.

his few highly theological lectures, like "The Mystical Ladder" for the *Journées romaines* [Days in Rome][8] of 1989, he concealed, as it were, his theology under his unique style of discourse and use of language. De Chergé mistrusted theological language, particularly in the field of theology of religions, which he knew very well was an area of ongoing research. He feared more than anything being boxed in by concepts or theories that might distort what spiritual experience allowed him to glimpse and occasionally formulate in other terms. He often reiterated that we must allow God to do something new; we must not settle too quickly for fixed concepts.

He knew the writers of the Cistercian tradition. Naturally, de Chergé was beholden in his way of thinking to Saint Bernard and to his fathers in monasticism. He owed a debt also to the great writers of the twentieth century. It is true that he quoted contemporary theologians only rarely (a fact that does not make the task of research any easier). But he knew what Karl Rahner wrote about the theology of religious encounter. When I was allowed into the library at Tibhirine, I picked up de Chergé's copy of Rahner's *Foundations of Christian Faith* and saw it fall open spontaneously in my hands to the page concerning non-Christian religions.[9]

De Chergé was also familiar with the thought of Teilhard de Chardin, who was a cherished companion, a mystic like him, and impelled to rethink Christology in terms of the scientific milieu in which he lived. In de Chergé's writings and talks there are quotations from Jürgen Moltmann and from Charles Péguy[10] who, de Chergé claimed, had written the best theological treatise on hope.[11] De Chergé was influenced also by the thought of

8. An initiative of the Dominican Order, begun in 1956, to promote Catholic-Muslim dialogue, this conference takes place every four years in Rome.

9. Karl Rahner, *Foundations of Christian Faith*, trans. William V. Dych (New York: Crossroad, 1997), 311–21.

10. Of interest is Anne-Noëlle Clément's study, "Péguy et de Chergé," *Cahiers de Tibhirine*, forthcoming.

11. "The best treatise on hope continues to be *La porche du mystère de la deuxième vertu* [*Portal of the Mystery of Hope*]." See Charles Péguy, *Portal of the*

Emmanuel Lévinas, whom he occasionally quoted and whose imprint can be discerned in his *Testament*. De Chergé's training at PISAI opened him up to an acquaintance with Muslim theology, Muslim mystics, and all those who, like Louis Massignon and Charles de Foucauld, were transformed by their encounter with Islam.

A Mystic

The other essential aspect of de Chergé's thought is the spiritual experience in which it is grounded. Incontestably, we are talking about a mystical experience that originates in several foundational experiences. Regular reading of his homilies or chapter talks is enough to convince one of this. Although we can detect certain conditions that strongly influenced Christian de Chergé's theology and without which it would be inconceivable, we must be careful, while attempting to explain it, never to uproot it from what constitutes, as it were, its soil. We would then risk no longer understanding it.

This experience does not reveal itself to the hurried reader. To be sure, sometimes it emerges in dazzling texts, some of which are beginning to be known by the broader public, like the *Testament*[12] or the homily for Holy Thursday 1995.[13] Usually, it reveals itself only partially at a first reading, and it is often necessary to return to a passage in a homily or in the chapter talks in order to see the progressive unfolding of an unexpected depth in words that have been counted and chiseled by experience long matured in what one imagines was continuous reflection.

Mystery of Hope (New York: Continuum, 2005). Christian de Chergé, *Dieu pour tout jour, chapitres du père Christian de Chergé à la communauté de Tibhirine (1985–1996)* [*God for Each Day: Chapter Talks of Fr. Christian de Chergé to the Community of Tibhirine*], 2nd ed., Les cahiers de Tibhirine (Montjoyer: Abbé d'Aiguebelle, 2006), 334.

12. An English version can be found on the Monastic Interreligious Dialogue web site: http://www.monasticdialog.com/a.php?id=497.

13. Found in Christian de Chergé, *L'autre que nous attendons, homélies du père Christian de Chergé (1970–1996)* [*The Other Whom We Await: Homilies of Fr. Christian de Chergé*], Les cahiers de Tibhirine (Montjoyer: Abbé d'Aiguebelle, 2006), 455.

De Chergé often chose to express in experiential terms what was undoubtedly a groundbreaking thought in some theological domain or other. He could speak at length about the Qur'an and its status without ever mentioning the word "inspiration," preferring instead to describe more precisely how he experienced it in relation to the Gospel. When he reflected, as he did at great length, on the relationship between the Christian and the Muslim scriptures, he did not advance any theory of the scriptures but rather allowed his reflection to play out before his listeners, leaving them free to make the journey themselves. But theology is there, operating and effective.

De Chergé's theology is first and foremost a spiritual experience of the emergence of the Word. It was about this experience that he spoke, never leaving it behind, and never forcing it to fit into the conventional words of theological tradition if he felt doing so might in any way damage, deform, or constrain the experience.

It is absolutely impossible to separate Christian de Chergé's thought from his spiritual experience. Commentaries that seek to explain de Chergé's thought without making constant reference to his experience are deficient and leave the reader unsatisfied. Obviously, linking theology and experience is a delicate undertaking. In the presence of a mystical experience caution is required. There are those who are tempted to oppose spiritual experience and theology, either to protect themselves from the theology of Christian de Chergé and its novelty by defining his work as spiritual, to protect themselves from dialogue with other believers, or to keep theology at a distance from spiritual experience under the pretext that theology would thus be more academic. This temptation must be resisted.

The biography of an author and the circumstances that form the context of his theology often furnish us with the keys for understanding the author's thought itself, but often we do not give them all the attention required. As far as Christian de Chergé is concerned, biography and context constitute the very soil that one cannot leave behind.

The experience of Tibhirine is a sign of the times offered to the whole Church at the start of the third millennium. John Paul

II's prophetic ministry in the area of interreligious dialogue is of a piece with the experience of Tibhirine. Little by little, I have become inwardly convinced that this little monastery of Atlas, surviving precariously in a stifled Algeria, is a sign for our time offered to all by the Spirit.

Chapter 3

The Foundational Experiences

The life, the vocation, and the thought of Christian de Chergé cannot really be understood without knowledge of the foundational experiences of his life. The most decisive experience was his encounter with Mohammed, a village policeman, during the Algerian war of independence. De Chergé belonged to the generation of men who lived through this war. For eighteen months, from July 1959 to January 1961, he was an officer in the S. A. S., *Sections Administratives Spécialisées* [Specialized Administrative Sections],[1] in the Djebel, north of Tiaret. It was there he met Mohammed, a family man, a simple person, and a devout Muslim. Their many conversations had a decisive impact on de Chergé. He let himself be transformed by the encounter, and a real friendship grew up between these two men.

Having reached the age of manhood, and confronted along with the rest of my generation with the hard reality of the

---

1. [Tr. note: An elite counterinsurgency force that attempted to win over the Muslim population by providing public health, education, and security services and by arming and training loyal Muslims (*harkis*). Christian's friend Mohammed was one such *harki*.] Christian de Chergé had just completed two years as a seminarian at the "Des Carmes" Seminary, a university seminary associated with the Institut Catholique de Paris.

conflict of that era, I was given the gift of meeting a mature man who liberated my faith by teaching it to express itself as a climate of simplicity, openness, and surrender to God, taking in quite naturally the relationships, the events, and the minutiae of daily life. Our dialogue was the expression of a peaceful and trusting friendship which had God for its horizon, above the fray. . . . Mohammed knew that I was a seminarian, and I watched him practice prayers and fasts with a cheerful heart. This illiterate man did not buy off his conscience with words; incapable of betraying one group for the sake of another, his brothers or his friends, he put his life at stake, despite his responsibility for his ten children.[2]

During a military skirmish, Mohammed intervened to spare his friend, insisting on de Chergé's attachment to Algeria and the Muslim people. Christian went unharmed, but the next day Mohammed was found beside his own well, murdered. Christian was deeply moved by the death of his friend. He let this event resound within him and gradually reveal its full meaning. He wrote several years later: "In the blood of this friend, I came to know that my call to follow Christ would have to be lived out, sooner or later, in the very country in which I received the token of the greatest love of all."[3] De Chergé heard there the call to bind himself to a people, to Algeria. And this bond with Algeria became integral to his calling to follow Christ.

Christian knew of the death threat against Mohammed, and he had told him he would pray for him. "I know that you will pray for me," Mohammed had said to him, "but you see, Christians do not know how to pray." This statement did not leave Christian unmoved. "I took this remark as a reproach directed at a Church that did not present itself, at least in a recognizable way,[4] as a community of prayer." The meaning of Mohammed's remark took on its full meaning in the dramatic event in which Mohammed

2. Christian de Chergé, "Prier en Église à l'écoute de l'Islam" ["Praying as Church While Listening to Islam"], *Chemins de dialogue* 27 (2006): 17–24; also published in the journal *Tychique* 34 (November 1981): 48–55.

3. De Chergé, "Prier en Église," 19.

4. [Tr. note: The French is *lisiblement* = "readably."]

made a gift of his life. "I knew at once that this consecration must flow into a common prayer in order to be truly a witness of the Church and a sign of the communion of saints."[5] Christian would become a monk in Algeria.

The Eucharistic Brother

This foundational event is not being recalled as a mere anecdote. It had the effect of a shock in the life of Christian de Chergé. Others before him, Louis Massignon (1883–1962), for example, had known events that effected a veritable conversion. Without equating the men and the eras, we can nevertheless say that both men, as a result of a defining event, became definitively engaged in a positive relationship with the Muslim faith. "And then there began a pilgrimage toward the communion of saints in which Christians and Muslims share the same filial joy. For I know that I am able to place firmly at this destination of my hope at least one Muslim, that beloved brother who lived, up to the moment of his death, the imitation of Jesus Christ."[6] De Chergé would feel the reverberations of Mohammed's death for the rest of his life.

His vocation clarified itself. He knew from that point on that he would live in Algeria, "the country in which I received the token of the greatest love of all." He repeated this in his *Testament*: "I would like my community, my Church, my family to remember that my life was given to God and to this country."[7] His vocation was to live in Algeria as a man of prayer in order to witness to prayer, and for this to be a true witness, he would have to witness to the Church. Through a Muslim, de Chergé received his vocation to be a monk in Algeria.

But the reflection does not end there. Mohammed "had given his life like Christ." He had imitated Christ. This act is celebrated in every Eucharist where Christians memorialize the gift that

5. De Chergé, "Prier en Église," 19.
6. De Chergé, "Prier en Église," 19.
7. Christian de Chergé, *L'invincible espérance* [*Hope Unconquerable*], ed. Bruno Chenu (Paris: Bayard, 1996, 2010), 221. See Appendix, p. 199, below.

Christ made of his life and where each person is invited to enter into this gift to the praise of the Father. Every Eucharist, Christian said, signified for him the gift of Mohammed's life: "And every Eucharist makes him infinitely present to me in the reality of the Body of Glory where the gift of his life took on its full dimension 'for me and for the many.' "[8] In the eucharistic gift of Mohammed, Christian recognized the gift of Christ himself. Of whom is de Chergé speaking in his final homily of Holy Thursday 1995—of Mohammed or of Christ? Or of both?

> He loved me to the end, to the end of me, to the end of
>   him. . . .
> He loved me in his way, which is not mine.
> He loved me graciously, gratuitously. . . . I might perhaps
>   have liked it to be more discreet, less solemn.
> He loved me as I do not know how to love: this simplicity,
>   this self-forgetting, this humble service without self-
>   gratification, without any self-regard.
> He loved me with the benevolent but inexorable authority
>   of a father, and also with the indulgent and somewhat
>   nervous tenderness of a mother.[9]

Christian learned from Mohammed the meaning of the Eucharist in its double movement. First, de Chergé's life was saved by the eucharistic gift of his friend; he received his life from him. And second, now he could, if he wished, enter in his turn into the gift of his own life. He began to understand the meaning of Eucharist. "He will understand later on," his mother had said of Christian at the time of his first communion.[10] "You will understand later on," Jesus had said to Peter when Peter refused to let his feet be washed. Christian began to understand: Another gave his life for him; Christ gave his life for him. He could, now that

---

8. De Chergé, "Prier en Église," 19.
9. Christian de Chergé, *L'autre que nous attendons, homélies du père Christian de Chergé (1970–1996)* [*The Other Whom We Await: Homilies of Fr. Christian de Chergé*], Les cahiers de Tibhirine (Montjoyer: Abbé d'Aiguebelle, 2006), 455.
10. De Chergé, *L'autre que nous attendons*, 359.

he had let his feet be washed, set out on the road to give, in his turn, his own life in the ordinariness of a monk's life.

But it was through a believer in another religion, through a believer in Islam, that Christian de Chergé received all of this. Here was the fundamental meaning of this encounter, a meaning that would bear fruit. De Chergé would live the rest of his life in the horizon of his meeting, through Mohammed, of Islam and of all Muslims. Dialogue with Islam would be part and parcel of his monastic vocation, a vocation he received through Mohammed, first through a peaceful and liberating friendship, then in the dramatic end of his friend's life. De Chergé would constantly return to draw on this foundational event as he advanced on the path of encounter and total gift. The experience would inform his thinking, and his theological thought would return to this foundational event again and again to be refreshed. The pilgrimage toward the communion of saints began in Tiaret.

The Brother of One Night

The second event, while not as decisive as the first, confirmed de Chergé's vocation. It took place one year before Christian's final monastic vows. Christian was praying a prayer of surrender after Compline in the semidarkness of the monastery church, he tells us, "between the altar and the tabernacle." A figure approached on his knees, murmuring, "*Allah Akbar!*" A brief glance and an exchange: "Pray for me," said the man to Christian, who recognized him as a guest at the monastery. Christian said, "Teach us to pray together," and their prayers intermingled, a single act of praise. A mutual friend of theirs arrived. Astonished to see them together in prayer he nevertheless joined them.

> To let His prayer call to both of you in the depths of a silence without any other voice. . . . Then together the *Fatiha*,[11] the *Magnificat* (which he recites word by word), the Our Father which he knows. . . . Praise. . . . Three hours long. . . . The

11. The *Fatiha*, *Surah* 1 of the Qurʾan, which constitutes the prologue, the overture, the liminal *surah*.

exuberant joy of each one! And what if God were laughing at the fine trick He just played after centuries of imprecations between brothers called to pray to Him?[12]

Christian understood what had happened. He would let it fully occupy its space in his life, though he would not write about it until later, in the text of his solemn profession.[13] There, he set out his itinerary in writing.[14] Here is his reading of the event:

> To confirm this calling, there were several inexplicable interventions in which God's hand could be recognized. Everything seemed to culminate on that day, in that encounter sought out by a Muslim guest in the quiet of an evening, after Compline. Our voices were joined and sustained by each other so as to blend into praises of the One from whom all love is born. This "event" is not a dream. It is a fact. As such, it incarnated the immense hope of my calling and made me live for the space of three hours what my faith knew was possible for ever and ever.[15]

This says it all. The fact that de Chergé included this event in his solemn monastic profession indicates the place that prayer among and with believers of other religions occupied in his monastic commitment. This shared prayer was constitutive of his calling. We are truly in the presence of an interreligious monastic vocation that has a particular relevance in the context of the post–Vatican II Church.

---

12. Christian de Chergé, *Sept vies pour Dieu et l'Algérie* [*Seven Lives for God and Algeria*], ed. Bruno Chenu (Paris: Bayard, 1996).

13. His solemn profession took place on October 1, 1976, the feast of Saint Thérèse of the Child Jesus. The encounter with "the brother" took place a year earlier, on September 21, 1975.

14. Christian de Chergé drew up a document, "The Meaning of a Call," which he gave to his brothers in community. He began with a Christian profession of faith colored by the *Fatiha*: "In the name of the God of tenderness and mercy, I profess." Point 1: "a call wholly oriented toward the vision of the living God"; point 2: The response, "a humble submission"; point 3: "The welcoming of the Word of God to which even the book of Islam provides an access," and so on. See Marie-Christine Ray, *Christian de Chergé, prieur de Tibhirine* [*Christian de Chergé: Prior of Tibhirine*] (Paris: Bayard, 1998), 112.

15. Ray, *Christian de Chergé*, 112.

"What my faith knew was possible for ever and ever." The expression is a curious one, but readers familiar with Christian de Chergé are not surprised by these suggestive expressions. What is "for ever and ever" is this communion of saints in which Christians are already united with the believers of Islam. This communion of saints, present even today, was accessible to de Chergé by faith; when Mohammed breached the barrier, de Chergé was able to commit himself to it with all his faith. It is present in the *Testament* when he speaks of his avid curiosity to see in the bosom of the Father the children of Islam.[16] And what is possible for ever and ever, starting right now, is common prayer.

Christian de Chergé, one year before his monastic profession, was given the gift to experience for three hours the proof of the reality that grounded his calling and of the immense hope that gave him life: the communion of prayer that he knew was already present, fulfilled in the bosom of the Father, and to which his life was consecrated. All that remained was for it to be realized, to become effective. "From now on, how could I not believe 'viable,' on the day that God alone wills, a community of prayer where Christians and Muslims (and Jews?) will welcome each other as brothers and sisters of the Spirit who already unites them in the night."[17] De Chergé believed in a communion of prayer, but also in a possible *community* of prayer among Jewish, Christian, and Muslim brothers and sisters. He would have the joy of experiencing this common prayer with the members of the Sufi confraternity in the framework of the "Ribât-es-Sâlam."[18] It was his vocation,

16. "This is what I shall be able to do, please God: immerse my gaze in that of the Father to contemplate with him his children of Islam just as he sees them, all shining with the glory of Christ, the fruit of his Passion, filled with the gift of the Spirit, whose secret joy will always be to establish communion and restore the likeness, playing with the differences" (de Chergé, *L'invincible espérance*, 223).

17. From the text of his solemn profession, in Ray, *Christian de Chergé*, 112.

18. *Ribât-es-Sâlam* means "bond of peace"; it designates the group founded at the instigation of Claude Rault, now the bishop of Sahara, originally for Christians to help them deepen their spiritual life through an integration of what they have discovered through encounter with Islam. Soon the group was joined by some Sufis from the *Alawiya* brotherhood. The *Ribât* continues to this day.

from that day on, to enter into this communion of prayer, to be someone "praying among others who pray."

The Meeting with the Emir Sayah Attiyah

Another event of great importance in de Chergé's journey was the meeting with the emir Sayah Attiyah on December 24, 1993. Neither foundational nor a confirmation of his calling, this meeting nevertheless oriented Christian as well as his community toward complete self-gift.[19]

The dramatic circumstances are well known. The emir appeared at the monastery on Christmas Eve with an armed band who had been wreaking havoc in the region the previous several days and had assassinated at Tamesguida (a village situated a few kilometers from the monastery) a dozen Croats who were building a tunnel in the Atlas Mountains. The emir demanded money and medicines and wanted Brother Luc, the physician, to come with them. Christian refused to comply with his demands and ended up explaining to the emir that this evening they were celebrating the birth of Jesus. "We are in the midst of our celebration of Christmas; for us this is the birth of the Prince of Peace." Sayah Attiyah replied, "Excuse me, I didn't know."[20]

Three or four days later, Christian wrote to Sayah Attiyah[21] asking to speak with him "man to man, believer to believer." Did

---

19. The diary of Brother Christophe illustrates this progressive detachment (Christophe Lebreton, *Le soufflé du don, journal de frère Christophe* [*The Breath of the Spirit: The Journal of Brother Christophe*] [Paris: Bayard, 1999], 74). Brother Christophe's poems have been published as *Aime jusqu'au bout du feu: Cent poems de vérité et de vie* [*Love to the Fire's Edge: One Hundred Poems of Truth and Life*] (Annecy: Monte-Cristo, 1997). His homilies appear in *Adorateurs dans le soufflé: Homélies du frère Christophe Lebreton pour fêtes et solennités (1989–1996)* [*Worshipers in the Breath of God: Homilies of Brother Christophe Lebreton for Feasts and Solemnities (1989–1996)*] (Montjoyer: Bellefontaine, 2009).

20. De Chergé, *L'invincible espérance*, 310. Concerning the visit, we also have the accounts of Brother Amédée and Brother Jean-Pierre in Bernardo Olivera, *How Far to Follow? The Martyrs of Atlas* (Petersham, MA: Saint Bede's Publications, 1997), 64–76.

21. Ray, *Christian de Chergé: Prieur de Tibhirine*, 186.

the letter ever reach him? Sayah Attiyah was later assassinated. Christian's prayer from that day on was: "Disarm me, disarm them."[22]

Surely a new stage had begun in the life of Christian de Chergé. With this background we are in a position to show how Christian de Chergé worked through a number of theological questions recurrent in the theology of world religions. We will emphasize his originality. For readers who are not familiar with the issues of the theology of religions, I will give a quick sketch according to topic of the various lines of response of contemporary theologians so that readers can find their bearings and situate Christian de Chergé in the broader field of current research. I will, as far as possible, make an effort to explain these issues simply, for the questions are sometimes complex, resigning myself in the process to the sacrifice of certain essential nuances. The first point to which I will give my attention is "the place of Islam in the plan of God."

---

22. [Tr. note: De Chergé, *L'invincible espérance*, 314.]

Chapter 4

The Place of Islam in God's Plan

Christian de Chergé could not but raise the question of the place of Islam, a religion born six centuries after Christianity, in the economy of salvation. This question is part of a larger one: from the point of view of Christian revelation, what is the place of other religions in the divine plan? Fundamental as it is to the theology of religious encounter, this question was given a whole new impetus by the Second Vatican Council and its Declaration on Non-Christian Religions (*Nostra Aetate*); by the meeting of leaders of world religions at Assisi on October 27, 1986; by certain initiatives of the public ministry of John Paul II;[1] and by theological reflection over the last few decades.

The question is not a new one—in a way, one could say that the apostle Paul was already haunted by it as he pondered the mystery of Israel (Rom 9–11)—but it is being posed today in a new way. Various answers have been put forward throughout history; it has to be admitted that they frequently amounted to a rejection, if not an outright demonization, of the religion of the other.

What Is the Place of Religions?

There is a wide variety of answers offered in contemporary theology. To be sure, the Catholic tradition is practically unanimous

---

1. For instance, the address to Muslim youth in Casablanca, August 19, 1985.

in no longer demonizing the religion of the other. *Nostra Aetate* has set the tone for the Church at present and in the future:

> The Catholic Church rejects nothing which is true and holy in these religions. She looks with sincere respect upon those ways of conduct and of life, those rules and teachings which, though differing in many particulars from what she holds and sets forth, nevertheless often reflect a ray of that Truth which enlightens all men.[2]

The council decree makes specific mention of the believers of Islam. It affirms that "[u]pon the Moslems, too, the Church looks with esteem,"[3] and calls to mind everything that unites the two traditions. And in the Dogmatic Constitution on the Church, *Lumen Gentium*, we read:

> But the plan of salvation also includes those who acknowledge the Creator. In the first place among these there are the Moslems, who, professing to hold the faith of Abraham, along with us adore the one and merciful God, who on the last day will judge mankind.[4]

Thus, Muslims occupy a special place in the Church's regard, second only to the Church's elder brothers and sisters in faith, the Jews, since Christians, Jews, and Muslims worship the same one and merciful God.

Building on the official teaching of the Church, which calls Christians to a positive view of other religions and of Islam in particular, theological reflection tries to comprehend and explain the place of religions and of non-Christian believers within the divine plan. As just affirmed, the spectrum of responses worked out over the course of the last few decades is broad. Some theologians view other religions as simple "evangelical preparations" anticipating

---

2. *Nostra Aetate* 2. All citations of documents from the Second Vatican Council are taken from *Vatican Council II: The Conciliar and Post Conciliar Documents*, ed. Austin Flannery (Collegeville, MN: Liturgical Press, 1975).

3. *Nostra Aetate* 3.

4. *Lumen Gentium* 16.

Christian revelation. Others, like Karl Barth, think that "religion is never true in itself,"[5] not even Christianity, whereas others, like Karl Rahner, view the religions as positive paths inscribed in God's plan.[6] Still others, like Raimundo Panikkar, consider that as there is "in Hinduism a living presence of Christ"[7] so Christ is likewise present in the various religious traditions. Some think that all religions are paths of salvation, while others, the so-called pluralists, affirm that all religions are of equal value. Then there are those who value orthopraxy above orthodoxy and for whom these debates are of little import: their point being that it is much more urgent that religions unite their efforts to bring about the reign of God by means of greater efforts for justice and peace. Obviously, these answers are not all of equal value or theological relevance, or even of equal fidelity to the Church's tradition of faith.[8]

The Place of Islam

When we ask specifically about the place of Islam, we find here also a wide variety of responses. Over the centuries there were periods when this religious tradition was subject to a veritable demonization as part and parcel of a clash of civilizations. Some have considered Islam to be a "natural religion," to use the expression of Jean Daniélou.[9] Others, taking up the position of John

---

5. Karl Barth, *Church Dogmatics*, vol. 1, bk. 2, trans. G. T. Thomson and Harold Knight (Edinburgh: T & T Clark, 1956), 325.

6. See Karl Rahner, *Foundations of Christian Faith*, trans. William V. Dych (New York: Crossroad, 1997), 156, 312ff.

7. Raimundo Panikkar, *The Unknown Christ of Hinduism* (London: Darton, Longman & Todd, 1967), 2.

8. For a review of these different theological opinions, the reader is advised to consult Jacques Dupuis, *Toward a Christian Theology of Religious Pluralism* (Maryknoll, NY: Orbis Books, 1997).

9. The concept of natural religion is complex, and some people continue to apply it to Islam. In this case, "natural religion" means a religion that has a human source. Conversely, "what makes a faith supernatural is its origin: receiving God from God, by believing in his revealed Word. . . . The attitude of Muslim faith is what we call supernatural. . . . For Vatican II has underlined this essential value of Muslim faith: 'they believe that God has

Damascene, thought it was a heretical version of Christianity.[10] The positive view of Islam of recent times owes much to the great orientalist Louis Massignon, who in Baghdad at the beginning of the twentieth century was brought back to the Christian faith by his encounter with Islam. Islam belongs to the heritage of Abraham, through Hagar and Ishmael,[11] Massignon reminds us; hence, it is not outside biblical revelation. The personal ties between Louis Massignon and Giambattista Montini, the future Pope Paul VI,[12] had important consequences at the Second Vatican Council: "When Vatican II undertook to speak of Islam, the memory of Massignon, who died in 1962 on the eve of the Council's opening, loomed large in the mind of Paul VI, as I can testify," writes Robert Caspar.[13]

Today the issue is framed in different terms. Instead of defining Islam's relationship to biblical revelation in order to determine its legitimacy, we start from the general or universal revelation that arises from the dialogue of God with humankind and seek

---

spoken to men'" (Robert Caspar, *Pour un regard chréien sur l'islam* [*Toward a Christian View of Islam*] [Paris: Bayard, 2006], 28–29).

10. John Damascene, *The Book of Heresies*, P.G. 94, cc. 763–73. According to John Damascene, Islam is the hundredth heresy. See the introduction to John Damascene, *Écrits sur l'islam* [*Writings on Islam*], SCh 338 (Paris: Éditions du Cerf, 1992), 70ff.

11. Ishmael is the biblical ancestor of the Muslims. He is the son of Abraham by the servant Hagar (Gen 16).

12. Louis Massignon had already formed ties with Pius XI over the Badaliya. [Tr. note: Badaliya (Arabic for "substitution") was a Christian movement founded by Massignon and Mary Kahil based on a commitment to the love of Muslim neighbors through prayer and loving service, thus imitating Christ's self-oblation for others.] Massignon wrote to Abd-el-Jalil: "He [Piux XI] blessed the oblation of my life and death for my Muslim brothers and sisters. . . . As for an official declaration by the Church on Al Hallaj, he adopted a wait-and-see attitude. (I am going to try to have drawn up a theological testimony on the juridical incorporation of Al Hallaj in the Church by the baptism of blood.) He stood up and blessed my particular 'way' and all my collaborators. He teased me, saying that by dint of loving them, I had become a 'Catholic Muslim' in order that Muslims might be loved, on account of me, in the Church" (Letter of July 24, 1934. Massignon, *Abd-el-Jallil, parrain et filleul* [*Godfather and Godson*], *1926–1962*, correspondence collected and annotated by Françoise Jacquin [Paris: Cerf, 2007], 108).

13. Caspar, *Pour un regard chrétien sur l'islam*, 185.

to understand the specific place of Islam within that universal revelation. Obviously, this raises many questions, in particular about prophecy or the status of the Qur᾽an. From the point of view of Christian revelation, is Mohammed a prophet? Certainly the Church fathers, especially Justin Martyr and Clement of Alexandria,[14] recognized the existence of prophets outside biblical revelation. As for Augustine, he saw Socrates as a prophet to the Greeks, a view that led Paul VI to affirm that "There is no doubt that the pagans also have their prophets."[15] Yves Congar, for his part, acknowledged the existence of an explanatory prophecy (*une prophétie explicative*) both within and outside the Church after the death of the apostles.[16] We must not be in too great a hurry to answer any of these questions.

What did Christian de Chergé think about these questions? He did not write a formal treatise on his conception of the place of Islam in the divine plan or discuss Islam in terms of the various theologies of religious encounter. Rather, he embraced Youakim Moubarac's opinion that "the theology of non-Christian religions has not yet outgrown its infancy."[17] While de Chergé kept abreast

14. Michel Fédou, *La voie du Christ* [*The Way of Christ*], Cogitatio Fidei Series 253 (Paris: Cerf, 2006). Michel Fédou gives a remarkable demonstration of how Justin of Rome and Clement of Alexandria elaborated their theological thought thanks to their engagement with the culture of their time. Justin was prepared to affirm that Socrates had a partial knowledge of Christ. As for Clement, he said that "philosophy is a work of providence" and that there were many paths of salvation: "Not only did He enumerate several ways of salvation for any one righteous man, but He added many other ways of many righteous" (*Stromata 1.5*; *Ante-Nicene Fathers*, vol. 2, ed. Alexander Roberts and James Donaldson [Grand Rapids, MI: Eerdmans, 1956]).

15. Paul VI, upon his return from Bombay, 1965.

16. Yves Congar, *Vraie et fausse réforme dans l'Église* (Paris: Cerf, 1950), 196–228; Yves Congar, *True and False Reform in the Church*, ed. Paul Philibert (Collegeville, MN: Liturgical Press, 2011).

17. Youakim Moubarac, *Approches chrétiennes de l'islam vu d'Orient* [*Christian Approaches to Islam as Seen from the East*] (Paris: Cerf, 1982), Islam et christianisme en dialogue, cited by Christian de Chergé, "Chrétiens et musulmans: nos différences ont-elles le sens d'une communion?" ["Christians and Muslims: Do Our Differences Have the Meaning of Communion?"], a reflection published in the *Letter of Ligué* 227 (1984–85): 21–37; and 228 (1985–86): 25–42,

of developments in theology,[18] he was determined not to abandon the plane of concrete life—not out of pragmatic skepticism, but, on the contrary, because of his personal commitment: "We believe we are called together, all of us, both to worship the One God and to share with all."[19] This is the ground de Chergé refused to abandon.

A Burning Question

Still, for de Chergé the question of the place of Islam in the divine plan was a "burning" (*lancinante*) one. During the 1989 Days in Rome conference whose theme was A Common Vision for Society, de Chergé said, "For the thirty years that I have held the existence of Islam as a burning question inside me I have had an immense curiosity to know the place that it occupies in the divine plan. Only death will provide me, I think, the answer I seek."[20] This questioning is so powerful that he returns to it a last time in his *Testament*, drawn up four years later, in more or less the same words: "[M]y avid (*lancinante*) curiosity will then be satisfied. This is what I shall be able to do, if God wills—immerse my gaze in that of the Father, and contemplate with him his children of Islam just as he sees them, all shining with the glory of Christ, the fruit of His Passion, and filled with the Gift of the Spirit."[21]

---

reprinted in Christian de Chergé, *L'invincible espérance* [*Hope Unconquerable*], ed. Bruno Chenu (Paris: Bayard, 1996), 111. In his correspondence with a childhood friend, Vincent Desprez, a monk at Ligugé, de Chergé spoke, in reference to an article he had written on mercy, of his trust in Father Moubarac and Father Caspar. See Vincent Desprez, "Christian de Chergé, lettre à un ami moine" ["Letter to a Monk Friend"], *Collectanea cisterciensia* 60 (1998): 212.

18. "Chrétiens et musulmans: nos différences" was written in 1984 (two years before the meeting in Assisi). De Chergé cites several authors: Geffré, Caspar, Masson, Talbi, le Gric. Their writings are from 1982–83, which demonstrates his interest and wide reading in the subject.

19. De Chergé, "Chrétiens et musulmans: nos différences," in de Chergé, *L'invincible espérance*, 111.

20. De Chergé, "Chrétiens et musulmans: pour un projet commun de société" ["Christians and Muslims: For a Common Vision of Society"], in de Chergé, *L'invincible espérance*, 170.

21. De Chergé, "Quand un à-Dieu s'envisage," the *Testament* of Christian de Chergé, *L'invincible espérance*, 224–24. [Passage quoted, 224. – Tr.]

The place of Islam, then, was always for de Chergé essentially a question. He gave no carefully argued response to it from any particular theological position so we would be false to him if we were to define him by or bring him into alignment with any one position. It is preferable to consider his original way of framing the problem. De Chergé's cautious attitude toward global answers and his rejection of a priori responses motivated his research and led him to a broader awareness of the question and to its effective application in the experience of dialogue.

This way of approaching the question has much to contribute to theological reflection and the life of the Church. It is not the a priori theological definition of the place of other religions in the plan of God that is the basis of interreligious dialogue. Rather, it is the experience itself of dialogue that lets the Christian make a statement about the place of other religions, in particular of Islam. To be sure, this statement will not be definitive. It remains partial, but its value lies in the fact that it is neither external nor a priori but arises from within the experience of encounter. Hence de Chergé did not begin with a determining theory about the place of other religions in the plan of God; he began from a posture of dialogue and so left open as a possibility whatever God wanted the dialogue partners to experience.

Hope

This is a dynamic stance. It inspires a real engagement, one that is not in the first instance the search for knowledge about religions or the search for an ethical attitude in the service of peace but rather is eschatological because it is a commitment to hope. "I am sure that I will decipher it [that is, the answer to the question concerning the place of Islam in the plan of God] in the dazzling Easter light of Him who presents himself to me as the only possible Muslim because he is all Yes to the will of the Father."[22] Hope is the ground of encounter. Dialogue is not in the first place the fruit of human reason, nor the effort to live together better, nor a

22. De Chergé, *L'invincible espérance*, 171.

path to peace, much less merely a political position. To be sure, it is all of those things, but none of those is its foundation. Even though certain contemporary currents of theology insist on the ethical aim of dialogue—an understanding among religions in order to promote justice and peace in the world—and although de Chergé recognized that this ethical aim has its place, nevertheless, in his view it was not the true *raison d'être* of dialogue, nor its goal, nor its foundation. For Christian de Chergé, the hope of the unity of Christians and Muslims in the heart of the Father is the only authentic basis of dialogue, the only path by which we can attain understanding in faith of the place of Islam.

Hope in Action

To the question "What is the place of Islam in the plan of God?" de Chergé has no answer besides a hope in an eschatological unity in the heart of the Father. This is not a distant hope located in a "beyond" and to be attained only in the future. De Chergé's eschatological hope is first of all the welcoming of a gift in the here-and-now that opens up a path of conversion:

> I am convinced that by letting this question haunt me, I am learning better to discover the expressions of solidarity and even participation existing today—including in matters of faith; not to let "the other" get fixed in some idea I might have of him, an idea that my Church may have passed on to me, or even that "the other" may say about himself.[23]

Not to fix the other in stereotypes, including his own, is so important for de Chergé that he will return to it a final time in his *Testament*: "I am also aware of the caricatures of Islam which a certain Islamism encourages. It is too easy to salve one's conscience by identifying this religious way with the fundamentalist ideologies of the extremists."[24]

---

23. De Chergé, *L'invincible espérance*, 171.
24. De Chergé, *L'invincible espérance*, 222; see Appendix, p. 200, below.

The Criterion of Hope

The criterion of hope is more important than any of the collective caricatures that we might have. It is more important even than ideas Muslims themselves might have of Islam. To take a stance in hope means to reject caricatures and to refrain from setting up categories, pronouncing peremptory judgments, and fixing our understanding to a given moment of history. At its core, the identity of Islam is unknown. It is not known by anyone, not even by Muslims. Islam is other than what is known of it. We cannot act as though we know what Islam is, nor can we speculate on its place in God's plan on the basis of the idea we have formed of it for ourselves. The historical instantiations of both Islam and Christianity fail to render the essence of either religious tradition; rather, to a certain extent, they betray them. No one can imagine what historical forms Islam and Christianity will take in future centuries, and thus we cannot determine their place in God's plan merely by reasoning on the basis of our observations of them.

But we can—and this is Christian de Chergé's choice—start from the opposite end. In a spirit of living faith we can start with God's plan as it is revealed in Christian revelation. In the new starting point Christians ground themselves in God's plan of unity: that all people be saved and gathered as God's children around God's table. This new starting point is, in the strict sense of the word, theological.

Muslim-Christian dialogue, then, is not determined by an a priori decision about the place of Islam in God's plan. Rather, it is dialogue that allows us to enter into the mystery of Islam, and, more broadly, of all other religions. In the same way, we understand Islam by starting not from our knowledge of it in its historical manifestations but rather from the mystery of God and his plan of unity. Faith in this mysterious plan of unity opens up a path for both parties of dialogue: a way of encounter, an exodus, a *hijra*, a true pilgrimage toward the communion of saints.

A Single Faith in the One God

Christians and Muslims can recognize a partial commonality of faith. "But the plan of salvation also includes . . . in the first place

. . . the Muslims: . . . they adore the one, merciful God."[25] Christians and the believers of Islam are joined in a common faith in the one, merciful God. This fundamental experience, common to the two religious traditions, grounds both Christianity and Islam in a common vocation: to bear witness, each of them separately and both together, to the mercy of God.

Christian de Chergé learned very early about the Oneness of God. He recounts the occasion on which his mother taught him this. As a child in Algeria he expressed curiosity about the Muslims he saw at prayer. His mother told him, "They are praying to God." He concluded, "I have always known that the God of Islam and the God of Jesus Christ do not make two."[26] The council's clear statement, "together with us they adore the one, merciful God," excludes the possibility of saying any longer that Muslims and Christians do not have the same God. To be sure, Christians are right to say that their theology of God is not the same as Muslims', but they cannot conclude that they do not have the same God without compromising the faith of both Christians and Muslims in the Oneness of God. "I believe in one God" are the words with which the Church's Creed begins. The conciliar document is insistent on this point of our common faith. "Together with us they adore."

A Single Faith in the Merciful God

Faith in the oneness of God is also common faith in a merciful God. De Chergé calls this fundamental convergence between Christianity and Islam "a common Word." Both traditions received it from God. Christians must understand this foundation of Islam, which is also the foundation of their own faith. Moreover, they need the faith of the believers in Islam in the mercy of God in order to discover, in a deeper way, the richness of their

25. *Lumen Gentium* 16.
26. Christian de Chergé, "Prier en Église à l'écoute de l'Islam" ["Praying as Church While Listening to Islam"], *Chemins de dialogue* 27 (2006): 18. See de Chergé, *L'invincible espérance*, 113.

own faith tradition. We cannot "confess as Christians the entire overwhelming richness of mercy if we are unable to listen with thanksgiving to those who profess it as the central mystery of their own faith life."[27] Mercy pervades the Qur'an. De Chergé notes 339 uses in the Qur'an of the root *rhm*, "mercy." The name *Al-Rahmân*, "the Merciful," is used fifty-seven times in the Qur'an, as in this quotation: "Your Lord is the Self-Sufficient, the Master of Mercy."[28] Christian de Chergé made a methodical and systematic analysis of all the *surah*s pertaining to the mercy of God and studied the encyclical of John Paul II, *Dives in Misericordia*, in reciprocal relation to the Quranic texts. In his correspondence with a friend, explaining that he had "taken up the study of mercy in the Qur'an in response to the recent encyclical,"[29] de Chergé deplored the fact that the encyclical makes no mention of mercy in the Qur'an because, as de Chergé puts it, mercy is "nuclear" to the Muslim faith. "Is it possible to speak in a Christian way about mercy without doing justice to all the 'keys'[30] it plays in the hearts and religious traditions of humankind? Are they aware in Rome that no Muslim can read the encyclical without feeling deeply ignored? . . . It is a word [*parole*] we have in common and it is our mission to bring it to birth."

This last sentence illuminates and explains de Chergé's reaction. The common word—faith in a merciful God—is not just any convergence of opinions between the two religious traditions. It is a shared word: the Word is one; mercy is one. "Mercy is the seal of the covenant between God and his creation. It marks each of

---

27. "Venons-en à une parole commune: chrétiens et musulmans, témoins et pèlerins de la miséricorde" ["Let Us Come to a Common Word: Christians and Muslims, Witnesses and Pilgrims of Mercy"], *Lettre de Ligugé* 217 (1983–81): 26–50; de Chergé, *L'invincible espérance*, 70.

28. [Tr. note: *Surah* 6:133, following the French text. According to the Saheeh International Version (Jeddah, Saudi Arabia, 1997): "And your Lord is the Free of need, the possessor of mercy."]

29. Private correspondence of February 21, 1981.

30. [Tr. note: *touches* = piano keys.]

his gifts."[31] Mercy is a common experience of a common word, the same experience of the one Word. "It is a shared word by which we confess, with a single surge of intensity, our congenital misery and its innate need for a liberating heart-to-Heart."[32]

In the Bible and in the Qurʾan alike, the mercy of God is expressed by means of maternal images. The root *rhm* is common to Hebrew and Arabic. *Rehem* signifies the maternal breast. God is like a mother. God has "bowels of mercy."

The Same Experience Offered to Both

In both the Bible and the Qurʾan God has manifested this mercy to his people despite their infidelities. Human beings come to know mercy if they have the intelligence to discover it in the gift of life, in nature, and in the rhythm of the seasons, but also in the gift of the Bible or the Qurʾan. Scriptural obedience is an experience of divine mercy. Human beings have the vocation to "reflect on the merciful presence of their Creator."[33] Humanity's path is therefore the path of conversion, in some sense a return to the mother's breast. The pilgrim to Mecca prays, "I come to you hoping in your mercy, lamenting the hardness of my heart, with an oppressed soul. . . . O Most Merciful, make us taste the freshness of your clemency and the sweetness of your pardon."

A Common Vocation

If all religions together have a common vocation to open humankind to transcendence, as the meeting at Assisi demonstrated magnificently, then the Muslim faith and the Christian faith have a particular common vocation in the service of mercy. De Chergé develops most of all the link between Islam and the Christian faith, but obviously the same holds true for the Jewish faith. Thus, the three Abrahamic monotheistic religions could bear witness to

---

31. De Chergé, *L'invincible espérance*, 84.
32. De Chergé, *L'invincible espérance*, 69.
33. De Chergé, *L'invincible espérance*, 90.

this mercy of God, in the first instance, in their mutual relations. A beautiful path of faith is offered for all of them. This common experience is a common vocation for the life of the world: "The world would be less of a desert if we could recognize for ourselves a common vocation: to multiply the fountains of mercy along the way. And how can this vocation be in doubt if we let the All-Merciful call us together to a single table, the table of sinners?"[34] For if there is one thing that unites Christians and Muslims, it is that they know, each in their own tradition, that they are sinners who can do nothing but turn to the mercy of God. They are seated together, says de Chergé, at the table of sinners:

> Day after day I learn . . . that the plan of God for Christianity and Islam remains constant: to invite us both to the table of sinners. The multiplied bread which it is given to us to break together is the bread of an absolute trust in the mercy of the All-Powerful. When we consent to meet in this sharing, doubly brothers and sisters because we are both prodigal and forgiven, it becomes possible for us—I affirm it—to listen to and recognize one and the same word of God offering us its richness of life, one and the same Word offered to the multitude in the remission of sins.[35]

Since the mercy of God holds such a position in Islam, how can one not acknowledge that, at least on this point, this religious tradition is a testimony to the one merciful God? When a common experience of mercy brings Christians and Muslims together, and when it is given to them to experience together "one and the same Word offered to the multitude in the remission of sins," then, with the prudence of someone who refuses to abandon the ground of experience, but rather giving his approval, de Chergé can say, "It is my profound belief that Islam is rooted in the tradition of Judeo-Christian revelation and that Mohammed was a prophet authentically inspired by the Spirit of the One and Living God."[36]

34. De Chergé, *L'invincible espérance*, 74.
35. De Chergé, "Prier en Église," 22–23.
36. De Chergé, "Prier en Église," 21.

Conclusion

Our question has been: what is the place of Islam in the plan of God? To this question, de Chergé had no precise or definitive answer, but far from constituting a dead end for him or paralyzing his search, this fact led him, on the contrary, to a commitment to dialogue, dialogue that had its source in his faith in the Father's plan of love and unity. Because of both his acceptance of his lack of knowledge and his faith in the Father's plan of unity, he refused to confine Islam to the idea people have of it, even to what Muslims say about it, or to what we see of it in its historical manifestations.

We will need to return to the question of dialogue, its starting point and aim, but already the encounter between Islam and Christianity reveals a common faith in the oneness of God and a common faith in the mercy of God, which makes both Christians and Muslims witnesses to the one merciful God. We have not answered the theoretical question, but an answer born of the encounter between Muslim faith and Christian faith is already being outlined. It tells us, if not *the* place of Islam in the plan of God, at least *a* place of Islam, characterized for the moment by living in and witnessing to the one merciful God.

As a matter of methodology, we affirm that the question remains open and cannot be closed too quickly by universal theological solutions. We note also that for de Chergé faith in eschatology was the prerequisite for establishing the path of encounter and progress along it. We consider decisive this eschatological aspect of the theology of religious encounter and will return to it later. Finally, we have seen that a common experience, namely, of mercy, has become a common vocation.

Chapter 5

The Dialogue with Islam

"Interreligious dialogue"[1] is the expression used to designate relations among persons of different religious traditions and, through them, among the religions themselves. On the one hand, interreligious dialogue cannot be reduced simply to a dialogue about the partners' respective religions. Dialogue concerns the whole of life. Conversely, though, interreligious dialogue cannot remain silent about the respective faiths of the dialogue participants. Dialogue among Christian and Muslim friends or neighbors, even if it takes the concrete form of interpersonal relations, cannot be reduced to these relations. It is called to open itself up to a positive consideration of the other's religious tradition.

The term *dialogue* was given a place of honor by Paul VI, particularly in his great encyclical on the Church, *Ecclesiam Suam*. The foundation of dialogue is revelation itself, which, in the words of Paul VI, "can likewise be looked upon as a dialogue. In the

---

1. On the topic of interreligious dialogue, see the principal texts of the magisterium: the encyclical of Paul VI, *Ecclesiam Suam*; John Paul II, *Redemptoris Missio*, 55–57; and Pontifical Council for Interreligious Dialogue, Dialogue and Proclamation: Reflection and Orientation on Interreligious Dialogue and the Proclamation of the Gospel of Jesus Christ, http://www .vatican.va/roman_curia/pontifical_councils/interelg/documents/rc_pc_ interelg_doc_19051991_dialogue-and-proclamatio_en.html (May 19, 1991).

Incarnation and in the Gospel it is God's Word that speaks to us. . . . Indeed, the whole history of man's salvation is one long, varied dialogue. . . . Child and mystic, both are called to take part in this unfailing, trustful dialogue; and the mystic finds there the fullest scope for his spiritual powers."[2] In his encyclical *Redemptoris Missio*, John Paul II says that "interreligious dialogue is a part of the Church's evangelizing mission";[3] nevertheless, he points out very clearly that dialogue cannot be used as a means to the end of proselytizing. Rather, the goal of dialogue is the discovery of the seeds of the Word:

> Dialogue does not originate from tactical concerns or self-interest, but is an activity with its own guiding principles, requirements and dignity. It is demanded by deep respect for everything that has been brought about in human beings by the Spirit who blows where he wills. Through dialogue, the Church seeks to uncover the "seeds of the Word,"[4] a "ray of that truth which enlightens all men";[5] these are found in individuals and in the religious traditions of mankind.[6]

The dialogue with Islam is rooted in Vatican II's declaration *Nostra Aetate*, which states that the Church has a high regard for Muslims and develops the bonds which unite the Muslim and Christian faiths. As we noted, the meeting at Casablanca (August 1985) and the speech of John Paul II before an audience of eighty thousand Muslims also provide firm anchorage for Muslim-Christian dialogue. On many occasions John Paul II invited Christians to give this dialogue a privileged place, second only to the special and

---

2. Paul VI, *Ecclesiam Suam* 58–108, in particular 70–71. [Tr. note: The actual text quoted is in 70.] Official English translation from Vatican web site, http://www.vatican.va/holy_father/paul_vi/encyclicals/documents/hf_p-vi_enc_06081964_ecclesiam_en.html.

3. John Paul II, *Redemptoris Missio* 55. Official English translation from Vatican web site, http://www.vatican.va/holy_father/john_paul_ii/encyclicals/documents/hf_jp-ii_enc_07121990_redemptoris-missio_en.html.

4. *Ad Gentes* 15.

5. *Nostra Aetate* 2.

6. *Redemptoris Missio* 56.

unique status of the dialogue between Christians and Jews. Jewish-Christian dialogue, whose uniqueness is beyond dispute, would lose its meaning if it did not open the way, in accordance with the very vocations of the people of Israel and the Church, to an encounter with all peoples, cultures, and therefore religions.

Christian de Chergé subscribed to the aims of Vatican II. In fact, he had a singular vantage point by comparison with those who, like Charles de Foucauld and Louis Massignon, found themselves equally shaken by their encounter with Islam but who lived before the council and paved its way. De Foucauld developed a spirituality of Christian presence in the world of Islam, the spirituality of Nazareth. De Chergé owed much to de Foucauld, but his own spirituality took the spirituality of Nazareth further. He and others have benefited from the council's reflections and from a more explicitly affirmed stance of dialogue both with individual Muslims and with Islam as a religion. Christian de Chergé and his brother monks were the heirs of de Foucauld and Massignon. They were also the beneficiaries of Vatican II and its declaration *Nostra Aetate*, as well as being contemporaries of John Paul II and his prophetic gestures.

Dialogue presupposes a going out from one's own self in order to reach the other. It can be understood as an *exodus* toward the other, in the faith that the other is being borne along by the same quest for God: "Our paths converge when one and the same thirst draws us to the same well."[7] Many people are familiar with this image of a well used by de Chergé in reference to a dialogue he had with one of his Muslim neighbors. With all its apparent simplicity, this real-life anecdote plumbs the depths of spiritual encounter:

> Since the day when he had asked me, quite unexpectedly, to teach him to pray, Mohammed made a habit of coming to talk with me regularly. He is a neighbor, and we have a long history of sharing. Often, I had to cut things short with him or else pass whole weekends without meeting with him, when guests were too numerous or too absorbing. One day, he found

7. Christian de Chergé, *L'invincible espérance* [*Hope Unconquerable*], ed. Bruno Chenu (Paris: Bayard, 1996), 74.

the perfect formula for calling me to order and demanding a meeting: "It's been a long time since we've dug our well!" The image stuck. We use it when we feel the need to share in depth.

Once, to tease him, I asked the question: "And at the bottom of our well, what will we find? Muslim water or Christian water?" He gave me a look, half-amused and half-rueful: "Come on now, we've spent all this time walking together, and you're still asking me this question! You know very well that at the bottom of that well, what we'll find is God's water!"[8]

This little parable speaks of the need each has of the other, and of the other believer. We all dig our well better if we are not digging alone. By the fact of his or her difference, the other is always inviting us to go deeper. Far from being an obstacle to Christian faith or luring Christians into a quicksand of relativism, religious diversity is, on the contrary, a spur to healthy emulation for all participants, with each staying faithful to his or her tradition. But this story makes another fundamental point that all can recognize in their own experience, namely, that no religious tradition, which is always partial and limited in its historical expression, can claim to encompass the Master of the Ages and the Lord of History. It is not religion that is absolute, not even the Christian religion; only God is absolute.[9] One cannot help being reminded of the bride's search in the Song of Solomon: "Have you seen him whom my soul loves?" she asks the sentinels at the city gates. Scarcely has she passed them when she finds Him whom her soul loves (Song 3:3-4). The bridegroom is not enclosed within the ramparts, nor can the city contain him. At the bottom of the well of encounter, the water is neither Christian nor Muslim: it is the water of God.

The Necessity of Dialogue

Dialogue is a necessity—so de Chergé tells us, taking up the very words of John Paul II: "I cannot help thinking that it is urgent,

8. De Chergé, *L'invincible espérance*, 183–84.
9. On this point, see Jean-Marc Aveline, *Paul Tillich* (Marseille: Chemins de Dialogue, 2007).

today especially, when Christians and Muslims have entered into a new phase of history, to recognize and develop the spiritual bonds that unite us."[10] Again, it is a matter of developing spiritual ties, not only ethical ones. Who should take the initiative? One of the objections often raised is this: Are the others also making overtures to dialogue? Aren't we always the ones taking the first step? The subtext is: Aren't we being naïve or idealistic? The objection comes up even in Christian's *Testament*: "Obviously, my death will appear to confirm those who hastily judged me naïve or idealistic: 'Let him tell us now what he thinks of it!' But these persons should know that finally my most avid curiosity will be set free."[11]

Though all agree that dialogue is a necessity, especially in view of the incomparable value of peace, many today, including Pope Benedict XVI, are also raising the issue of reciprocity. It would be a mistake to see this as a new direction taken by this pontificate, concluding that interreligious dialogue, particularly with respect to Islam, has seen its day, or even finding in it grounds that are *ecclesiastically correct* to justify attitudes far from the Gospel. Two comments: already in several places John Paul II had demanded such reciprocity from Muslims. For instance:

> Particular care will therefore be taken so that Islamic-Christian dialogue respects on both sides the principle of religious freedom with all that this involves, also including external and public manifestations of faith. . . . Christians and Muslims are called to commit themselves to . . . raising their voices . . . against the lack of reciprocity in matters of religious freedom.[12]

10. De Chergé, *L'invincible espérance*, 71. Quotation from John Paul II, Address to the Catholic Community of Ankara (November 29, 1979), 3, translated from the official French version, Vatican web site, http://www.vatican.va/holy_father/john_paul_ii/speeches/1979/november/documents/hf_jp-ii_spe_19791129_ankara-turchia_fr.html.

11. De Chergé, *L'invincible espérance*, 223; see Appendix, pp. 200–201, below.

12. John Paul II, *Ecclesia in Africa*, Post-synodal Exhortation (1995), 66. Official English version from Vatican web site, http://www.vatican.va/holy_father/john_paul_ii/apost_exhortations/documents/hf_jp-ii_exh_14091995_ecclesia-in-africa_en.html.

The second comment is on the level of epistemology. Interreligious dialogue has a political dimension as well as a theological dimension. The reciprocity being required is a political necessity, especially for religious minorities, and forms a condition for the establishment of a lasting peace. It is part of the responsibility of the magisterium of the Church to appeal for this reciprocity.

Reciprocity is also highly desirable from the theological point of view, but it cannot be an a priori condition of dialogue. It must always be kept in mind that, according to Christian revelation, the first initiator of dialogue is God himself. God continues to offer it to us, without counting the cost, without stopping to evaluate humankind's response to the divine offer of a covenant. Unwearied, disregarding any offences committed, God continues to offer this covenant of love to all people. The Church must remember that God's faithfulness does not depend on how much the Church is able to reciprocate it, or on how adept the Church is at reading the signs of the times, or on how docile it is to the Spirit. This is a great mystery. That is why the divine initiative calls us in our turn to enter into this dialogue of love, to become participants in it, by becoming unconditionally men and women of dialogue.

If there is a reciprocity whose claim we cannot avoid, it is our response to God who took the first step, who brought it to fulfillment in God's Son, and who invites the Son's disciples to walk the path of dialogue along with him. Reciprocity, highly desirable though it is, can never be an a priori rule governing relations between spouses, parents, and friends. It would be out of bounds scrupulously to monitor that for each party's advance there was a matching response from the other. As much as it is politically legitimate to look for reciprocity between religions, reciprocity cannot be a theological condition of interreligious dialogue on the part of the disciples of Christ. De Chergé says:

> "We're always the ones going first." Now stop! As though we weren't beholden in the first instance to the tremendous initiative taken by the One who loved us to the end. Therefore we must avoid at all costs this payback mentality. It still haunts us in a thousand ways. Approaching the other and approach-

ing God is one and the same thing, and I can't get out of doing either. Both require the same generosity.[13]

As it happens, it is not always the Christians who take the initiative—hence the appeal from 138 international Muslim leaders addressed to the pope and all leaders of the Christian Churches on the basis of "a common word between us and you." The text of this appeal has no hint of polemics. Emphasizing how precious peace is and how great is the responsibility for peace of the world's two most populous religions, the basis on which the appeal is argued is theological: "We have in common the love of God and the love of the neighbor."[14]

Thus, dialogue is a necessity not only for the sake of peace between peoples and within the pluralist societies in which we live but because we need dialogue in order to dig our own well and because it is a response to the divine initiative. It can never be done without self-emptying and without risk. There is no such thing as an encounter without risk.

> It seems to me that the Spirit wants to break down at any cost the walls of our convenient entrenchments and to leave us empty-handed and open-hearted, ready to receive and to give, to let Christ make his way, his Paschal mystery, done his way,

13. Christian de Chergé, "L'échelle mystique du dialogue" ["The Mystical Ladder of Dialogue"], *Islamochristiana* 23 (1997): 7. [Tr. note: The word translated "generosity" is *gratuité*, emphasizing the grace and spontaneity involved. Regrettably, the English word "gratuity" has certain unwanted connotations.] A version of this text can also be found in *L'invincible espérance*, 167–204.

14. *A Common Word between Us and You*, an open letter and appeal from Muslim religious guides to Benedict XVI and to the principal representatives of the Christian Churches, dated October 13, 2007. [Tr. note: The quotation cited above does not appear in those words in the letter. The following two passages come closest: "Thus the Unity of God, love of Him, and love of the neighbor form a common ground upon which Islam and Christianity (and Judaism) are founded." "We as Muslims invite Christians to come together with us on the basis of what is common to us, which is also what is most essential to our faith and practice: the *Two Commandments* of love." Both are found in the Summary & Abridgement preceding the actual letter.]

the way of the "son of man," that no dogmatic formula can contain. . . . An availability to God and to the other who is different from oneself that leaves wide open and endless the way of Love, which is to say, of our common future.[15]

Dialogue Is Existential

On the other hand, de Chergé is very suspicious of *theological* dialogue or, more precisely, of theology's claim, whether openly acknowledged or not, to control dialogue, to set out its rules and terms, and to define its very nature. He is equally suspicious of a canonical discourse on Islam that might box in, however slightly, this religious tradition. He was deeply affected by the request of the Sufis of the Alawi Order and by the experience of the *Ribât*.[16] The Sufis had said, "We do not want to engage in a dogmatic discussion with you. In dogma or theology there are many barriers that are man-made. But we feel that we are called to unity. We wish to let God create something new between us. This cannot happen except in prayer. That is why we have wanted to have this prayer meeting with you."[17] Theological reflection is still at the stammering stage. Therefore, rigid theological definitions are not appropriate at the starting point of dialogue; instead, we should leave space for what the Spirit has to say to us and to teach us today. The royal road to this end is prayer and contemplation.

> I remain convinced that Father Eyt saw things clearly when he emphasized the (current) limits of theology in the matter of the encounter between religions, as well as the need to plunge into contemplation in order to be able subsequently to make progress. Not to remain stuck in positions that are still apologetic, but to go forward, is a source of suffering, even if you do rediscover the ineffable freedom of the Spirit.[18]

15. Christian de Chergé, unpublished letter to a friend.
16. See chapter 3 n. 18.
17. De Chergé, *L'invincible espérance*, 172.
18. Christian de Chergé, unpublished letter to a friend.

It has to be acknowledged that we of the Christian faith do not really know what interreligious dialogue is, nor where the Spirit is leading one side or the other. The danger for those who have some knowledge of Islam would be to enclose this religious way within the limited knowledge they have of it; for theologians, it would be to attempt to arrive at definitive answers on the basis of what they have understood up to this point about the mission of the Church. How can space be left for the One God except by immersing oneself with courage in the way of contemplation and the way of encounter, without confining God in one's reasoning, for "it is always from beyond our reason that God comes to us, whatever our respective faiths may be."[19]

For de Chergé, dialogue must be, in the first instance, existential. For the monks of Atlas, *existential dialogue* meant daily life and work done in common with neighbors and with the people of the region; for Brother Luc, the doctor of the Atlas community, it meant the dispensary; and for all, the frequent meetings and visits at the monastery. This is what allowed de Chergé to write:

> Dialogue is essentially characterized by the fact that we never take the initiative. I would happily call it existential. It is often the fruit of a long co-existence and of shared concerns, sometimes very concrete ones—which is to say that it is very rarely at a strictly theological level. In fact, we tend to avoid this kind of narrow-minded jousting.[20]

Existential dialogue is at once concrete and spiritual. There are people who have managed to find fault with one or another of its aspects. Some claimed that its spirituality was naïve—a criticism de Chergé takes up in his *Testament*—that the concreteness of existential dialogue, anchored as it was in the experience of a handful of villagers of the Atlas Mountains, would lead to a distorted conception of Islam. But such criticisms were condescending toward both the spiritual life and these Muslim neighbors of Atlas. It is difficult to fault someone for having a partial experience. After

19. De Chergé, "L'échelle mystique," 12.
20. [Quotation not attributed in original. – Ed.]

all, every experience is partial, but at least it has the advantage of being specific, concrete, and lived out in real time. In its particularity, experience resists generalizations.

The realities of everyday life do not oblige us to concede, as people sometimes assume, that there are better things to do in life than discuss religion and that we are better off building a new world together, working to improve the quality of life, and liberating people from various forms of poverty.[21] To ignore the spiritual dimension of each individual is unthinkable:

> Existential dialogue, then, concerns at once the work of the hands and the work of the Spirit, the everyday and the eternal—so great a truth is it that we cannot welcome the man or the woman who comes asking for our attention except in their concrete and mysterious reality as children of God, "created beforehand in Christ Jesus" (Eph. 2:10).[22] We would cease to be Christians, or quite simply, human beings, if we were to mutilate others in their hidden dimension, for the sake of a so-called "purely human encounter," which refers—let us be clear about this—to an expurgated humanity *purified* of any personal, and therefore unique, relation with the Wholly Other. Dialogue, then, means to keep our feet firmly planted on the ground (or even in the manure) but our head exploring the heavens.[23]

De Chergé could not have made himself any clearer. Interreligious dialogue neither privileges nor excludes any dimension of human beings: not their concrete humanity, not their capacity for intellectual reflection, not their spiritual dimension. Too

---

21. This is a firmly held position in the field of the theology of world religions, set in opposition to the stance that goes by the barbarous name of *soteriocentrism*.

22. [Tr. note: The French is "créés par avance dans le Christ," but the "beforehand" belongs in every other translation, including the Vulgate and GNT, to the good works, not to our creation. The whole verse is as follows: "For we are what he has made us, created in Christ Jesus for good works, which God prepared beforehand to be our way of life."]

23. De Chergé, "L'échelle mystique," 2.

often dialogue is seen as a matter of theological discussions or, conversely, as a common effort in service of society. The danger lies in reducing dialogue to a single dimension when, in fact, it is an encounter among persons in all dimensions of their humanity. De Chergé shares with us his belief in existential dialogue:

> I am most powerfully convinced that a life like ours, so concrete and at the same time so dependent on the faith of Muslims, can be a witness that existential dialogue is the interreligious dialogue *par excellence*. For the experiences and perspectives it affords rattle the bars surrounding an approach to dialogue that is too exclusively dogmatic.[24]

The Conditions of Dialogue

A certain number of conditions must be met for existential dialogue to occur. De Chergé often insisted on the need for humility: "Every dialogue between believers of good faith should always begin with a joint recognition that God is calling us to humility. This means, it follows logically, that we renounce any claim to be better or superior; it also means that we are striving for a form of personal authenticity without which we could not even dream of laying claim to the Truth."[25] His reflection on humility was steeped in the Rule of Saint Benedict. Humility is a ladder that you climb up by climbing down.[26]

All dialogue worthy of the name requires a good deal of interest in the other and great respect for his or her faith. Interreligious dialogue demands respect and delicacy not simply by the very nature of dialogue but because the other's faith is a gift from God, even if I do not truly understand this gift and it remains

---

24. De Chergé, unpublished letter to a friend, 1984.
25. De Chergé, "L'échelle mystique," 12.
26. See commentaries on the Rule of Saint Benedict on humility; Christian de Chergé, *Dieu pour tout jour, chapitres du père Christian de Chergé à la communauté de Tibhirine (1986–1996)* [*God for Each Day: Chapter Talks of Fr. Christian de Chergé to the Community of Tibhirine*], 2nd ed., Les cahiers de Tibhirine (Montjoyer: Abbe d'Aiguebelle, 2006), 259–321.

very mysterious from my viewpoint. This gift that is given to the other is, in a certain sense, a gift that is given to me: "The faith of the other is a gift from God, albeit a mysterious one. Therefore it commands respect. . . . And this gift given to the other is also intended for me, to urge me in the direction of what I have to profess. To neglect it is to fail to contemplate the work of the Spirit and our share of this work."[27] Seeing the faith of the other as a gift from God for him or her and for me prevents me from disregarding it or displaying indifference toward it. It is a work of the Spirit, whom I can contemplate at work in the heart of the other believer and hence also in my own heart.

Humility in dialogue disposes us to learn from the other: "We can truly expect a new thing each time we make the effort to discern [humility's] 'signs' at the 'horizons' of worlds and hearts by becoming listeners, and also students, of the other—of Muslims, in this case."[28] Dialogue does not consist in evaluating the faith of the others, calibrating it to the precise measure of my own beliefs, wishing to establish comparisons and criteria, measuring distances, or projecting hostile images that all too easily become lethal realities. The proper attitude of dialogue consists in becoming a pupil in another's school, and doing this with a view to discerning the signs of a reality that we do not yet understand, that we do not truly know, and that is the mystery of unity and mercy woven through both religious traditions. Christians can affirm that they need Muslims in order to live out their own faith. De Chergé made his own the words of Pope John Paul II in a speech given in the Philippines in 1981: "My dear friends, I want you to be convinced that Christians, your brothers and sisters, need you and need your love."[29] We must correctly situate this need at its

---

27. De Chergé, *L'invincible espérance*, 183.

28. De Chergé, *L'invincible espérance*, 173.

29. De Chergé, *L'invincible espérance*, 182. The speech was given to representatives of the Muslim community at Davao airport, the Philippines, on February 20, 1981. The quotation was translated from paragraph 5 of the official Italian version: http://www.vatican.va/holy_father/john_paul_ii/speeches/1981/february/documents/hf_jp-ii_spe_19810220_davao-comunita-musulmana_it.html.

proper level: it exists not solely at the level of a policy of cordial
and peaceful relations but at the level of faith.

Dialogue Is a Mystical Ladder

De Chergé borrowed from John Climacus the image of the mystical ladder,[30] an image that has greatly influenced the spiritual and
monastic traditions. He applied the ladder image to dialogue, thus
demonstrating the extent to which dialogue, for him, was a royal
road for contemporary mysticism. Dialogue is made up of two
parallel poles, the two "respective fidelities," by which we are to
understand the two religious traditions. De Chergé also described
these two upright poles as "our respective faiths." The space between the base and the summit of the ladder, the intermediary
space, represents the spiritual world, as indicated by the angels
who go up and down it in the story of Jacob's ladder. This spiritual
world lies midway between the worlds of heaven and earth, the
mystery of God and the world in which humankind evolves. These
two worlds are not in opposition to each other; on the contrary,
they converge toward union in a New Man. The ladder is vertical.

The ladder is "fixed in the ground," and between the two uprights, rungs unite these two fidelities: "Between the pillars of
Islam and the essential observances of every form of consecrated
life, there are obvious correspondences which are like successive
rungs for a common ascent."[31] The rungs of a ladder are deeply
fixed into each of the two uprights of the ladder, making it possible to climb. These rungs, which belong to both the Christian
and the Muslim faiths, are astonishingly numerous. De Chergé
takes the time to list them: "gift of self to the Absoluteness of God,
regular prayer, fasting, sharing, alms, conversion of the heart,
unceasing mindfulness of the Presence, trust in Providence, the
imperative of boundless hospitality, and the call to spiritual combat and to a pilgrimage which is also an interior one."[32]

30. De Chergé, "L'échelle mystique."
31. De Chergé, "L'échelle mystique," 11.
32. De Chergé, "L'échelle mystique," 11.

It is noteworthy that he does not list *common beliefs*, as does, for example, the document *Nostra Aetate*; instead, he lists *common religious practices*. Indeed, it is these practices, more than beliefs, that form the rungs by which all can progress. The ladder metaphor shows each one the need for the other's faith. If one upright of the ladder was missing it would not be a ladder at all.

Each rung joins the two uprights. Dialogue is neither a matter of agreement nor a conversation. Dialogue is a mystical ladder; that is, it is the means by which we—whichever tradition we belong to—manage to walk toward the communion of saints, to live out the paschal mystery or the *hijra*. "How can we not recognize in this the Spirit of holiness, whose coming or going, whose descending or ascending, no one knows? Its task is always to cause 'to be born from above' (Jn 3:7), to draw onto an upward path."[33] In the meetings of the *Ribât*, these different rungs were often assigned as topics for reflection between sessions.

The top of the ladder rests in the beyond. This fact can be viewed in two ways. First, the point of contact is in God. "Our ladder is well secured in our common clay. Between the two uprights we have seen rungs set across which it is less our business to count than to climb. And here we are, beyond the horizon, sure of finding in God that firm support, that 'mighty Rock' of which the psalms sing."[34] The other point of the ladder's contact is the communion of saints. This concept had great significance for de Chergé. Here he does not use the precise phrase, but he speaks of the assembly of the elect and "the heavenly Jerusalem in which everyone was born."[35]

The metaphor of the ladder is richly suggestive. Its antecedents in the spiritual tradition make it an even more meaningful and powerful introduction to the essence of dialogue, which is mystical. The text Dialogue and Proclamation spells out four levels of dialogue: the dialogue of life, the dialogue of action, the

---

33. De Chergé, "L'échelle mystique," 11.
34. De Chergé, "L'échelle mystique," 11. [Tr. note: See Ps 62:7.]
35. Psalm 87:5. See chapter 8, where the theme of the communion of saints is developed.

dialogue of theological exchange, and the dialogue of religious experience. These levels of dialogue demonstrate the diversity of forms it takes but do not explain the nature of dialogue or its aim. What de Chergé wrote is in the same vein as what Paul VI said in *Ecclesiam Suam*: dialogue has a "transcendent origin." It is a royal road along which the Spirit of Holiness is leading believers today.

Fruits of Dialogue

Christian de Chergé acknowledged, along with Moubarac, that emulation is the poor cousin of dialogue. But given that a tree is judged by its fruits, one of the essential fruits of dialogue is the conversion of both parties, the product of surrender and humility, by which we accept that we do not know where the Spirit is leading us, but we do accept to walk the path of slow transformation. (Henri le Saux, in a Christian-Hindu context, underwent and wrote about a similar experience of surrender, exodus, and the paschal mystery, particularly in his *Journal*.) "From the moment that we give ourselves over, mutually and deliberately, to the slow and transformative letting-go that comes out of a shared lifetime, we live anew as an Easter, an exodus, and a *hijra* (why not?), the spiritual adventure of Abraham."[36] Conversion is the goal of dialogue, "a mutual conversion in which God engages us (rung by rung), according to our fidelities in the coming of his kingdom."[37] De Chergé also declared that in his vocation to live at Notre Dame de l'Atlas

> I would need to learn to understand and to contemplate Islam at its most authentic, that is to say, in its submission to God, and to do that with no other desire than for a mutual conversion destined to lead us, if it please God, both us and them,

36. De Chergé, "L'échelle mystique," 8.
37. De Chergé, "L'échelle mystique," 12. [Tr. note: De Chergé is quoting (with his own addition of "rung by rung") from the pastoral letter of the Conference of North African Bishops of May 4, 1979, "Chrétiens au Maghreb: le sens de nos rencontres" ("Christians in the Maghreb: The Meaning of Our Encounters"), 10.3.]

toward the appointed place of each in the great assembly of all the living.[38]

Conversion must not be confused with change of religion: "Conversion is a dynamic process, a way of being meant to remain active. It is a 'tropism': we turn toward God the way a plant turns toward the sun. Change of religion may bring about an important shift in focus, but it does not exhaust the whole meaning of conversion, and it may well turn out that it is not even a part of the meaning of conversion."[39] All, of whatever religion, are called equally to conversion: "Because all are called to conversion, the conversion of others matters to me, and mine to them. The conversion of sinners is a necessary prelude to the communion of saints."[40] Again, de Chergé located the starting point of conversion not in sin, not even in humankind, but in God.[41] Conversion thus becomes a human dynamic, inscribed in our very nature, an innate "turning" toward God, and not an enforced reparation for our sinfulness or a challenge to our moral resolve.

Conclusion

Interreligious dialogue is a term that gives rise to ambiguity. It is often understood as a specific activity. *Dialogue and Proclamation* reminds us that its forms can be diverse, and in this sense, it is first of all existential. Christian de Chergé applied this understanding of dialogue to his concrete experience of life at Tibhirine, which included both working side by side and having conversations about prayer with the other. He showed that dialogue is at its core an interior disposition of humility that turns toward others, to the

---

38. Christian de Chergé, "Prier en Église à l'écoute de l'Islam, réponse à la revue *Tychique*" ["Praying as Church While Listening to Islam: A Reply to the Journal *Tychique*"], Pentecost 1982, *Chemins de dialogue*, 27.

39. Chapter talk for Friday, May 23, 1986; de Chergé, *Dieu pour tout jour*, 122.

40. Chapter talk for Wednesday, June 4, 1986; de Chergé, *Dieu pour tout jour*, 125.

41. Christophe Purgu, "Processus de conversion" ["Processes of Conversion"], *Chemins de dialogue* 24 (2004): 155–72.

faith of others. It is a mystical ladder by which both parties, by climbing similar rungs, allow themselves to be converted toward the One God. This way of understanding dialogue is available to all those, Christian and Muslim, who wish to use this ladder. It is fixed in the earth, in the religious diversity in which we are immersed. It has its points of contact in God and the communion of saints, which, from this very moment, is being incarnated through this dialogical way of being.

Chapter 6

Reading the Qur'an

Christian de Chergé was a diligent reader of the Qur'an in Arabic. He considered engaging with the Qur'an part of his personal vocation. He devoted himself to textual study of the Book, and in writing his homilies he drew inspiration from particular *surahs*. He frequently mentions doing *lectio divina*[1] with the Qur'an. It was a practice that "has allowed me, as the Christian that I am, to have an authentic spiritual experience in and through what others have received as properly their own for the sake of cultivating within them a taste for God: the call to prayer, the spontaneous prayerful utterance, the act of sharing . . . and the Quranic verse: I definitely believe a genuine *lectio divina* of the Qur'an is possible, above all in classical Arabic, which is so near to the original milieu of our own Scriptures."[2]

Others before him had translated, read, and meditated on the Qur'an or the scriptures of other religious traditions.[3] How are

---

1. *Lectio divina:* a meditative and prayerful reading of Holy Scripture.

2. "Address by Christian de Chergé to the General Chapter, 1993," in Christian de Chergé, *Sept vies pour Dieu et l'Algérie* [*Seven Lives for God and Algeria*], ed. Bruno Chenu (Paris: Bayard, 1996), 9.

3. Peter the Venerable, abbot of Cluny, had a Latin translation of the Qur'an made in the twelfth century, and this translation was the official one up until modern times. See, in a Hindu context, the works of Henri Le Saux (Abashiktananda), e.g., *Hindu-Christian Meeting Point: Within the Cave of the Heart* (Delhi: ISPCK, 1976).

Christians able to read and receive other scriptures?[4] Can they consider them inspired? The Roman Catholic International Theological Commission has pronounced upon this subject, restricting the use of the term "inspiration" to the Jewish and Christian scriptures alone. The document *Dominus Iesus* took the same position: "The Church's tradition, however, reserves the designation of *inspired texts* to the canonical books of the Old and New Testaments, since these are inspired by the Holy Spirit."[5] However restrictive it may be, this document follows *Nostra Aetate* in recognizing in other sacred texts "a ray of Truth." Thus it affirms that God "does not fail to make himself present" among world religions, including in "the sacred books of other religions."[6] Even though the use of the term "inspiration" is restricted, the question remains: may Christians consider the Qurʾan, if not *the* Word of God, at least *a* Word of God?[7] As Robert Caspar puts it, a Christian "can no longer think, as in former times, of a diabolical origin, or even a purely human origin" of the Qurʾan.[8]

Lectio divina with the Quranic text cannot be isolated from the consideration of other constitutive elements of the Muslim religious tradition, for instance, the call to prayer, hospitality, and

4. On this delicate question, read the reflections of the GRIC, Groupe de Recherche Islamo-Chrétien [Muslim-Christian Research Group], *Ces Écritures qui nous questionnent* [*These Scriptures Which Interrogate Us*] (Paris: Éditions du Centurion, 1987); *Le dialogue des Écritures* [*The Dialogue among Scriptures*], ed. Isabel Chareire and Christian Salenson, with contributions by Paula Bony, Isabelle Chareire, Michel Guillaud, Gilbert Jouberjean, Jean Massonnet, Colette Poggy, and Christian Salenson (Brussels: Éditions Lessius, 2007).

5. International Theological Commission, Congregation for the Doctrine of the Faith, "Declaration '*Dominus Iesus*' on the Unicity and Salvific Universality of Jesus Christ and the Church," 2000, Vatican web site, http://www.vatican.va/roman_curia/congregations/cfaith/documents/rc_con_cfaith_doc_20000806_dominus-iesus_en.html.

6. *Dominus Iesus* 8.

7. Claude Geffré, *De Babel à Pentecôte* [*From Babel to Pentecost*], Cogitatio Fidei Series 247 (Paris: Éditions du Cerf, 2006), 153–65. Jacques Dupuis, *Vers une théologie chrétienne du pluralisme religieux* [*Toward a Christian Theology of Religious Pluralism*], Cogitatio Fidei Series 200 (Paris: Éditions du Cerf, 1997), 357–84.

8. Robert Caspar, *Pour un regard chrétien sur l'islam* [*Toward a Christian View of Islam*] (Paris: Bayard, 2006), 102.

pilgrimage. De Chergé thought of his relation to the Qur'an as analogous to his relationship to Muslim prayer. He wrote more than once about the invitation to prayer made by the muezzin[9] that every call to prayer comes from God. He claimed that his *lectio divina* with the Qur'an was a genuine spiritual experience. Moreover, in order to underline its Christian authenticity, he specified that this was a gift that had been given to him: "It is given to me as the Christian that I am."

As we have seen, for Christian de Chergé the Qur'an is "what the other has received as properly his own to cultivate within him the taste for God." Let us pause here. When he says that the Qur'an is "what the other has received as properly his own," he means by "the other" the Muslim community. The Qur'an belongs to that community. Christians cannot appropriate it for themselves. Consequently, the exercise of a certain restraint is called for in the presence of the gift that the other has received. Others can be assiduous readers of the Qur'an as long as they do not forgot that this scripture is not their own. The phrase "as properly his own" prohibits the annexing of this scripture. It also guards against a melding of the Christian Scriptures and the Quranic texts together or putting them on the same level. On the other hand, recognizing the Qur'an as a gift to the other is an invitation to show respect for these texts. Who was their author? From whom did the other receive the Qur'an—from the Prophet or from God himself? Everything indicates that this gift came not solely from the Prophet but from God himself.

For de Chergé, *lectio* with the Qur'an was a common practice. Thus, returning from the Assekrem where he had gone for a long three-month retreat, he noted, "Long 'one-on-ones'[10] and also long

9. "Bell and muezzin sound in unison or in succession in the same enclosure, and it is difficult not to receive the call to prayer, from wherever it comes, as a reminder of the communion which prevails in the heart of the One to whom we turn with the same surrender" ("Chrétiens et musulmans, pour un projet commun de société" ["Christians and Muslims, for a Common Vision of Society"], in de Chergé, *L'invincible espérance*, 191).

10. [Tr. note: Literally, "longs 'seul à seul'"—"long alone-to-alones." Compare the famous phrase of Plotinus, "alone with the Alone," repeated by, among other Cistercians, William of Saint Thierry.]

lectio divina of both the Bible and the Qurʾan, since that is the call
that I carry and to which I have to respond from the interior of a
heart that wants to listen."[11]*Lectio divina* with the Qurʾan was part
of his response to his monastic vocation in the land of Islam. He
acknowledges, moreover, that he is not the only one to take an
interest in the scriptures of others:

> Our Sufi friends like to quote the Gospel, which they were
> keen to read. So many parables and sayings find a vibrant
> echo in the Muslim milieu so familiar to us! Could we not let
> the Book of Islam resound, in the stillness of an interior listen-
> ing, with the desire and the respect of these brothers who draw
> from it their taste for God? Or are we bound to continue turn-
> ing a deaf ear to the other's message while contesting on prin-
> ciple its unique connection with the Wholly Other?[12]

Christian de Chergé is fond of saying that the Sufis read the Gospel: "They are keen to read it." Thus the Christian Scripture, the
Gospel, can be an eloquent scripture for Muslims too. The Quranic
texts are not to be confused with the Christian Scriptures, but this
does not prevent recognizing that they can have a "unique connection with the Wholly Other."

De Chergé urges a peaceful listening to the other's scripture, a
respectful listening, with the same desire as these brothers "who
draw from it the taste for God" approach the Qurʾan. The term
"desire" is not insignificant; it qualifies the reader's relationship
with Scripture, and through Scripture, with the Word, orienting
the reader to receive these scriptures in a spirit of a desire to welcome the Word. It is impossible to turn a deaf ear. The expression
is not insignificant for an attentive reader of the Rule of Saint
Benedict. From its opening lines, "Listen, my son, . . . incline the
ear of your heart,"[13] the Rule is an invitation to give ear.

---

11. Correspondence with a Friend, letter of March 8, 1980. Unpublished.
12. "Chrétienes et musulmans, pour un projet commun de sociéte," in de
Chergé, *L'invicible espérance*, 167.
13. [Tr. note: Compare the opening words of the Rule's prologue 1: "Listen,
O my son, to the teachings of your master, and turn to them with the ear of

The Qur'an has a "unique connection with the Wholly Other," de Chergé says. For him, this assertion cannot be contested. To those for whom the case is already closed, for whom the Qur'an cannot, on principle, be scripture having a connection to the Wholly Other, de Chergé opposes his own "genuine spiritual experience" in contact with this Book, an experience grounded in his own vocation and in his readiness to listen to what the Spirit has to say to us. The connection between the Qur'an and the Wholly Other is "unique" in relation to the Christian Scriptures, with which the Qur'an cannot be identified. But just as de Chergé does not take a position on the place of Islam in the plan of God, except to say that he knows and believes that there is one—in the order of revelation—so it is with the Qur'an. Though the Qur'an has a "unique connection with the Wholly Other," for the time being it is impossible to specify the nature of this connection. The fact that we cannot know precisely the nature of this connection between the Qur'an and the Wholly Other, far from being a reason for discouragement, is an invitation to enter into the spiritual experience of reading it.

Intertextuality

There are many examples showing that Christian de Chergé read the Bible and the Qur'an together. There is, for instance, his commentary on the Bread of Life passage in chapter 6 of the Gospel of John in which de Chergé holds in the background the Quranic *surah* of the Table Spread with Food.[14] In the *surah*, the apostles

---

your heart" (*The Rule of Saint Benedict*, trans. Terrence G. Kardong [Collegeville, MN: Liturgical Press, 1996]).]

14. "The disciples said, 'O Jesus, Son of Mary, can your Lord send down to us a table [spread with food] from the heaven?' [Jesus] said, 'Fear Allah, if you should be believers.' They said, 'We wish to eat from it and let our hearts be reassured and know that you have been truthful to us and be among its witnesses.' Said Jesus, the son of Mary, 'O Allah, our Lord, send down to us a table [spread with food] from the heaven to be for us a [feast] for the first and the last of us and a sign from You. And provide for us, and You are the best of providers'" (*The Holy Qur'an*, Surah 5, 112–14; Saheeh International Version [Jeddah, Saudi Arabia, 1997]). ["Festival" altered to "feast." – Tr.]

make a request of Jesus, namely, that his Lord send down a table spread with food. They want assurances, but Jesus appeals to them to have faith. Jesus invokes God, asking him to send down a "table spread with food" to be "a feast" and "a sign." According to de Chergé in his commentary on the discourse on the Bread of Life in John 6, Jesus sees the lack of bread, that is to say, the insatiable hunger of the human heart and the human inability to satisfy that hunger. And the key to de Chergé's explication is borrowed from the *surah* by means of a subtle play on words: God *provides*. . . . He sees [*vide*] for [*pro*].[15] "Provide for us the necessities of life."

In this commentary de Chergé is explicating at one and the same time both the Quranic and the biblical text, thus explicating one by means of the other. He is not opposing the texts or demonstrating the superiority of one over the other. Nor is he comparing them, by highlighting in turn what each one says or by seeking out the originality of each. Neither is he looking for the unity underlying these two texts by focusing on how they can be shown to be saying the same thing in different ways. Instead, he makes them play off each other, so that one aids the reader in understanding the other, and vice versa.

De Chergé shows how a Christian can read the texts of another religious tradition. His way of reading reminds us that texts held sacred by other religious believers have something to tell us because of the relationship they may have to the Wholly Other. They do not bring a new revelation, which would be contrary to the Christian revelation, but they do allow us to read more deeply our own sacred texts. This way of reading has enormous significance for the way we relate to another religious tradition where we find the same typology: we can oppose religious traditions, we can try to compare them, we can search for what is original or specific to each, or we can search for their unity at the expense of their difference. But we can also establish a dialogic relationship among them and believe that each of us, from the heart of our own religious tradition, can be enriched by the encounter with the other.

15. [Tr. note: In French, the point of the play on words is obvious: "Dieu pourvoit. . . . Il voit pour."]

Thus, Christian de Chergé was making neither a Christian interpretation of the Quranic text nor a Quranic interpretation of the Christian text. He was letting the texts respond to each other. This way of proceeding is, strictly speaking, a genuine dialogue of the two Scriptures by which each one helps draw out the beauty and the meaning of the other.

Where did Christian de Chergé learn to read like this? The answer is obvious: in his monastic tradition. This way of reading is typical of *lectio divina*, particularly as it is practiced in the Cistercian tradition. This is what Saint Bernard did, following a great many Church fathers: he passed from one text to another, practicing a form of intertextuality within the biblical corpus. This method is the application of a traditional way of reading to texts belonging to another religious tradition. It is a truly Cistercian reading of the Qur'an.

A Word That Is One

What is the link between this Islamic scripture and the Word?

> The Word of God is present to Christians and Muslims as a viaticum, provisions for the crossing of the desert. The Scriptures are the treasure where the Christian loves to seek day and night for the new and the old. *Ausculta, o fili!*[16] "Listen, my son." As we have noted, these are the first words of the Rule of Saint Benedict. The Qur'an opens with the reciprocal command: *Iqra!* Recite! Every Muslim hears it as spoken to him- or herself. And so for Christians as well as for Muslims there begins one and the same Exodus beyond the letters engraved in stone.[17] "Incline the ear of your heart," adds Saint Benedict.[18]

16. [Tr. note: Compare Ps 1:2: "Happy are those who[se] . . . delight is in the law of the LORD, and on his law they meditate day and night"; Matt 13:52: "Therefore every scribe who has been trained for the kingdom of heaven is like the master of a household who brings out of his treasure what is new and what is old"; the Latin text of RB Prol 1: "*Obsculta, o fili, praecepta magistri, et inclina aurem cordis tui*" (Kardong, *Rule of St. Benedict*).]

17. [Tr. note: *la lettre figée*—"the fixed letter." Cf. 2 Cor 3:7.]

18. Christian de Chergé, "L'échelle mystique du dialogue" ["The Mystical Ladder of Dialogue"], *Islamochristiana* 23 (1997): 1–26, at 11.

De Chergé makes a distinction between Scripture and the Word. The Scriptures are different in the two traditions but the Word of God is offered to both. The Word is One. Thanks to this Word, both Christians and Muslims can make their life's journey, can make their exodus by crossing the desert. The Word is a "viaticum," a word used by Christians to speak of the Eucharist offered at the time of a Christian's final passover. How do we feed on this Word? For Christians, it is by dipping into the biblical Scriptures, this "treasure" where, according to Scripture itself, the promise is made that we will find "both new and old."[19] For Muslims, it is by listening to or reciting the Qurʾan. De Chergé does not use the term "scripture" here to describe the Qurʾan and is careful not to establish a symmetrical relationship between the Bible and the Qurʾan. Nevertheless, both texts have as their function to open us up to the Word that lies "beyond the letters engraved in stone." The Word does not appear in its immediacy to anyone. It reveals itself only to those who, having set out on the road for one and the same exodus, open their hearts to receive it beyond "the letters engraved in stone."

De Chergé admits that he has often experienced the Qurʾan as the Word: "Quite often I have seen arising from the Qurʾan, in the course of an initially difficult and disconcerting reading, a shortcut of the Gospel, as it were, which then becomes a true path of communion with the other and with God."[20] The verb "arise" suggests an event, an occurrence of the Word. The Word is always an event because "the Word is living," in the expression of the Letter to the Hebrews.[21] The term "arising" also evokes the resurrection. De Chergé suggests that this experience is frequent, as though it were a normal function of the Qurʾan to allow for the Word to arise. There is an opposition between the laborious effort of the reader of the Qurʾan, whose reading is described as "arduous and disconcerting," and the spontaneity of the Word that the reader "sees arising."

19. [Tr. note: Compare Matt 13:52.]
20. Christian de Chergé, "L'échelle mystique du dialogue," 11.
21. Heb 4:12.

If this interpretation is accurate, then we must conclude that, although Christian de Chergé does not reduce his reading to an interpretation of the Qur'an according to the Gospel, the Gospel remains his criterion of discernment for the reception and authentication of the Word of God through the Qur'an.

If we take note of the fact that for de Chergé the Qur'an can lead to an experience of an "arising" of the Word, then we should take a further step: "Could not the Risen Christ, who fulfills all the Scriptures, give a full meaning [*un sens plénier*] to that scripture, without in any way changing its face? Unthinkable, unless we approach the Qur'an with a heart that is poor and undefended, ready to listen to the traveler who has come from elsewhere, on the road to Emmaus."[22]

It is not the case that the New Testament fulfills the Old. Rather, the New Testament allows us to understand the Old, while the Old Testament, in its turn, allows us to understand the New. Scriptures are not fulfilled by other Scriptures. It is Christ, the Word of God incarnated in Jesus of Nazareth, who is the fulfillment of all the Scriptures, the Old as well as the New Testament. And if the risen Christ is indeed the fulfillment of all the Scriptures, could we not say along with Richard Caspar, "The Qur'an's emphasis on a truth about the mystery of God, God's unity and transcendence" does not oppose but rather "gives to the mystery of the incarnate God its full sense [*son plein sens*]"?[23] Christian de Chergé does not offer us a developed response. He is content to pose the question and to indicate a path that can bring us to an answer, the road to Emmaus to be traveled with "a heart that is simple and undefended."

And so we would move from the experience of a Word that is One for both Christians and Muslims, a viaticum for the exodus, by way of the Christian Scriptures and the reading of the Qur'an, to the fulfillment of the Scriptures, of all the Scriptures, by the risen Christ who would also give a fuller meaning [*sens plénier*] to the Qur'an.

22. "Chrétiens et musulmans: projet commun de société," in de Chergé, *L'invincible espérance*, 178.

23. Robert Caspar, *Pour un regard chrétien sur l'islam* [*Toward a Christian View of Islam*] (Paris: Bayard, 2006), 105.

The Oneness of the Word [*Verbe*]

Given that the experience of the Word [*Parole*] is common to
both traditions, may we not affirm that both the Bible and the
Qurʾan refer us to the One Word [*Verbe*]? "For all, the Word [*Verbe*]
is One." Both the Qurʾan and the Bible refer to the One Word
[*Verbe*] of God, though they do so in different ways. Christ is made
manifest as a theophany of the Word [*Verbe*] becoming incarnate
in a human nature like ours. "And the Word [*Verbe*] became flesh
and lived among us, and we have seen his glory, the glory as of
a father's only son, full of grace and truth" [John 1:14]. In Islam,
there is a theophany of the Word [*Verbe*] adopting a human language in the Qurʾan. "For all, the Word [*Verbe*] is One."

For Muslims, too, the Word [*Verbe*] is one. We find the parallel
statement: "If humankind and the *jinns* were to come together
to produce something like the Qurʾan, they would not produce
anything like it, even if they were to help each other."[24] The affirmation of the oneness of the Word [*Verbe*] exceeds the unique
affirmation peculiar to the Christian faith. In the Qurʾan the Word
of God [*Verbe de Dieu*] is one of the titles belonging to Jesus because he is the fruit of the creative Word [*Parole*] in the womb of
Mary.[25] "So on the one side, there is the Only Son. On the other, the
Book is one. Both participate in divine oneness without creating
plurality within God."[26] Christian de Chergé spoke of a double
theophany of the Word [*Verbe*]: in Christianity a theophany of
the Word [*Verbe*] that becomes incarnate in a humanity like our
own; and in Islam, a theophany of the Word [*Verbe*] in the human
language of the Qurʾan. For both, the Word [*Verbe*] is One.

The thought is bold and subtle. The incarnation of the Word
[*Verbe*] and the word [*parole*] of the Qurʾan are asymmetrical. We
must be careful to preserve this asymmetry. De Chergé spoke of
theophany in both cases, but in the case of the Qurʾan, he spoke of

24. *Surah* 17:88; "Chrétiens et musulman, nos differences," in de Chergé,
L'invincible espérance, 127.

25. Robert Caspar, *Traité de théologie musulmane*, vol. 2 (Rome: PISAI, 1987,
1989), 110.

26. Caspar, *Théologie musulmane*, 127.

adoption into a human language and not of incarnation. He avoided saying that the Word [*Verbe*] is incarnated in the Qur²an as the Word [*Verbe*] is incarnated in the Son. He established a symmetrical relationship neither between the incarnation of the Word [*Verbe*] according to Christian revelation and the theophany of the Word [*Verbe*] according to the Qur²an, nor one between the Bible and the Qur²an. De Chergé reached the very threshold of difference, but a difference that did not separate, for its meaning was grounded in the fact that for both Christians and Muslims, the Word [*Verbe*] is One.

And the Difference?

The difference is clearly stated, but "seeing things differently does not mean not seeing different things," and "to speak otherwise of God is not to speak of another God." This difference does not threaten unity; de Chergé was suspicious of any separatist tendency. He alerts us "to the danger that exists of coming into contradiction with God when an overly univocal conception of the ways of the One and Only leads people to denounce as impious any way of approaching divine difference other than the one their own faith privileges."[27] Difference is neither a pretext for denouncing the other nor an end in itself; it finds its end and fulfillment in the unity which is proclaimed and, most of all, "offered as a sign of the One." We will have more to say on this subject.

> Therefore we are going to leave behind, more or less, the familiar landscape of our religious certainties and the language in which we are used to expressing them in order to examine the Islamic tradition and above all the entire language [*parole*] of the Qur²an. We will have to re-examine the verses of the book where difference is proclaimed, sometimes severely denounced, yet more often offered as a sign of the Only One and even as a road toward Him "for those who understand."[28]

27. De Chergé, *L'invincible espérance*, 128.
28. "Nos différénces ont-elles le sens d'une communion?" ["Do Our Differences Have the Meaning of a Communion?"], in de Chergé, *L'invincible espérance*, 117.

Christian de Chergé introduces us to an inter-reading of the Qur'an and the Bible. He claims to have a genuine experience of the Word [*Parole*] that is an experience of the Oneness of the Word [*Verbe*]. Experience precedes reflection at the same time as it evokes it unceasingly, without ever bringing reflection to fixity or closure.

These few reflections on Christian de Chergé as reader of the Qur'an and on the place of the Qur'an in God's plan are undergirded by the question of revelation. Universal revelation, a vaster topic than biblical revelation, is, strictly speaking, the self-communication made by God to humankind since the beginning of time. God has not ceased to speak to humankind, to pursue with them "a varied and astonishing conversation,"[29] in the beautiful words of Paul VI, and this dialogue of salvation continues unceasingly within cultures and religions. Religions participate in this universal revelation. The God who makes God's self known within cultures does not fail to do so within religions too. Religions have a partial participation in the universal plan of salvation.

Biblical revelation is not therefore exclusive; instead, it brings out the full meaning of universal revelation. In it is found the culmination of all revelation, for "God spoke to our ancestors in many and various ways . . . but in these last days he has spoken to us by a Son" (Heb 1:1-2). In the Word made flesh all revelation finds its fulfillment: the risen Christ fulfills in his flesh all the Scriptures. This reflection upon Scripture and the Word leads us to ponder and meditate on the risen Christ, for "there is no other name under heaven given among mortals by which we must be saved" (Acts 4:12).

---

29. Paul VI, *Ecclesiam Suam* 72.

Chapter 7

A Greater Christ

One of the major problems raised in the theology of the encounter of religions is the question of the unique mediation of universal salvation by Christ. The Christian faith affirms that Christ is the sole mediator between God and humankind and the only Savior. Scripture says, "For there is one God; there is also one mediator between God and humankind, Christ Jesus, himself human, who gave himself a ransom for all" (1 Tim 2:5-6). Similarly, it affirms, "[T]here is no other name under heaven given among mortals by which we must be saved" (Acts 4:12). It must be admitted that many Christians have no clear idea what this means. What does it mean to be saved? Saved from what? What does it mean to say that Christ saved us? These legitimate and relevant questions are outside the scope of this study. Let us note simply that we have here a central affirmation of Christian faith. In other words, to renounce this affirmation would amount to a grave compromise of the Christian faith.

Now this affirmation collides with the fact that other world religions, including Islam, also present themselves as paths of salvation. Moreover, with Christian de Chergé we have been invited to believe that Islam has a particular place in the plan of God and to recognize in the Qurʾan a particular presence of God's Word [*Parole*]. Unless we deny, then, all meaning to other religions—their teachings, their rituals, their texts, and their practices—which would put us in contradiction with the Second Vatican Council, we are bound to say that in a certain way they participate in the plan of God who desires everyone to be saved. But, again, doesn't this recognition contradict the Christian affirmation of faith that Christ is the unique Savior? Can Christians claim to be in dialogue with other religions if Christians insist from the outset that Jesus is the only Savior? Are there not other mediations of salvation, perhaps other mediators?

It is a difficult question. If Christians hold firmly to their belief that Christ is the unique Savior, then we are still obliged to attempt an account of how all human beings in the history of humankind are saved by Jesus Christ when the incarnation took place in a particular moment of time, in a particular geographic location, and that many people are unaware of this historical fact.

This paradox has the potential to open a path to a broader, deeper, even different, understanding of Christ. People who set out on this path with faith and in the context of the Church will not fail to discover, through the Holy Spirit, an unexpected Christ, a "greater Christ" [*un Christ inattendu, un "Christ plus grand"*], a discovery that will transform their relationship with him.

We are at the very heart of the Christian faith here, and, as the International Theological Commission acknowledges, "Christianity's major difficulty has always been focused on the 'incarnation of God,' which confers upon the person and action of Jesus Christ the characteristics of uniqueness and universality with respect to the salvation of humanity."[1] How can the incarnation, a particular event inserted into history and therefore into what is relative, have universal scope? Is it possible for the Absolute to insert itself into the relativity of history? Theologians have tried to address this question. As one might suspect, the theological positions are diverse and are not always in alignment with the faith of the Church.[2]

---

1. *International Theological Commission*, vol. 2: *Texts and Documents 1986–2007*, ed. Michael Sharkey and Thomas Weinandy (San Francisco: Ignatius Press, 2009), 152.

2. Joseph Doré, "La présence du Christ dans les religions non-chrétiennes" ["The Presence of Christ in Non-Christian Religions"], *Chemins de dialogue* 9 (1997): 13–50.

Some, for example, affirm that Christ is certainly a mediator but explain that this mediation could have been performed in other times and places by other religious figures in the history of humanity. For them, Christ would be a mediator, and for Christians the greatest one, but still only one among others. Others credit Jesus Christ with a normative value, that it to say, they make him the ultimate reference. Others still, like Raimundo Panikkar, think that while Jesus is the Christ, the Christ is not Jesus.[3] This sentence is subject to various interpretations. It could mean that the Christ was incarnated in Jesus of Nazareth, but he could also have been incarnated in other individuals. This position relativizes the unique character of Jesus Christ, and so people speak of relativism with respect to the Christian faith. Or else it could mean that, although the Word of God was incarnated in the man Jesus of Nazareth, the Word was made manifest in many ways before being incarnated at a given point in time, as Scripture attests, "Before Abraham was, I am [*ego eimi*]" (John 8:58), and continues to manifest itself in the affirmation that "Christ is present in our midst." We do not intend to make an inventory of christological positions but simply to situate the theological context of Christian de Chergé's thought.[4]

As fundamental and as complex as the christological question may be, it is not unresolvable. Scripture shows that Christ is the Word by which all things were made: "All things came into being through him, and without him not one thing came into being" (John 1:2). He recapitulates everything in himself. He is the "New Man" (Eph. 2:15, NJB[5]). The Word is the Light "which

---

3. "Jesus is the Christ, but the Christ cannot be totally identified with Jesus" (Raimundo Panikkar, "A Christophany for Our Times," *Theology Digest* 39 [1992]: 9).

4. For elaboration of the various christologies, see, for instance, Monique Aebischer-Crettol, *Vers un oecuménisme interreligieux: jalons pour une théologie chrétiennes du pluralism religieux* [*Toward an Interreligious Ecumenism: Signposts for a Christian Theology of Religious Pluralism*], Cogitatio Fidei Series 221 (Paris: Cerf, 2001); and Jacques Dupuis, *Toward a Christian Theology of Religious Pluralism* (Maryknoll, NY: Orbis, 1997), 180–201.

5. [Tr. note: The Jerusalem Bible follows the French in using the masculine noun, which seems to make Salenson's point better. The NRSV uses the inclusive term "humanity."]

enlightens everyone . . . coming into the world" (John 1:9).[6] The Christian tradition early on declared that there are "seeds of the Word [*Verbe*]"[7] outside the visible boundaries of the Church, and thus Christ is also present, in a certain fashion, in other cultures and religions. Religions are inseminated by Christ. The Council of Quercy affirmed as early as 853 that "as no man is, or has been, or ever will be, whose nature will not have been assumed in Him [sc. Christ Jesus], so there is, has been, or will be no man, for whom He has not suffered."[8] The Second Vatican Council also stated, in the spirit of Saint Irenaeus, that the Son of God united himself with every person: "[W]e must hold that the Holy Spirit offers to all the possibility of being made partners, in a way known to God, in the paschal mystery."[9]

The christological question may not be unresolvable, but, beyond an exclusively theoretical answer, any satisfying resolution calls for a rigorous development and deepening of faith in Christ that goes beyond the necessarily limited idea that any single individual might have of Christ. This demand to go beyond in the area of Christology is not the least of the opportunities offered by religious diversity. "And who do you say that I am?" Christ never stops asking this question, unceasingly calling his Church and each of its members to see "where he lives."

What does Christian de Chergé have to say about this key question in the theology of religious encounter? In considering the similar question of the place of Islam in the plan of God we saw that the exclusion of a priori answers created an even greater opening for a quest in faith, by way of existential and spiritual

---

6. [Tr. note: The French Bible follows the older syntax; compare the KJV, in which "coming into the world" modifies "everyone"; in newer translations, such as the NRSV, it modifies "the light."]

7. *Saint Justin Martyr: The First and Second Apologies*, trans. Leslie William Barnard, Ancient Christian Writers Series 56 (Mahwah, NJ: Paulist Press, 1997), 1:46, 2:7.

8. In *The Sources of Catholic Dogma*, trans. Roy J. Deferrari (St. Louis, MO: B. Herder, 1957), 127.

9. *Gaudium et Spes* (Pastoral Constitution on the Church in the Modern World), December 7, 1965, 22.5.

dialogue, in faith, with Muslims and with Islam. The same holds true for faith in Christ.

De Chergé's entire Christology was restructured by his decision to take Islam seriously. For example, when he commissioned a crucifix for the monastery's chapel he gave precise specifications for its design. However many points of commonality there are between the Christian and Muslim faiths, the crucifix remains a stumbling block. According to Islam, Christ, though he was fixed upon the cross, did not die: "[T]hey did not kill him. They did not crucify him; it only appeared to them to be so."[10] We know that the most common explanation of this passage, though not the only one, states that there was a substitution for Jesus on the cross while God raised Jesus up to heaven. Sensitive to this Muslim interpretation, de Chergé chose to display on the cross, as was already done in the Roman era, a Christ already resurrected, through whom the glory of the Father was made manifest.[11]

This design was not a simple accommodation or from a desire not to shock, still less a way of passing over the Christian faith in silence. Rather, de Chergé's own meditation was shaped by the Christ of glory, more precisely, by the Christ of the ascension. Thus, without eliding the death of Christ on the cross, de Chergé demonstrates its deep meaning. One could make a similar point concerning the discussion de Chergé had with a Muslim friend about the cross, a discussion he recounted in a magnificent homily for the feast of the Triumph of the Cross:

> "And what about the cross?" I was asked this recently by one of our Sufi friends. "What if we were to talk about the cross?"
> "Which one?" I asked him.

---

10. Qurʾan, *Surah* 4:157. [Tr. note: This version is translated directly from the French text. The Saheeh International Version translates the latter part differently: "but [another] was made to resemble him to them."]

11. The original crucifix is found in the choir of the Abbey of Our Lady of Aiguebelle. It is a theology lesson in itself. Anne-Noëlle Clément undertook an exploration of the meaning of this icon; the results are found in her article, "La croix de Tibhirine" ["The Cross of Tibhirine"], published in *Chemins de dialogue* 24 (2004): 133–45.

"The cross of Jesus, obviously."

"Yes, but which one? When you see an image of Jesus on the cross, how many crosses do you see?"

He hesitated, then:

"Perhaps three. Two for sure. There is the one in front and the one behind."

"And which is the one that comes from God?"

"The one in front," he said.

"And which is the one that comes from men?"

"The one behind."

"And which is the more ancient?"

"The one in front. It's like this: men could not have invented the other except that God had already created the first."

"And what is the meaning of this cross in front, of this man with his arms outstretched?"

"When I stretch out my arms," he said, "it is in order to embrace, to love."

"And the other?"

"It is the instrument of love that is distorted and disfigured, of hatred fixing in death the gesture of life."

The Sufi friend had said: "Perhaps three?" This third cross, wasn't it I, wasn't it he, making the effort which drew both of us to separate ourselves from the cross "behind," the cross of evil and sin, in order to cling to the one "in front," the cross of victorious love?[12]

De Chergé will henceforth see the cross in a different light.

It is impossible, in light of that account, not to think differently of the way of the cross.[13] As we have seen, de Chergé did not grapple with theological questions in theoretical ways, and he did not take explicit positions in the debates current among theologians. Nevertheless, his writings reveal that he did have a definite point

---

12. "Homélie pour la fête de la croix glorieuse, 14 septembre 1993," in Bruno Chenu, ed., *Sept vies pour Dieu et l'Algérie* [*Seven Lives for God and Algeria*] (Paris: Bayard, 1996), 105; also in *L'autre que nous attendons, homélies du père Christian de Chergé (1970–1996)* [*The Other Whom We Await: Homilies of Fr. Christian de Chergé*], Les cahiers de Tibhirine (Montjoyer: Abbé d'Aiguebelle, 2006), 402.

13. Christian Salenson, *Prier 15 jours avec Christian de Chergé, prieur des moines de Tibhirine*, Praying 15 Days Series (Paris: Nouvelle Cité, 2006), 39–40.

of view, a personal response born of his openness to existential dialogue and of his spiritual experience. What follows here is an introduction to de Chergé's Christology, starting from several of his writings on Christ as mediator, and a suggestion of some consequences his approach might have for the Christian faith.

Affirmation of and Faith in the Salvific Mediation of Christ

In the *Testament*, de Chergé vigorously affirms the unique salvific mediation of Christ: "God willing, I will be able to immerse my gaze into that of the Father to contemplate with him his children of Islam, all shining with the glory of Christ."[14] This sentence synthesizes a great deal of de Chergé's thought and experience. Some remarks are called for. First of all, the expression "children of Islam" captures our attention. Muslims have a share in salvation not simply on an individual basis; it is precisely *as* "children of Islam" that they are saved. De Chergé is very careful to describe them as the "children" of Islam; they remain in the bosom of the Father, which implies the part the religion of Islam has in their salvation.

It is because they are in the bosom of the Father, illuminated by Christ and through his mediation, that Muslims' salvation is accomplished. Fundamentally, the children of Islam are saved by virtue of the mediation of Christ. They are not saved by virtue of belonging to their own religion, but neither are they saved outside of their religion, just as Christians are not saved by membership in their Christian religion, for there is one and only one salvific mediation, which is Christ, and that holds true also for Christians.

This allows us to clarify the question: are the different religions all paths of salvation? In a certain sense, no religion, from the point of view of Christian revelation, is a path of salvation, not even Christianity, for, again, there is only one "name by which we must be saved" (Acts 4:12). But it is necessary to add immediately that this salvation is not given independently of the

14. De Chergé, *L'invincible espérance*, 223.

religious tradition to which each person belongs. It is from this point of view that one can then say that religions are also, in a certain sense, paths of salvation.

De Chergé describes the mediation of Christ in terms of illumination: "All shining with Christ." The children of Islam are illuminated by the one and only Light, namely, Christ. When Christians recite the Nicene Creed, they say of Christ that he is "Light from Light." The reference to the prologue of the Gospel of John is clear: the Word [*Verbe*] is the true light "which illumines everyone coming into the world" (John 1:9).[15] *Everyone*, and so not only those who believe in Jesus Christ. The One Light, who is Christ, embraces all religions and all cultures.

To this illumination by Christ is added a brief phrase: "fruit of his passion." The saved children of Islam are the fruits of the passion of Christ. This affirmation reinforces further the uniqueness of the mediation of Christ. The theme of illumination pointed us to the Word of God and to the prologue of the Gospel of John. It is impossible to dissociate this approach to Christ, Word of God, from his incarnation in Jesus of Nazareth and the event of the cross.

Salvation in Christ is rendered effective by the gift of the Spirit. The children of Islam, illuminated by the glory of Christ, are "filled with the gift of the Spirit." "They have been given the gift of the Spirit just as we have been," says the apostle Peter of his experience in his meeting with the God-fearer Cornelius (Acts 10). This experience is ongoing; it is lived by all the apostles of all times, no matter what their states of life or their vocations. All who risk themselves in the encounter with the other, "taking nothing for their journey" (Mark 6:8), discover that the gift of the Spirit has been given to others as well as to them. It is by the gift of the Spirit that fills the heart of every person that one can let oneself be transformed in Christ, for "the Word of God takes bodily form in the shadow of the Spirit."[16]

---

15. [Tr. note: This version follows the Latin Vulgate. See n. 6 above.]

16. Chapter talk for October 27, 1986, in *Dieu pour tout jour, chapitres du père Christian de Chergé à la communauté de Tibhirine (1985–1996)* [*God for Each Day: Chapter Talks of Fr. Christian de Chergé to the Community of Tibhirine*], 2nd ed., Les cahiers de Tibhirine (Montjoyer: Abbé d'Aiguebelle, 2006), 144.

So salvation in Christ is to be understood in a trinitarian perspective: filled with the Spirit, illuminated by Christ, existing in the gaze of the Father. Thus Christian de Chergé witnesses to his faith when he writes, "And the believer—I am thinking of the Muslim—who turns toward God with all his fervor, and who no longer wants anything except what God wants, with a heart that is surrendered and free at the same time—this believer is led by the Spirit to the Son, to the place of the Son, even if he does not know it."[17] Clearly de Chergé is thinking of his friend Mohammed, who was configured to Christ—"in the place of Christ"—in the gift he made of his life.

"My Most Burning Curiosity Will Be Set Free"

This sentence from the *Testament* precedes the one just commented on: "My most burning [*lancinante*] curiosity will be set free. This is what I shall be able to do, God willing: contemplate his children of Islam." It is the Father's will that the salvation of the children of Islam is by Christ's mediation. This is an object of Christian faith. According to de Chergé it cannot be apprehended as the result of scholarly reasoning. We must believe without seeing, and believing creates the desire to see. De Chergé expresses this desire to see as his wanting "to immerse one's gaze." The universal mediation of Christ is an object of faith. As such, it must be embraced both by those who might be tempted by relativism as they think of other possible mediations besides Christ (a relativism against which the magisterium rightly puts us on guard) and by those who hold aloof from the encounter between religions, finding the project naïve and idealistic. Both positions betray a lack of faith in the mediation of Christ.

---

17. Chapter talk for June 6, 1992, in de Chergé, *Dieu pour tout jour*, 398. The reader will recognize here an echo of Karl Rahner and of Justin Martyr: "And those who lived with the *logos* are Christians, even though they have been thought atheists: as, among the Greeks, Socrates and Heraclitus, and people like them; and among the gentiles, Abraham, and Ananias" (Justin Martyr, *The First Apology*, 46).

All Peoples Are United in the Heart of Christ

What de Chergé says in his *Testament* about the children of Islam must be broadened to include other religions and all cultures. The "children of Islam" are in the gaze of the Father, illuminated by Christ, and filled with the Spirit, but also "all peoples are united in the heart of Christ." The verb tense is the present indicative. Right now all peoples are united in the heart of the Father, even though this mystery remains hidden and can be glimpsed only in faith and a hope correctly understood. "Let the peoples praise you, O God; let all the peoples praise you" (Ps 67:3).

This cultural broadening that characterized Christian de Chergé's approach to religion is important for the theology of religious encounter. Dialogue with Islam was a part of de Chergé's vocation, but his belonging to the culture of Algeria was equally decisive for his calling. Just as there is always a risk of reducing universal Christian revelation to biblical revelation, forgetting that God has spoken to humankind since the beginning, so also there is a great risk of thinking that revelation can be confused with the history of religions. For Christian de Chergé, God's self-revelation is not limited to the religious history of human beings. It extends to the entire history of the human race. De Chergé put this belief to the test in the covenant that bound him to Algeria. "I would like my community . . . to remember that my life was given to God and to [Algeria]," he reminds us in his *Testament*. "The unity of all peoples in the heart of Christ seems still more obvious when we commit ourselves loyally to listening to another people." We will return to this aspect when we speak of the Church. Those who keep vigil in hope, the eschatological watchers, must live and experience this unity of all peoples in Christ. One of the charisms of the monastic life is presence to all the peoples of the earth, including "the house of Islam," because the aim of monasticism is to signify that already in Christ the praise of all the peoples is rising toward God. Each monastery can do this only by "committing itself loyally to listening" to a people. The unity of all peoples in the praise rising toward the Father is an eschatological sign and, as such, it is a sign manifested in a privileged way by the monastic life.

Faith in the present unity of all peoples in the heart of Christ, together with the hope born of that faith, go hand in hand with the understanding of the Church's mission advanced by Vatican II and its recognition of the sacramental nature of the Church. We will to return to this topic later.

Which Christology?

As we have tried to demonstrate, Christian de Chergé was deeply committed to his belief in the mediation of Christ. How did he express his understanding of this mystery? Again, the easiest thing is to start with a significant quotation, one we have already commented upon in the preceding chapter: "Christ is received as a theophany of the Word becoming incarnate in a humanity similar to our own. In Islam, there is also a theophany of the Word adopting a human language in the Qur'an. For all, the Word is One."[18]

In a word, de Chergé's Christology is essentially a Christology of the incarnate Word: the Word is incarnate in the man Jesus. De Chergé speaks more often about the incarnation than he does about the resurrection, and when he speaks of the resurrection, he privileges the image of the ascension. But the incarnation is the focal point of his Christology. The incarnation of the Word in Jesus of Nazareth fulfills all the manifestations of the Word in history. De Chergé echoes the Letter to the Hebrews: "Long ago God spoke to our ancestors in many and various ways" (Heb 1:1). It is well known that the fathers of the Church favored this Christology of the *Logos*. The Christology of de Chergé is prefigured in an early creed, a Credo before the Credo, found in Irenaeus of Lyon:

> The Word of God, the Son of God, Christ Jesus our Lord, was shown forth by the prophets . . . according to the manner in which the Father disposed, and through Him were made all things whatsoever. He also, in the end of times, for the recapitulation of all things, is become a man.[19]

18. See above, p. 74.
19. Irenaeus, *Proof of the Apostolic Preaching*, trans. Joseph P. Smith, Ancient Christian Writers Series 16, ed. Johannes Quasten and Joseph C. Plumpe (Westminster, MD: The Newman Press; London: Longmans, Green & Co, 1952), 51.

In Islam, there is also a Word [*Verbe*]. There is, then, a theophany of the Word [*Verbe*] in both Islam and Christian revelation. But although there is theophany of the Word in both, in Christianity this theophany of the Word is "incarnation" into a humanity like ours. This is not the case in Islam. De Chergé does not confuse the *manifestation* of the Word with its *incarnation*, nor does he separate them, for incarnation, which is a manifestation of the Word, fulfills and "recapitulates" all other manifestations. But the incarnation of the Christ in Jesus of Nazareth is not the only divine manifestation of the Word. "The Word is handed over to the many, and it is the work of the Spirit to watch over this seed at work in our hearts."[20] The incarnation of the Word in Jesus of Nazareth is not the end: "The goal and the very meaning of the Incarnation is not primarily [*n'est pas d'abord*] that the Word should become flesh, but that our flesh should be brought into the divine milieu of the Word."[21] Note the influence of Teilhard de Chardin: the expression "divine milieu" is directly borrowed from him.

The Greater Christ [*Le Christ plus grand*]

Christ is therefore greater than what Christians might believe they have grasped of him. Two extremely important quotations, deliberately chosen by de Chergé, offer an entry point into his thought. One is from the Second Vatican Council: "The Lord is the goal of human history, the focal point of the desires of history and civilization, the center of mankind, the joy of all hearts, and the fulfillment of all aspirations."[22] The other is from Teilhard de Chardin: "I believe that the Church is still a child. Christ, by whom she lives, is immeasurably greater than she imagines."[23] Both quotations are Teilhardian. The thought of Teilhard de Chardin influenced the conciliar document; it also without question influenced Christian de Chergé. It can be surmised that the Christol-

20. Homily for August 2, 1994, in *L'autre que nous attendons*.
21. Homily for July 19, 1994, in *L'autre que nous attendons*.
22. *Gaudium et Spes*, 45.2.
23. Pierre Teilhard de Chardin, "On My Attitude to the Official Church," in *The Heart of Matter*, trans. René Hague (London: Collins, 1978), 117–18. Quoted by de Chergé , "L'échelle mystique du dialogue," 8.

ogy of Teilhard de Chardin, of considerable originality within its twentieth-century context, allowed and encouraged de Chergé to move toward a Christology of the *Logos*.[24]

Teilhard de Chardin worked out his Christology in the context, even under the constraint, of his scientific thinking, challenged by contemporary scientific thinking on the evolution of the world and of its species. In taking up the challenge, Teilhard de Chardin was led to develop a Christology of the "Cosmic Christ."[25]

De Chergé did his thinking with Islam constantly on his mind and in his heart. The conception of Christ he developed necessarily was influenced by his cultural horizon. He found in Teilhard de Chardin the encouragement and the opening he needed. To be sure, Christian de Chergé made little reference to the Cosmic Christ of Teilhard de Chardin, but, like Teilhard de Chardin, he had an understanding of Christ as the Universal Christ. The Christ of de Chergé was always a universal Christ with a mystical body whose outlines were never fully drawn. Thus the ascension is of central importance. Christ appears as "an elevated Christ, higher than all universes, and an extended Christ, expanding to the ends of the earth, a double movement revealed in the crucifix, turned toward the Father and handed over to the multitude."[26] This conception of Christ is a far cry from a reduction to what Teilhard de Chardin called a "little classroom Christ."[27] Christian de Chergé expressed his Christology in a formulation that is synthetic and so suggestive that Teilhard de Chardin would not deny it: "God is greater, *Allah Akbar*. Christ is also greater, inconceivably greater," he wrote, commenting on Matthew 11:27 ("No one knows the Son except the Father"). The affinity between Teilhard de Chardin

24. The "greater Christ" is a quotation from Teilhard de Chardin found in "L'échelle mystique du dialogue," published in 1989. But the "greater Christ" already appears in de Chergé's correspondence in 1979: "The Other calls me to see God and his Christ as greater," an unpublished letter to a friend, September 2, 1979.

25. Gustave Martelet, *Teilhard de Chardin: prophète d'un Christ toujours plus grand* [*Prophet of an Ever Greater Christ*] (Brussels: Lessius, 2005), 40.

26. Homily for Ascension Day, in *L'autre que nous attendons*, 367.

27. "Un petit Christ d'école"; Gustave Martelet, *Teilhard de Chardin*, 56.

and de Chergé—an affinity not so much of thought, since their cultural horizons were different, but of willingness to be open to a radical cultural or religious difference—is found in other areas as well, such as the understanding of the Eucharist, eschatology, and the communion of saints.

The Christology of Christian de Chergé, like that of Teilhard de Chardin, is a Christology of the incarnate Word. As such, it is unique in the context of the christologies of the latter half of the twentieth century that have, overall, emphasized the person of Jesus. In Joseph Moingt's remarkable work on Christology, particularly in the preface to the first volume, *L'homme qui venait de Dieu*,[28] the author gives a very interesting account of his personal journey, one that perfectly describes the transmutation in Christology in the last century. Moingt relates what a radical change it was for him to move from a Christology of the incarnate Word, which he was heir to, to a Christology giving priority to the person of Jesus of Nazareth, a shift he unhesitatingly describes as a deconstruction of the Christology of the incarnate Word toward a reconstruction of a Christology based on the man Jesus and his message.

But now, paradoxically, we are in the presence of another Christological approach, one that was made necessary for Teilhard de Chardin by his cultural context and for de Chergé by his involvement in the encounter with Islam. Teilhard de Chardin and de Chergé were, to a certain extent, each exceptions, but both too, though in different ways, were in unique cultural situations. Each was obligated to swim against the stream of the theological reflection of their respective eras as they thought through their faith to reclaim a Christology of the incarnate Word. (The same could be said of Raimundo Panikkar who continued to hope for a Christology less exclusively Western to respond to the challenge of Asian culture.[29])

---

28. Joseph Moingt, *L'homme qui venait de Dieu* [*The Man Who Came from God*], Cogitatio Fidei Series 200 (Paris, Cerf, 1993), 7–20.

29. Raimundo Panikkar, *Christophanie pour notre temps* (Arles: Éditions Actes sud, 2001); *La plénitude de l'homme* (Arles: Éditions Actes sud, 2007).

Religious diversity compels us to reexamine our Christology and perhaps even to advance beyond its current state. Without sacrificing any of the benefits of the christological reflection of the twentieth century with its emphasis on Jesus of Nazareth, the universality of the mediation of Christ calls for a new stage in thought. In his fine book on Teilhard de Chardin, with its title relevant to our concerns, *Teilhard de Chardin, prophète d'un Christ toujours plus grand* [*Teilhard de Chardin, Prophet of an Ever Greater Christ*], Gustave Martelet says that what "we need today to recognize about the mystery of Christ [is] its immensity, lest we see it unjustly marginalized."[30] Jean-Marc Aveline raised the same question in his work on the issue of Christology in the theology of world religions, in particular in his conclusion and his critical evaluation of the thought of Paul Tillich.[31] The experience of Christian de Chergé and his theological thought confirm this need, if the preceding remarks are correct. This is one of the contributions of Christian de Chergé to the theology of religious encounter. It is time to raise again the question of the contemporary relevance of the traditional *Logos* Christology. Perhaps we need to draw once more on the patristic writings on the *Logos*.[32] Here, for instance, is what Origen had to say:

> What is our Savior? He is the brightness of God's glory. It is not that the brightness of His glory was once for all [*hapax*] generated and is now generated no more, but just as light produces brightness, so is the brightness of God's glory generated. . . . If then the Savior is continually being generated . . . the Savior is continually being begotten of the Father. Likewise, if you too have the spirit of sonship, God continually begets you in Him, in every deed, in every thought, and so

30. Gustave Martelet, *Teilhard de Chardin*, 57.

31. Jean-Marc Aveline, *L'enjeu christologique en théologie des religions* [*The Issue of Christology in the Theology of Religions*] (Paris: Cerf, 2003).

32. Michel Fédou, *La voie du Christ: genèses de la christologie dans le contexte religieux de l'antiquité au début du IVe siècle* [*The Way of Christ: Origins of Christology in the Religious Context of Antiquity to the Beginning of the Fourth Century*], Cogitatio Fidei Series 253 (Paris: Cerf, 2006).

begotten you come to be a continually begotten son of God in
Christ Jesus.[33]

Consequences

Now it is time to draw out the implications of a universal mediation of Christ founded on a theology of the incarnate Word.
It is not enough to say that the mediation of Christ extends to
the children of Islam and leave it at that. It remains necessary to
work out the consequences of this universal mediation of Christ
for Christians. It is not enough to say, correct though it is, that we
must not relativize the Christian faith and so affirm the universal mediation of Christ. We must go further, which is to say, as
Church, we must accept a face of Christ that comes to us precisely
through this universal mediation across cultures and religions.

First Consequence: Receiving the Christ of Islam

Given that salvific mediation operates within Islam, and given
that Christians cannot claim to know everything about the Christ
who transcends religious boundaries, Christians must receive
also the Christ of Islam. What does it mean to receive the Christ
of Islam? Certainly, it means to receive with good will what the
Qurʾan says about Christ: "I am sure that the Christ of the Qurʾan
has something to do with the Christ of our faith," says de Chergé.[34]
It is also necessary to receive what Islam as lived and practiced
can tell us about Christ: "In order to enrich our partial knowledge
in this moment, we need what others can add through what they
are, what they do, and what they believe."[35]

But in order to be able to receive Christ from another religious
tradition, we Christians must willingly live the paschal mystery

33. Origen, "In Jerem. Hom." ["Homily on Jeremiah"], 4. 4; *Selections from
the Commentaries and Homilies of Origen*, trans. R. B. Tollinton (London: SPCK;
NY and Toronto: Macmillan, 1929), 23–24, altered.

34. Unpublished correspondence, letter of July 4, 1981.

35. Christian de Chergé, "Pour un projet commun de société," in de Chergé,
L'invincible espérance, 174.

from our understanding of Christ. Like the apostles, we must be willing to lose Christ, the knowledge we have of him, and then to find him again. "We must lose Christ, let him die in the humanity so much like ours in which we have clothed and sometimes disguised him [*maquillé*], in order to let him be reborn, other and yet identical, in this surplus of humanity, in which our place is marked out, and the other's also."[36] Our knowledge of Christ is partial; if it is absolutized, it becomes constricting. "In order to enter in truth into dialogue, we will have to accept, in the name of Christ, that Islam has something to tell us on behalf of Christ."[37]

Second Consequence: Receiving Islam from Christ

Christ helps us to understand Islam. De Chergé is not afraid to write that the Son is the only true Muslim, for he was nothing but "Yes" to the will of the Father. In the words of the apostle Paul, "For the Son of God, Jesus Christ, whom we proclaimed among you, Silvanus and Timothy and I, was not 'Yes and No'; but in him it is always 'Yes.' For in him every one of God's promises is a 'Yes'" (2 Cor 1:19-20). For Islam, true religion is, at its core, this primordial obedience that constitutes the eternal covenant between God and humankind. This is why the Qur'an says, "Religion in the sight of Allah is Islam" (*Surah* 3:19).

> Here we are in the heart of Islam. Humankind entered into religion through this "Yes" which was at the prelude to their history, which made them, through their entire being, worshippers of the ways of God. . . . It is exactly here that we have to allow the whole of Jesus' life to breathe gently, in order to detect the echo of worship that characterizes humanity: he was only "Yes" to God [2 Cor 1:19].[38]

Thus, with great audacity and assurance, de Chergé uttered this formula, which Muslims do not contest: "Christ is the only Muslim" because he was only "Yes" to God. But in recognizing this,

36. Unpublished correspondence, letter of June 7, 1981.
37. Unpublished correspondence, letter of June 12, 1981.
38. [Quotation not attributted in original. – Ed.]

de Chergé recognized the validity of what he calls "the heart of Islam," and he reveals its relevance for Christianity by recalling the words of the apostle Paul. So Christ not only is the only Muslim but also, by acting thus, fulfills Islam by his total obedience. He exercises fully his universal mediation. Christians and Muslims can jointly recognize themselves as called to this fidelity to the ways of God. Assuredly, this "Yes" constitutes one of the rungs common to both Muslims and Christians on the mystical ladder.

Christ, the one mediator, is the mediator of the prayer of Islam. De Chergé confesses that as a disciple of Christ, "I have a vocation to unite myself to Christ, through whom every prayer rises, and who offers to the Father, mysteriously, this prayer of Islam along with the prayer of every upright heart."[39] We will return to this topic of the mediation of prayer.

39. Chapter talk for November 28, 1989, in de Chergé, *Dieu pour tout jour*, 304.

Chapter 8

Communion of Saints and Community

Once positive consideration is given to other religions and it is recognized that religions have a place in the plan of God, this question arises: what is the mission of the Church in such a situation? Questions of ecclesiology are the objects of numerous reflections on the part of theologians involved in religious encounter. The magisterium has intervened several times, in particular in conciliar documents[1] and encyclicals[2] or, again, in the declaration of the Congregation for the Doctrine of the Faith, *Dominus Iesus*.[3]

A Brief Review of Some Ecclesiological Questions

A Christian theology of religious encounter is duty-bound to consider the Church's own mission in the Father's salvific plan,

---

1. Obviously, the document *Nostra Aetate* (Declaration on the Relation of the Church to Non-Christian Religions), October 28, 1965, but also *Lumen Gentium* (Dogmatic Constitution on the Church), November 21, 1964, paragraph 16, and *Gaudium et Spes* (Pastoral Constitution on the Church in the Modern World), December 7, 1965, especially paragraph 22.

2. In particular, Paul VI, *Ecclesiam Suam*, and John Paul II, *Redemptoris Missio*.

3. Congregation for the Doctrine of the Faith, "Declaration '*Dominus Iesus*' on the Unicity and Salvific Universality of Jesus Christ and the Church," 2000.

while leaving open the question of the mission of other religions and of Judaism in particular. Frequently when the question of "the mission of the Church" has been addressed, it has been as though the Church alone had received a mission, forgetting even the vocation of Israel and its role in history. This forgetting distorts Christians' understanding of the unique mission of the Church.

The Church is ordered in its entirety to the plan of salvation. It is the universal salvific will of the Father that determines the particular place of the Church in the mission of salvation. The Second Vatican Council took great care to place the mission of the Church within the trinitarian mission: the plan of the Father and the mission of the Son and that of the Spirit.[4] Faithful to the tradition, it affirmed the necessity of the Church for salvation, and without denying the adage *extra ecclesiam nulla salus,* "outside the Church there is no salvation," *Dominus Iesus* restored its proper meaning, stepping back from the exclusivist interpretation of the Council of Florence in 1442.[5] In the words of the International Theological Commission:

> One speaks of the necessity of the Church for salvation in two senses: the necessity of belonging to the Church for those who believe in Jesus, and the necessity, for salvation, of the ministry of the Church which, on mission from God, must be at the service of the coming of the kingdom of God.[6]

The nature of the Church is to be missionary; hence, the understanding of mission has consequences for the understanding of the mystery of the Church. The Church no longer recognizes itself in the definition of Robert Bellarmine, who thought that the Church

---

4. The term "mission" was not applied to the Church until the modern era. This word has been traditionally reserved for the mission of God, as Karl Barth reminded his audience in the lecture "Theology of Mission at the Present Time," *Les cahiers du monde non-chrétien* 4 (1932).

5. "Decree for the Jacobites," Council of Florence (1442); *The Sources of Catholic Dogma,* 230.

6. International Theological Commission, "Christianity and the World Religions" (1997), 65, http://www.vatican.va/roman_curia/congregations/cfaith/cti_documents/rc_cti_1997_cristianesimo-religioni_en.html.

was like the republic of Venice,[7] an organized and hierarchical society. Moreover, there was a time when the documents of the magisterium, in particular *Mystici Corporis*,[8] practically identified the Catholic Church with the Church that is the Body of Christ, but the pure and simple identification of the two would obviously make impossible any ecumenical initiative and all interreligious dialogue. Therefore, desirous of promoting the cause of ecumenism, the council fathers, in the dogmatic constitution *Lumen Gentium*, decided to emphasize the notion of the People of God.[9] They did not by any means set aside the image of the Body of Christ, but the notion of the People of God allowed them to disengage from the improper restriction of the term "Church of Christ" to "the Catholic Church," thus opening up the position of previous magisterial documents.[10]

The dogmatic constitution on the Church, *Lumen Gentium*, affirms that non-Christians are ordered, in their own manner, to the one People of God. The distinction among different groups is noteworthy. In the first place are the Jews; in the second place, the Muslims. The fact that the council reserves a particular place for the Muslims helps give a privileged place to Islamic-Christian dialogue, though one not comparable to Jewish-Christian dialogue, given that Jewish revelation is constitutive of Christian faith. Next come those who do not know the Gospel of Christ and who do not know the Church and, finally, those who do not know God. These distinctions are not merely concentric circles,[11]

7. [Tr. note: "The Church is an association of men which is just as visible and tangible as the association of the Roman people or the kingdom of France or the Republic of Venice" (*De Controversiis Christianae Fidei* [1588], 2.3.2). The translation is found in Avery Dulles, *Models of the Church* (New York: Doubleday, 1987), 16.]

8. *Mystici Corporis* [*Christi*] [*The Mystical Body of Christ*], an encyclical promulgated by Pius XII in 1943.

9. See Maurice Vidal, *Cette Église que je cherche à comprendre, Entretiens avec Christian Salenson et Jacques Tessier* [*This Church Which I Seek to Understand, Conversations with Christian Salenson and Jacques Tessier*], Publications Chemins de dialogue (Marseilles: Éditions de l'Atelier, 2008).

10. Specifically, *Mystici Corporis*.

11. An image used in *Ecclesiam Suam*, 96ff.

for that would display a fundamentally ecclesiocentric understanding.[12] This way of understanding the ordering of the rest of
humankind to the unique People of God is not grounded in vary-
ing degrees of membership in the Church; rather, it is grounded
in the universal call to salvation, a call that includes the vocation
to the unity of a unique People of God that transcends the visible
boundaries of the Church.

Gaudium et Spes puts its own stamp upon the question. It de-
clares forcefully that everyone, in a manner known to God, is
associated with the paschal mystery. This being the case,

> when non-Christians, justified by means of the grace of God,
> are associated with the paschal mystery of Jesus Christ, they
> are also associated with the mystery of his body, which is the
> Church. The mystery of the Church in Christ is a dynamic real-
> ity in the Holy Spirit. Although the visible expression of be-
> longing to the Church is lacking to this spiritual union,
> justified non-Christians are included in the Church, "the Mys-
> tical Body of Christ" and "a spiritual community" [*Lumen
> Gentium* 8].[13]

Hence, non-Christians are related to the unique People of God on
several accounts; by living in the paschal mystery, they participate
"in a manner known to God" in the Mystical Body of Christ. As
for the visible Church, its vocation is to be a universal sacrament
of salvation.

We set aside the debates that have gone on, especially provoked by the document *Dominus Iesus* and, more recently, by the
document of the Congregation for the Doctrine of the Faith on
the oneness of the Church of Christ and its relation to the Roman
Catholic Church, concerning the interpretation of the council's
phrase *subsistit in*.[14] The question of the phrase's interpretation

---

12. Maurice Vidal, "Dialogue au coeur de la mission: perspectives ec-
clésiologiques d'*Ecclesiam suam*," *Chemins de dialogue* 4 (1994): 49–63.

13. "Christianity and the World Religions," 72.

14. The phrase appears in *Lumen Gentium*, 8; see also Congregation for
the Doctrine of the Faith, "Responses to Some Questions Regarding Certain Aspects of the Doctrine on the Church," official English translation

is the question of the status of other churches.[15] The council must always be interpreted in terms of the will of the council fathers. The council fathers affirmed that the Church of Christ *subsists in* the Catholic Church, taking care, motivated by a deliberately ecumenical concern, not to restrict the Church of Christ to the Catholic Church. As regards the theology of the encounter of religions, all the current debates highlight the necessity of the notion of the People of God preferred by the council, even if this notion cannot on its own do justice to the totality of the mystery of the Church.

Another aspect of the issue merits particular attention. It concerns the *kingdom of God* and the progressive distinction in magisterial documents between the Church and the kingdom of God.[16] This distinction is clear in the encyclical *Redemptoris Missio*: the Church is in the service of the kingdom, which it announces and in which it is itself also a participant. "The Church is not itself its own end, for it is ordered to the Kingdom of God of which it is seed, sign and instrument. While it is distinct from Christ and the Kingdom, the Church is indissolubly united to both."[17]

Ecclesiological questions are complex and necessary in the theology of religions, but in return, the theology of religions demands an ecclesiology equal to the challenges raised by the encounter with other believers and their religious traditions and that would lead the Church to define precisely its unique ministry.

---

available from the Vatican web site, http://www.vatican.va/roman_curia/congregations/cfaith/documents/rc_con_cfaith_doc_20070629_responsa-quaestiones_en.html.

15. Notable in this connection is the exchange of correspondence between the Metropolitan Damaskinos and Cardinal Joseph Ratzinger: Joseph Ratzinger, *Faire route avec Dieu, l'Église comme communion* [*On a Journey with God: Church as Communion*] (Les Plans-sur-Bex, Switzerland: Éditions Parole et Silence, 2003), a translation of *Weggemeinschaft: Kirche als Kommunio* (Augsburg: Sankt Ulrich, 2002).

16. Jacques Dupuis gives his reading of the evolution of the relation between the Church of Rome and the kingdom of God in *Toward a Christian Theology of Religious Pluralism* (Maryknoll, NY: Orbis, 1997), 333–42.

17. John Paul II, *Redemptoris Missio*, 18.

The Ecclesiology of Christian de Chergé

What is the ecclesiology of Christian de Chergé? The following quotation can set the stage for our discussion: "The consecrated community is by vocation a sign of communion: of the communion in the Church, of the communion of the whole people of God dedicated, in Christ, to appearing as an evolving mystery, the mystery of the communion of saints, in which it will disappear as the stream loses itself in the ocean."[18] Christian de Chergé distinguishes two levels of the Church: the ecclesial community, which can take various organizational forms, and the communion of saints. We have mentioned above the importance of the notion of the People of God for Vatican II. What de Chergé calls "the communion of saints" is close to what the council means by the expression "People of God." He says: "The . . . whole people of God" is "an evolving mystery, the mystery of the communion of saints." His favorite term for speaking of the Church is "the communion of saints," but with de Chergé the term has undergone a transformation with respect to the classical definition as it is understood by Vatican II: the communion between the heavenly Church and the earthly Church.[19] Because the concept of the communion of saints is key in the thought of Christian de Chergé, it is through this concept that we shall gain entry into the mystery of the Church.

The Communion of Saints

We must return again to Mohammed. His death revealed to Christian de Chergé the mystery made present of the communion of saints. Christian de Chergé said that with this event he "began a pilgrimage toward the communion of saints where Christians and

---

18. Chapter talk for 19 January, 1995, in Christian de Chergé, *Dieu pour tout jour, chapitres du père Christian de Chergé à la communauté de Tibhirine (1985–1996)* [*God for Each Day: Chapter Talks of Fr. Christian de Chergé to the Community of Tibhirine*], 2nd ed., Les cahiers de Tibhirine (Montjoyer: Abbé d'Aiguebelle, 2006), 512.

19. *Lumen Gentium* 49–50.

Muslims, and so many others along with them, share the same joy of sons and daughters." For de Chergé Mohammed was the ever-present sign of this: "For I know that I am able to place firmly at this destination of my hope at least one Muslim, that beloved brother, who lived up to the moment of his death the imitation of Jesus Christ. And every Eucharist makes him infinitely present to me in the reality of the Body of Glory where the gift of his life took on its full dimension 'for me and for the many.' "[20] Besides, one and the same faith in the communion of saints unites Christians and Muslims, and that is one of the reasons why de Chergé favored this notion. "This final mystery, of primary importance to us, points out the place of meeting without indicating the way that leads there." Thus, both Christians and Muslims must allow themselves to be led by this common faith: "Thus we let ourselves be moved, and the Spirit of Jesus remains free to do its work among us, making use of our differences, even those that shock us. We recognize the Spirit working. We receive from prolonged silent prayer, side by side, notably with our Sufi friends, a feeling of fulfillment, all the more trustworthy for being known as deeply shared. God knows it much better than we do."[21]

The communion of saints defines the Church as a Mystical Body or the People of God. In his reflection on the Church, de Chergé started from the vision of the book of Revelation: "I saw the holy city, the new Jerusalem, coming down out of heaven from God" (Rev 21:2). He did not start with a notion of the Church as a sociological or historical reality. The Church is the assembly of those called by Christ, the Mystical Body, the spiritual community. It is the heavenly Jerusalem "in which everyone was born" (Ps 87:5).[22] The Church is "the community which the Eternal gathers to himself." Yet it is impossible reductively to identify "the

20. Christian de Chergé, "Prier en Église à l'écoute de l'Islam" ["Praying as Church While Listening to Islam"], *Chemins de dialogue* 27 (2006): 19.
21. Christian de Chergé, *Sept vies pour Dieu et l'Algérie* [*Seven Lives for God and Algeria*], ed. Bruno Chenu (Paris: Bayard, 1996), 72.
22. [Tr. note: "Everyone" follows the French translation of the Bible de Jérusalem.]

community which the Eternal gathers to himself" with the Church or the Jewish people or the Muslim *Umma.*

> Faced with the constant temptation to reduce the community which the Eternal gathers to himself to those congregations which our temples, made with human hands, manage to collect for better or worse, Jews, Christians, or Muslims, we will need always to enter into the vaster design which continually explodes the paltry boundaries of our quick exclusions and our intransigences; for truly God "desires everyone to be saved" [1 Tim 2:4].[23]

The liturgical feast of the Church preferred by de Chergé, even more than Pentecost, was the Solemnity of All Saints. We possess five homilies of his for All Saints.

> We are a people on the move between heaven and earth, astonished to discern this evolution of communion whose web the Holy Spirit is weaving among all people; for all, absolutely all, have been marked with the seal of sanctity in the image and likeness of thrice-holy God: this is our faith, but only the truly poor in spirit understand.[24]

This communion of saints is the community that the Eternal gathers to the Eternal's self. It is the work of the Spirit of God. It knows none of the boundaries we have been so quick to draw. We have the assurance, given that "God desires everyone to be saved," that it gathers together men and women who, in different ways, have tried to follow a path of salvation.

The communion of saints is here; it is present and on offer now, even if it remains hidden from sight. Mohammed is in the communion, along with countless other Muslims. Even though it

23. Christian de Chergé, *L'invincible espérance* [*Hope Unconquerable*], ed. Bruno Chenu (Paris: Bayard, 1996), 147.

24. Homily for November 1, 1976, *L'autre que nous attendons, homélies du père Christian de Chergé (1970–1996)* [*The Other Whom We Await: Homilies of Fr. Christian de Chergé*], Les cahiers de Tibhirine (Montjoyer: Abbé d'Aiguebelle, 2006), 9.

will be seen in full light only beyond death, it is a beyond that is present, a beyond that is coming toward us. We can see its signs, smell its fragrance:

> In the present reality of the communion of the "elect," both Christians and Muslims think we will be able to rejoin in oneness of heart these brothers and sisters who were once "Muslims" or "Christians" . . . who share, *in fact*, the same joy of God after having lived, up to the moment of their death, an authentic fidelity to the norms of their different faiths.[25]

Who belongs to the Church? The council, in *Lumen Gentium* and *Gaudium et Spes*, avoided speaking only of "belonging," preferring to talk of relation to the People of God or of participation in the paschal mystery, yet we may ask, "Who are all these people?" "Who are these, robed in white, and where have they come from?" (Rev 7:13) asks the witness in the book of Revelation.

> We too ask: All these people robed in white, where are they from? Wherever can they be coming from? And if we were told: twelve thousand from paganism, and twelve thousand from Judaism, and twelve thousand from Christianity, and twelve thousand from Islam, etc.? We would leap out of our seats! What's this! And the Master would reply: is your heart narrow because my heaven is broad and because it has many dwelling places? A mystery, this universal call, for us who are trying to stand even now before the throne of the Lamb.[26]

Communion of Saints, a Present Reality

It is present and it is coming, since it remains as yet hidden from our eyes: "a communion of saints still on its way since it is under this veil of a sign, the sign of pilgrimage."[27] De Chergé loved the image of the mystical ladder deeply planted in the earth

25. De Chergé, *L'invincible espérance*, 164.
26. Christian de Chergé, "L'échelle mystique du dialogue" ["The Mystical Ladder of Dialogue"], *Islamochristiana* 23 (1997): 11.
27. Homily for May 31, 1993, *L'autre que nous attendons*, 394.

and leaning on the Rock, on God, "between heaven and earth."
We have our feet firmly on the ground, and even in the dung,
he says, and at the same time our head is in heaven, exploring.
The communion of saints is real now, truer than what is visible
of the Church or other faith communities, more real than what
we believe to be real.

Work of the Spirit

This communion is the work of the Spirit. "Since the Spirit
began to circulate freely between heaven and earth, there is no
longer any visible boundary among people."[28] We should not
hinder the work of the Spirit by setting up defenses where we
find differences or being overly cautious about fixed positions
that can so rapidly become murderous. Once again, it is only by
faith that we can enter. "The communion of saints is a mystery
of permanent praise and adoration. . . . This mystery is truly
incarnate, since side by side with us brothers and sisters—non-
Christians, Jews or Muslims—recognize themselves in this hymn
of praise. Is there anything preventing it from being here and now
the song of a communion that so many other transitory aspects
would render illusory?"[29]

De Chergé always proceeds with the same intuition and the
same stance, that of the seeker in faith. We know little about the
plan of God and the ways of its fulfillment in history. Hence, it is
necessary to let the Spirit of God do its work and not to want to
enclose it in theological positions that are too narrow and incapable of evolution, or could even pose an obstacle to the work of
the Spirit. To enter into this mystery, one must be poor in spirit.
The poor in spirit are "those whose joy is to be welcoming and
readily to share everything they have and are, without holding
anything back for themselves, for all of it, they know, is the gift

---

28. Homily for November 1, 1981, de Chergé, *L'autre que nous attendons*, 49.
29. [Tr. note: The author did not identify the source of this quotation nor
of the one in the following paragraph.]

of the Holy Spirit. . . . This simplicity should exclude from our horizon big words that weigh us down so much."

"[B]ecause we are turned . . . toward the communion of saints . . . we cannot claim to be converted by ourselves: we need others (all others), in order to complete what is missing in our conversion, and they need us."[30] In the Spirit and by it we are already in this great communion of saints, even while we are still on pilgrimage toward it. Our participation in the communion of saints is stronger than many of the differences that may seem to us, from a human viewpoint, insurmountable. The reality of the Church, its mystery, is the communion of saints.

The Ecclesial Community

At this point, we may wonder: what is the mission of a particular ecclesial community, whether the monastic community, or the local diocesan Church, or the universal Church? The ecclesial community is to be understood and evaluated in light of the mysterious reality of the communion of saints. It is not so much the Church that clarifies the communion of saints; it is the communion of saints that clarifies the nature and singular mission of the Church. "It is up to us visibly to signify along with all the other mysteries of the Kingdom this *beyond* of the communion of saints, where Christians and Muslims share the same joy of sons and daughters."[31]

For de Chergé, this is the primary function of the Church. Theological discourse about the Church as sacrament is not enough unless at the same time there is constructed an ecclesial life that goes along with it. "And how are we to go about [constructing an ecclesial life] other than by loving freely, from this moment on, those whom a mysterious plan of God is preparing and sanctifying by way of Islam, and by living with them a Eucharistic sharing of the whole of our daily life?"[32] The Church best signifies the

---

30. Chapter talk for August 4, 1986, de Chergé, *Dieu pour tout jour*, 142.
31. De Chergé, *L'invincible espérance*, 187.
32. De Chergé, *L'invincible espérance*, 187.

communion of saints when it lives out freely the encounter with other believers. It goes without saying that we should not limit the sign of the communion of saints to Islam or interreligious dialogue. But undoubtedly there is to be found there a strong and concrete sign of the Church's faithfulness to its mission. John Paul II said precisely this to the cardinals and members of the Curia after the meeting at Assisi,[33] suggesting that their reading of this encounter be an "exegesis of the events"[34] offering a superlative illustration of the sacramental mission of the Church as it was defined by the Second Vatican Council. "Moreover," says de Chergé,

> it seems to me that in responding to the urgent necessity of incarnating this reality of communion which so utterly transcends us we exorcise most effectively the odor of proselytism and of the fixation that tends to reduce conversion to the move from one religion to another. When there is in fact such a move, it is because God has shifted the action beyond any human mediation—and that too commands respect.[35]

Christian de Chergé used a key phrase to describe his understanding of the Church. He called it "incarnation of the mystery of the communion of the saints." He also referred to the Church as "continuous incarnation." Again, this expression must be properly understood.[36]

> The Church of Pentecost, charged with the single mission of gathering all together in the living Christ, must also witness to this other mysterious saying of Jesus: "In my Father's house there are many dwelling places" [John 14:2]. How then can the Church be shocked by this omnipresent reality of differ-

---

33. "To the Roman Curia at the Exchange of Christmas Wishes," December 22, 1986, official version only in Italian on Vatican web site: http://www.vatican.va/holy_father/john_paul_ii/speeches/1986/december/index.htm.
    34. [Tr. note: "*una lezione dei fatti*" is so translated by the English edition of *L'Osservatore Romano*, January 5, 1987.]
    35. De Chergé, "L'échelle mystique," 18.
    36. See Raimundo Pannikar, *Christophany: The Fullness of Man* (Maryknoll, NY: Orbis, 2004), [176–79; see 128, 169 – Tr.].

ence which invites her to discern the marks of the Spirit working to enlarge the space of its heart?[37]

The incarnation of the communion of saints is seen in the way the Church embraces this mystery of difference, of which religious diversity is one of the most vivid expressions but by no means the only one. "Like all the mysteries of the Kingdom, the mystery of the communion of saints depends on the disciples of Christ to provide the channel for its incarnation. Therefore we must signify this union of the beyond by means of the quasi-sacrament of loving harmony among us from this very moment."[38]

The visible Church is the communion of saints incarnated in community. De Chergé described this community as "the community of saints in labor pains." That is the title of the third part of his "The Mystical Ladder." How does this community live? Monk that he is, de Chergé goes back to prayer and work, *ora et labora*, "the two pillars of Benedictine life."[39] They are "also the pillars of existential dialogue." We will return to the question of prayer. Suffice it for the moment to say that prayer is a fundamental attitude of dialogue. Not the least of the contributions of the theology of religions is its renewed call for an examination of the Church's priestly mission throughout the whole of its ecclesial life. As for work, it is not reducible to acts of labor; rather, in the writings of Christian de Chergé, work stands for a "prolonged co-existence." The brothers of Tibhirine had made the choice to form a labor cooperative with the people of Tibhirine. This choice reflected their wish to live on equal terms with their neighbors, something that probably would not have been possible within a system of hired labor.

---

37. De Chergé, *L'invincible espérance*, 116–17.

38. De Chergé, *L'invincible espérance*, 164.

39. [Tr. note: "les deux mamelles (the two teats)"—a French expression derived from a comment by the pro-agriculturalist, anti-manufacturing Duc de Sully (1560–1641), minister of Henri IV: "Labourage et pâturage sont les deux mamelles de la France (Agriculture and pastoralism are the two teats of France)." It defies direct translation into English.]

The Monastic Community

The monastic community is a particular form of Church, an *ecclesiola* [little Church], within which a profound unity binds the members together. De Chergé expressed this forcefully in relation to the White Fathers of Tizi Ouzou, all four of whom were assassinated.[40] "Those whom God had joined in one and the same consecrated life were not divided by death." He went on to articulate the very meaning of religious community: "The sign that they have left us remains expressive of the ultimate meaning of every religious community, which is to anticipate the communion of saints."[41]

His remarks apply to every Church community, starting from the *ecclesiola* formed by the couple or the family. Once we realize the dysfunctionality that mars so many religious communities and Christian communities in general, we understand how much easier it is to talk about relationship than to live it. Many religious communities probably have to struggle to believe that they incarnate and anticipate the communion of saints. Obviously, this pilgrimage toward the communion of saints presupposes a true conversion. "The common life continues to be a slow conversion during which the communion of saints is worked out, a difficult combat founded on the faith that one day the face of God will be all in all and that it is imperative for us from this very moment to seek out this all, this face of God in every person."[42]

A few days before the monks of Atlas were kidnapped, during the penultimate community chapter, Christian de Chergé said to his brothers, "Community is possible only among those who are open to the contemplation of the wonders of God hidden in each person, signs of the One God written upon our faces as so many differences promised to the communion of saints, even if, neces-

40. The White Fathers of Tizi Ouzou—Alain Dieulangard, Jean Chevillard, Charles Decker, and Christian Chessel—were assassinated on December 27, 1994. See Robert Masson, *Jusqu'au bout de la nuit: L'Église de l'Algérie* (Paris: Cerf, 1998), 115–45.

41. Chapter talk for February 18, 1995, de Chergé, *Dieu pour tout jour*, 517.

42. Chapter talk for August 13, 1986, de Chergé, *Dieu pour tout jour*, 143.

sarily, for a little while these things are difficult for us to see."[43]
Conversion is one of the principal *raisons d'être* of interreligious
dialogue. All are called to conversion: "Because all are called to
conversion, the conversion of others is the necessary prelude to
the communion of saints."[44] Solitary conversion is impossible: "It
is because we are turned toward the communion of saints (the
heavenly Jerusalem) that we cannot claim to convert by ourselves:
we need others (all others) in order to complete what is lacking
in our conversion, and they need us."[45]

Thus, in its various communities, the visible Church presents
itself to us as "the great sacrament of the communion of saints,"
the sacrament of the people of God gathered in the heart of the
Father, to which, in fact, all people are called by universal redemp-
tive grace. This is why, in the very words of the Second Vatican
Council, the Church must examine "with greater care the relation
which she has to non-Christian religions," remember that "all men
form but one community," and be the sacrament of this "single
community whose existence preceded all divisions and that is
destined to rise up in the full daylight of the final resurrection."[46]
This vision of the Church is not without consequences for pastoral
theology.

43. Chapter talk for March 12, 1996, de Chergé, *Dieu pour tout jour*, 548.
44. Chapter talk for June 4, 1986, de Chergé, *Dieu pour tout jour*, 125.
45. Chapter talk for August 4, 1986, de Chergé, *Dieu pour tout jour*, 142.
46. De Chergé, *L'invincible espérance*, 152.

Chapter 9

The Quasi-Sacrament of Difference

The religious and cultural diversity that will continue to mark our societies raises yet again the question of otherness, for the state as much as for the Churches. On this topic Western culture has often found itself in difficulty. As evidence of this difficulty it is enough to mention the fate of the Jews from the Middle Ages to the present, the conquest of the New World with the genocide of indigenous populations, and colonization. Today, we can legitimately take the ideology of globalization to task for its lack of respect for cultures. There are also, of course, the challenges presented by the difference between the sexes, man and woman. The course of history seems to suggest that we are incapable of coupling the concepts of equality and difference. In the name of equality, we end up denying all difference, and in the name of difference, we deny equality. How are we to think about difference? How are we to think about religious difference in particular? How are we to think about difference in some way other than exhorting each other to a respect of differences or to a weak and forced tolerance?

For that matter, how are we to think about difference in its relation to unity as a theological gift and not simply as a socio-political fact to be managed as best we can? For, again, according to de Chergé, "the Church of Pentecost, charged with the single mission

111

of gathering all together in the living Christ, must witness also to that other mysterious saying of Jesus: 'In my Father's house, there are many dwelling-places' [John 14:2]."[1] In the Gospel of John, Jesus rightly says that there is only one flock and only one shepherd. But he also says—and this is given much less commentary—that there are many sheepfolds (John 10:16).

The Very Fact of Difference

Difference can be seen in creation, where the similarity among creatures is the fact that they are different one from the other. The Bible speaks of the diversity of animal and plant life, created and called to develop "according to their kinds."[2] The believer is invited to recognize, in and through this difference in the profusion of creation, the work of the Creator.

> Indeed [there] are signs for those of understanding / Who remember Allah while standing or sitting or lying on their sides and give thought to the creation of the heavens and the earth, saying, "Our Lord, You did not create this aimlessly; exalted are You!" [*Surah* 3:190-91]

De Chergé alludes poetically to the covenant with Noah. The rainbow associates the one and the many. "The diversity of colors testified to [God's] inner richness, but it was the uniqueness of the polychromatic curve that spoke of the Wholly Other's penchant for the multitudinous."[3]

Difference presents itself to us not only in the wonders of creation but also in all realms of human life, in particular across the spectrum of religious diversity. It is impossible to say that we are all alike without betraying ourselves and revealing our inability to cope with difference. A Muslim is not a Christian, nor is a Chris-

---

1. Christian de Chergé, *L'invincible espérance* [*Hope Unconquerable*], ed. Bruno Chenu (Paris: Bayard, 1996), 117.
2. [Tr. note: The New International Version translation, quoted above, conveys the sense wanted here better than NRSV's "of every kind."]
3. De Chergé, *L'invincible espérance*, 121.

tian a Muslim, an observation that is worth repeating in a culture that insists on reducing everything to the same level. Difference presents itself to us as a fact. But what is its meaning? Where is it leading us? Is it an obstacle to unity that must be overcome by trying to reduce, or even to eliminate, difference? If in differences there are things that cause separation, the question becomes, for Christian de Chergé, "What is the meaning on the divine level of that which separates us on the human level?" It is common to recognize a divine meaning in that which unites us. But what if what separates us also had a meaning in God? "And what if difference derived its meaning from the revelation God makes to us of Who He is? What would prevent us from conceiving it as we conceive faith itself, namely, as a gift from God?"[4]

Posing the question in these terms forces us to leave behind a certain number of familiar habits of thought. De Chergé's question suggests that difference may be not so much an impediment on the road to unity as a gift from God. The fact of difference cannot be understood except in terms of its ground, and its ground is unity. In order to consider difference as mystery, we must first of all consider the mystery of unity.

Division

In the course of history, difference has often been distorted by shattered unity. The division of Christians largely contributed to the birth of Islam. The Qurʾan capitalized on the division of Christians. Mohammed Abduh writes:

> At the moment when Islam appeared, people were divided on religious questions while at the same time remote from the true faith—except for a small number; they quarreled and excommunicated each other and believed that as a result they were in the bosom of God. [. . .] Islam rejected all that and declared formally that religion is One, in all eras.[5]

---

4. De Chergé, *L'invincible espérance*, 112.
5. De Chergé, *L'invincible espérance*, 138.

Notwithstanding this declaration, division continued and deepened still further in the course of history, especially, in the West, at the time of the Reformation. Division perverts difference.

A Plan for Unity Mysteriously at Work

De Chergé places his faith in the "plan for unity mysteriously at work in the world," through which is formed the one People of God. He finds affirmation of this single community in the council document *Nostra Aetate*: "All men form but one community. This is so because all stem from the one stock which God created . . . and also because all share a common destiny, namely God. His providence, evident goodness, and saving designs extend to all men."[6] John Paul II reiterated this vigorously:

> There is only one single divine plan for every human being that comes into this world [cf. Jn 1:9], one single origin and end, whatever the color of their skin, the historical and geographical horizon within which they live and act, the culture in which they have been raised and in which they express themselves. The differences are of lesser importance in comparison with the unity which, in contrast, is radical, fundamental and determinative.[7]

We find this same idea in the Qurʾan, in this well-known *surah*:

> Had Allah willed, He would have made you one community. But He wished to test you by means of the gift He has given you. Seek to surpass each other in your good works. To Allah is your return all together, and He will then inform you concerning that over which you used to differ. (*Surah* 5:48)

---

6. *Nostra Aetate* 1.

7. John Paul II, "To the Roman Curia at the Exchange of Christmas Wishes," December 22, 1986; *Chemins de dialogue* 20 (2002): 165. Only in Italian on the Vatican web site: http://www.vatican.va/holy_father/john_paul_ii/speeches/1986/december/documents/hf_jp-ii_spe_19861222_curia-romana_it.html.

Unity is "radical, fundamental and determinative." These three adjectives must be taken very seriously in a theology of religious encounter. If unity is *fundamental*, then all reflection must be referred to the first foundation, namely, the unity of the human family. The *root* of the theology of religions is found in this unity, and that makes it radical in the etymological sense of the word. But if unity is *determinative*, then nothing should be said or done against this unity. The task henceforth is to inhabit what presents itself to us as a mystery—that is, radical, fundamental, and determinative unity—and only then to think about religious plurality, about the encounter of believers, and about the theology of religious encounter, never departing from this mystery of unity. Religious difference itself is then revealed to be something not exterior, an obstacle, but interior, a manifestation of the mystery of unity. That is why we do damage to unity when we relativize or, worse still, when we deny differences, but we do just as much harm when we make a radical opposition between difference and the unity that it is the function of difference to reveal.

The fundamental unity of the human race has its source in the oneness of God. The absoluteness of the One is strongly affirmed in both Christianity and Islam. The two are united in speaking of oneness, but each conceives of this oneness in a somewhat different way: "this oneness . . . is something we proclaim differently."[8] Christians believe in the Trinity, but in such a way that trinity does not in any way contradict divine unity, notwithstanding, no doubt, what the prophet Mohammed learned from the Christian sects extant at the birth of Islam. Discourse concerning the oneness of God is itself characterized by difference. We recall de Chergé's observations: "seeing things differently does not mean that one is not seeing the same things,"[9] and "speaking otherwise of God is not speaking of another God."[10] The Wholly Other leaves open the possibility of speaking otherwise of God. Our common faith in the oneness of God bears the imprint of our

8. De Chergé, *L'invincible espérance*, 125–26.
9. De Chergé, *L'invincible espérance*, 127.
10. De Chergé, *L'invincible espérance*, 128.

difference. Christian de Chergé takes up a metaphor borrowed from Meister Eckhart. Each blade of grass is different from every other, and yet they are all similar. Their differences witness to their unity. "Could we not imagine that the difference which identifies someone as belonging to Christianity or Islam is rooted in the One God from which it proceeds?"[11] Thus both unity and difference have their origin in God, and difference is oriented toward unity.

Differentiated Unity

De Chergé attributed to the Holy Spirit the ability to use difference to establish communion and reestablish likeness: "filled with the gift of the Spirit whose secret joy will always be to establish communion and restore the likeness, playing with the differences."[12] Spirit creates not only communion; it creates difference too. Or, rather, it creates unity by making and playing with differences. It even seems that it finds its happiness where we sometimes find distress. The Spirit acts by means of difference to permit both sides, both created in the image of God, to rediscover likeness. De Chergé alludes to the lovely passage in the Wisdom of ben Sirach in which all things are said to come in pairs and each exists to highlight the beauty of the other.[13]

Difference is part of the mystery of unity. In Christian revelation, unity and difference are inscribed from the beginning in the creation of man and woman. Unity is signified in and by difference. It is only together and by means of their recognized differences, loved and displayed, that man and woman signify, both one and the other, in a differentiated manner, the unity of God. Man and woman are images of God, both together and one by means of the other. Difference presents itself as that which best signifies the One God. The difference between man and woman, far from being an obstacle to surmount in order to arrive at unity, originates in

---

11. De Chergé, *L'invincible espérance*, 126.
12. De Chergé, *L'invincible espérance*, 223.
13. Sirach (= Ecclesiasticus) 42:24-25: "All things come in pairs, one opposite the other, and he has made nothing incomplete. Each supplements the virtues of the other."

unity itself. A couple expresses its unity in God by manifesting its differences. It is the path by which man and woman, and, equally, the believers of different religions, recover the likeness of their origin.

Obviously, this is a far cry from the quest for a uniformity that is merely a caricature of unity, whether in the couple, in society, or in the Churches. Uniformity does not witness to unity. On the contrary, it is a witness against unity. On the other hand, "if differences really come from unity, they must logically tend to return to it."[14]

De Chergé accorded to difference a "quasi-sacramental function." Difference is a sacrament of unity in God. John Paul II, explaining in his speech to the cardinals and members of the Curia that there are two kinds of difference, noted in particular that "there are the differences in which are reflected the genius and spiritual riches given by God to the nations."[15] Everyone is directed back to mystery by the encounter with difference. Obviously, it is impossible for either Christians or Muslims to deny part of themselves or to put a part of their own faith under a bushel. It is not by reducing difference that we advance toward unity or that we best signify it. On the contrary, when differences are kept clearly in view, they can become the path to a communion that intends unity, a communion that God alone can conceive of, which cannot be achieved by our efforts.

Hidden Unity

Unity is a plan mysteriously at work. This is another way of saying that unity remains in part hidden from view. But it is not to say that unity is to be relegated to the end time, in an eschatology understood exclusively as "last things," in a historical future.

> The various monotheisms ascribe to every word of God the meaning of a reiterated call to the fulfillment of this plan; and

---

14. De Chergé, *L'invincible espérance*, 157.
15. John Paul II, "To the Roman Curia," 166.

each one of us will feel invested with a more and more universal responsibility, in proportion to the size of the single community that must be restored.[16]

This is the hidden unity of the beginning and the end of the human family, but it is also the unity of the paschal mystery. It is the same paschal mystery at work in the world, making human beings pass from this world to the Father. No matter what their beliefs, all people are invited by the Spirit of God, "which has been poured into all hearts" (see Rom 5:5), to pass from death to life. Thus, the mystery of unity manifests itself not only in the works of creation or in the diversity of cultures and religions but also in the paschal mystery, which is offered to each person. "This unity as yet hidden belongs to the faith of both [Muslims and Christians]."[17]

Unity Deferred[18]

This unity, which is in part mysteriously present, is deferred because we are cruelly divided. Nevertheless, we have in common "the shared hope of a deferred unity." Both sides, Christians and Muslims, believe that the unity that remains hidden even in the differences will one day be made fully manifest. As for this common hope:

> Is it not already an authentic bond? All we would need to do would be to welcome it together as a call of the Spirit which presides at each encounter in order to seek from it new bursts of self-transcendence toward an ever greater truth. By surrendering itself entirely to this hope the Church would be doing no more than penetrating further into its own mystery which is, in this world, to signify the communion of saints beyond all the tensions of its own members.[19]

16. De Chergé, *L'invincible espérance*, 147–48.
17. De Chergé, *L'invincible espérance*, 153.
18. [Tr. note: The French verb *différer* means both "to differ" and "to defer"—a play on words made famous by Jacques Derrida.]
19. De Chergé, *L'invincible espérance*, 154.

A crisis of identity in the Church would prevent the Church from fully living out its mission of signifying the communion of saints "accomplished" in the heart of the Father. If the Church of Christ subsists in the Catholic Church, then it is the Church's business less to talk about unity than to live unity and to signify to all peoples that they are oriented toward the one People of God.[20] Both Christians and Muslims are on the way of the cross, the way of exodus, the way of *hijra*. Difference itself is calling us to mutual emulation. Imagining Christians and Muslims as two pilgrims, and invoking the story in Luke's gospel of the encounter on the road to Emmaus, De Chergé wrote, "However different the roads, the joy that seems to burn in their hearts, in each of them, might well make them converge upon the same inn, there where eyes are opened in the sharing of one bread kneaded with love for the multitude."[21] Difference, then, presents itself as a road to Emmaus and in a convergence that remains as yet hidden from our eyes, for our eyes are prevented from recognizing the Paschal Lord, but we can already now *intend* him in the breaking of the bread, "for you and for the multitude."

Conclusion

Given that unity is what grounds difference, difference in its turn can become the quasi-sacrament of unity in God. Difference presents itself to us with the function of signifying transcendent unity, in particular through sharing and trustful mutual understanding. Difference, then, holds the path of a communion in God. This communion expresses itself both in a common work for justice and peace and in a common yet diversified response to a single call to prayer that comes from God.

Difference conceived as an expression of unity, a unity that is greater and other than we can conceive it, opens us to the mystery of God and God's knowledge. It prevents believers from making an idol of their own religious traditions, their own formulas of

20. *Lumen Gentium* 16.
21. De Chergé, *L'invincible espérance*, 116.

faith; from constructing for themselves an identity based on opposition; and from an obsessive effort to affirm their uniqueness.
Difference as a differentiated expression of unity allows us to
let others take their place in the plan of God. True dialogue then
becomes the requirement for each participant to rely on the particular grace and different gifts of the other, even if this results in
being challenged and rubbed raw. This view of difference as an
expression of unity comes with the promise of a deeper understanding of the mystery of God. De Chergé quotes this magnificent passage from the emir Abd-El-Kader. It neatly sums up the
theme of this chapter:

> He said to me: "And I, who am I?"
> I answered: "You are the Perfect One, the One Who is Tran-
> scendent with respect to everything that can enter the mind."
> He replied: "You do not know me!"
> I said to him without fear of showing disrespect: "You are the
> One in Whose likeness are all contingent creatures. You are
> the Lord and the Servant, the One and the many. . . . In you
> are united contraries and opposites."
> He said: "Enough. You know me! Praise Us for what We have
> taught you about Us for you cannot know Us by anyone other
> than Us. Nothing leads to Us except Ourself."[22]

22. Emir Abd-El-Kader, *Écrits spirituels* (Paris: Éditions du Seuil, 1982), 86.

Chapter 10

Eschatology

Both the Christology and the ecclesiology of Christian de Chergé lead us to ask, what is the unifying feature of his theology of religious encounter? It seems to us that *eschatology* is the epicenter of his theology. All de Chergé's thinking was worked out from the perspective of an already-accomplished realization of the plan of the Father to be "all in all" and to gather around the table of the kingdom "a great multitude that no one could count, from every nation, from all tribes and peoples and languages" (Rev 7:9).

De Chergé contemplated the question of the place of Islam in the plan of God in his vision of the children of Islam in the bosom of the Father. To the question about the meaning of interreligious dialogue, his response was that, far from being reduced to a sociopolitical necessity, it is a participation in the life of the Trinity. As for Christology, Christ himself eludes those who have the mission to witness to him ("Do not hold on to me" [John 20:17]) and reveals himself as the "ever greater" Christ. And as for ecclesiology, the Church is the heavenly Jerusalem "in which everyone is born," the community gathered by the Eternal One, which the visible Church has a vocation to signify by incarnating the Body of Christ, which transcends all the limits of our exclusions.

As a mystic, Christian de Chergé lived each day a theology of religious encounter that had its focal point, its point of equilibrium, in eschatological thinking. In this he was truly a monk. As he himself recognized:

If the monk believes he has something to say here, it is less as an effective builder of the city of men . . . than as someone committed to practicing a way of being in the world that makes no sense outside what we call hope of "the last things."[1]

This is eschatology. But to say that de Chergé was truly a monk is not a way of discarding his thought and setting it aside as valuable for only those who have embraced his state of life. We share the opinion of Raimundo Panikkar, who wrote, "[T]he monk is the expression of an archetype which is a *constitutive dimension of human life*"[2] inasmuch as the monk is oriented toward the ultimate goal of human life and toward the associated experience of its absence. "Not everyone can or should enter a monastery, but everybody has a monastic dimension that ought to be cultivated."[3]

We have tried to show—and this will become even more apparent in the final part of the book—this eschatological way of thinking rooted in monastic experience is not idealistic; instead, it is observably fruitful. It was the way Christian de Chergé and his brothers were able to live authentically in dialogue, modify their understanding of their vocation in the land of Islam, enter into a spirit of universal brotherhood, and end by giving their lives for love and fidelity. This leads us to form the hypothesis that only a theology of religious encounter that is centered in eschatological thinking can make the claim to honor both religious diversity and fidelity to the mystery of Christ. We have come to the conclusion that a theology of religions is necessarily a theology of hope—although we still need to explicate the meaning of this expression. This perspective seems to us to be the only one equal to the task of rescuing the theology of religious encounter from the dilemma that confronts it—namely, relativism, which fails to respect the whole of Christian faith, and dogmatism, which avoids the fact of religious diversity altogether. Our immersion in the

1. Christian de Chergé, "L'échelle mystique du dialogue" ["The Mystical Ladder of Dialogue"], *Islamochristiana* 23 (1997): 3.

2. Raimundo Panikkar, *Blessed Simplicity: The Monk as Universal Archetype* (New York: Seabury Press, 1982), 11.

3. Panikkar, *Blessed Simplicity*, 14.

writings of Christian de Chergé has persuaded us that eschatology is the heart of the theology of religious encounter and that this is far from the least of Christian de Chergé's contributions to Christian theology as a whole. We think that this perspective is also the only one that can really ground—not politically, but theologically—interreligious dialogue.

While this intuition needs to be confirmed from the writings of Christian de Chergé, it also needs to take into account the reflection on eschatology that has so strongly characterized twentieth-century theology. A brief summary of recent theological reflection on eschatology will help us understand where and how Christian de Chergé is situated within the spectrum of contemporary theologies.

From the Last Things to the God Who Comes

From the scholastic period until at least the latter part of the nineteenth century, eschatology was understood as a theology of the "last things": human beings are destined for eternal life in the beatific vision beyond death. While in their earthly embodied existence, they must strive to live well and die well in order to be found worthy, on the day of their death, to enter into the kingdom of God, identified with this afterlife. In their present life, human beings live in the hope of this life-beyond-death. This is the object of hope.

It was owing to Rudolf Bultmann in particular that this view of last things has been challenged and given a theological reappraisal. For Bultmann, the eschatological event existed not any longer in the past or at the end of history but in the present, here and now. "Jesus Christ is the eschatological event, not as an established fact of past time but as repeatedly present, as addressing you and me here and now, in preaching."[4] The decisive event has taken place; it happens anew continuously in preaching and in authentic Christian existence. The eschatology of a distant future

4. Rudolf Bultmann, *The Presence of Eternity: History and Eschatology*, Gifford Lectures 1955 (New York: Harper and Brothers, 1957), 151–52.

is interpreted as existentially present, and we move from a "future eschatology"—by which is meant the "last things"—to a "present eschatology." The eschatological moment is here:

> [D]o not look around yourself into universal history; you must look into your own personal history. Always in your present lies the meaning in history, and you cannot see it as a spectator, but only in your responsible decisions. In every moment slumbers the possibility of being the eschatological moment. You must awaken it.[5]

There has been no lack of criticism of this understanding of eschatology. It has been faulted for neglecting future eschatological fulfillment in the afterlife, and thus for seriously compromising the Christian faith. However justified these criticisms may be—a matter open to question—it remains true nonetheless that Bultmann's contribution changed the direction of theology. By bringing eschatology into the present, Bultmann emphasized the role of authentic existence. His theology stimulated the thinking of numerous theologians, among the latter Jürgen Moltmann who elaborated a theology of hope.

Unlike Bultmann's eschatology, Moltmann's "does not collapse the future into the present. Instead, the future really has a future."[6] To be sure, Bultmann freed us from an eschatology conceived uniquely in terms of "last things," but without the future, what would become of history? For Moltmann, eschatology is a tension between the present and the future. "Eschatology is the doctrine of Christine hope," deliberately oriented toward the future. We cannot speak of an "adventist eschatology" (Moltmann)[7] as distinct

---

5. Bultmann, *The Presence of Eternity*, 155.

6. [Tr. note: An untranslatable play on synonyms: "Le futur a réellement un avenir." The second word for "the future" can be parsed as *à-venir*, "to-come" (as Salenson will do later). The source is Jean-Marie Glé, "Le retour de l'eschatologie" ("The Return of Eschatology"), *Recherches de Science Religieuse* 84, no. 2 (1996): 231.]

7. [Tr. note: Moltmann uses the phrase *Adventus Dei* = "coming of God"; see Rev 1:4, "(God) who is and who was and who is to come." Moltmann's *Zukunft* (= "future") is defined not by time but by the Parousia, the "universal

from both a "futurist eschatology" (the scholastic "last things") and a "presentist eschatology" (Bultmann). Moltmann's future is grounded in a guaranteed and stable promise founded in the resurrection of Jesus Christ. Thus, faith in the promise, rooted in the resurrection, is the foundation of hope. In promises, the hidden future is already proclaimed, acting even in the present by means of the hope that it awakens.

Moltmann himself underwent an evolution between his books *Theology of Hope* and *The Crucified God*.[8] His earlier conception of hope [*espérance*], while it successfully met the contradiction of bringing eschatology into the present, was marked by the optimism [*espoir*],[9] the enthusiasm [*élans*], and the positive outlook that characterized the 1960s and 1970s. Due at least in part to subsequent sociopolitical conditions in the world, it became apparent that the category of assurance [*promesse*] was not sufficient.

Thus, while each had something important to offer theological reflection, neither the scholastic eschatology of "last things" nor Bultmann's eschatology of the present nor even Moltmann's theology of hope appeared sufficient.

God Who Comes

Lex orandi, lex credendi [the law of prayer is the law of belief], says the old adage. In the Christian liturgy we pray not to the God who is, who was, and who will be but to the "God who is, who was, and who comes." The theological frame of reference

---

advent" of Jesus Christ. Jürgen Moltmann, "Theology as Eschatology," *The Future of Hope*, ed. Frederick Herzog (New York: Herder & Herder, 1970), 1–50, esp. 12–13.]

8. Jürgen Moltmann, *Theology of Hope: On the Ground and the Implications of a Christian Eschatology*, trans. James W. Leitch (New York: Harper and Row, 1967); *The Crucified God: The Cross of Christ as the Foundation and Criticism of Christian Theology*, trans. R. A. Wilson and John Bowden (New York: Harper and Row, 1974). [Jürgen Moltmann, *The Coming of God: Christian Eschatology*, trans. Margaret Kohl (Minneapolis: Fortress Press, 1996). Ed.]

9. [Tr. note: *espérance* implies a more spiritual quality and is used for the theological virtue, whereas *espoir* is more worldly, implying ordinary expectation or wish for good things.]

is not so much the future as it is Advent. Advent, as a category of liturgical time, cannot be reduced to a waiting for something that is supposed to come. The expression "God who comes" is not the liturgical rehearsal of the long wait of the patriarchs and prophets, nor is it an exhortation to prepare for the imminent end of the world or the day of our death, much less the signal that we are about to celebrate the feast of Christmas. Advent, this "God who comes," designates a present mystery: Today, here and now, God comes. Today, here and now, eschatology is realized. "See, now is the acceptable time; see, now is the day of salvation" (2 Cor 6:2). Hope is not, therefore, merely a virtue that projects us toward a "time" beyond time but also a virtue that projects us into the beyond within this present moment, into "a beyond under the banner of time," in the lovely formulation of Christian de Chergé that in a way summarizes his eschatology.[10]

Before further exploring de Chergé's theology of hope, we need first to acknowledge its dependence on Charles Péguy.

Hope in Péguy

Anne-Noëlle Clément has discovered that Christian de Chergé was a devoted reader of Charles Péguy and that his understanding of hope was influenced by Péguy.[11] We have a clear attestation of this from Christian de Chergé himself who wrote that "the best theological treatise on hope continues to be Péguy's *Porche du mystère de la deuxième vertu* [*Portal of the Mystery of the Second Virtue*]."[12]

A perusal of the writings of Péguy reveals the extent of his influence on de Chergé. The titles of the latter's homilies for the

---

10. *Un au-delà sous le signe du temps.*

11. Anne-Noëlle Clément, "Péguy et l'espérance," *Cahier de Tibhirine* (Monjoyer: Abbaye Notre-Dame d'Aiguebelle, forthcoming).

12. Chapter talk for August 11, 1990, in Christian de Chergé, *Dieu pour tout jour, chapitres du père Christian de Chergé à la communauté de Tibhirine (1985–1996)* [*God for Each Day: Chapter Talks of Fr. Christian de Chergé to the Community of Tibhirine*], 2nd ed., Les cahiers de Tibhirine (Montjoyer: Abbé d'Aiguebelle, 2006), 334.

Easter Triduum 1994—"The Martyrdom of Charity," "The Martyrdom of Innocence," and "The Martyrdom of Hope"—correspond to Péguy's "mysteries": "The Mystery of the Charity of Joan of Arc" and "The Mystery of the Innocents." Christian de Chergé borrowed from Charles Péguy, and Péguy's influence has penetrated even the cadence of the language.

Relevant to our purposes, in *Le porche du mystère de la deuxième vertu*[13] Péguy effects a reversal by shifting the origin of hope to God. It is not so much that the human creature turns toward God in hope; rather, God turns toward the human creature. God is the first to hope. And what does God hope? That not one of these little ones should be lost [see Matt 18:14]. For the human creature, then, to hope is to enter into God's hoping. Péguy wrote, "A religion that is resigned to considering some brothers and sisters eternally lost and that would not miss them eternally is profoundly self-centered on the question of salvation and therefore already bourgeois and capitalist."[14] Christian de Chergé's comment on this passage illustrates the attitude of someone animated by God's love: "Wanting all people to be saved and already *seeing* them as such."[15] Thus Péguy's theological treatise on hope supplies a position: God's hope that goes in search of the lost sheep so that not one is lost. The content of this hope is the salvation of all human creatures, with the sinning and the pardoned at the same table.[16] It is Péguy, then, who introduces us to the eschatology and theology of hope of Christian de Chergé.

"A Beyond under the Banner of Time"

As suggested above, this phrase of de Chergé nicely serves as a summary of his eschatology. In an Easter Vigil homily de Chergé

---

13. Charles Péguy, *Le porche du mystère de la deuxième vertu* (Paris: Gallimard, 1986); Charles Péguy, *The Portal of the Mystery of Hope*, trans. David Louis Schindler (Grand Rapids, MI: Eerdmans, 1996).

14. Péguy, *Le porche du mystère*, quoted by de Chergé, chapter talk for July 28, 1990, *Dieu pour tout jour*, 331.

15. De Chergé, *Dieu pour tout jour*, 331.

16. Anne-Noëlle Clément, "Péguy et l'espérance."

described the women in Mark's gospel entering "into a space beyond death."[17] They are projected outside themselves. The witness who has come from elsewhere takes the place of the Crucified One and "they enter ardently, into this space beyond death that will give to their faith the dimension of hope."[18] We will return later to hope in the proper sense of the word.

Eschatology is expressed here as "a space beyond death" that exists not only for the Crucified and Risen One but also for the women who are in a way themselves also beyond death. They are "in the world" but they are no longer "of the world." Speaking of himself and his brother monks, it is they, says Christian, who are in a way "beyond that horizon that is blocked by the threat of death, since it is Christ who goes before us."[19]

Eschatology can be defined as a place "beyond death," but not only or even primarily beyond physical death, as in the theology of last things. This "beyond death" is [given] to us to live in today. In a way, we are no longer of this world. We are projected, like the women at the empty tomb, into a place "beyond death" where, it must be clear to us, it is given to us to live "under the sign of time," that is to say, in the here and now, the existential dimension of life. The second part of this definition of eschatology is essential. Death, from this perspective, is not simply bodily death on the last day. It is death to self. It is a matter of living without leaving the here and now. Living "under the banner of time" is now the criterion of validity for living "beyond death."

De Chergé also uses the image of the mystical ladder to describe this Beyond. As we have seen, the mystical ladder "leans into the Beyond";[20] its solid point of support is found in God, the "mighty Rock." God is beyond what we can know of him, because "in order that the two uprights of our ladder should stay

---

17. [Tr. note: "cet au-delà de la mort"—"this beyond-death."]

18. De Chergé, "Le martyre de l'espérance," Easter Vigil Homily, April 2–3, 1994, in Christian de Chergé, *L'invincible espérance* [*Hope Unconquerable*], ed. Bruno Chenu (Paris: Bayard, 1996), 240.

19. De Chergé, "Le martyre de l'espérance," Easter Vigil Homily, April 2–3, 1994, in de Chergé *L'invincible espérance*, 242.

20. [Tr. note: *Sic*: "vers l'au-delà"; de Chergé "L'échelle mystique,"17.]

firmly attached to God"—for the ladder is composed of the two religious traditions, Islam and Christianity—"it is important that God be what each of us, from our respective faiths, say God is, and more than that for all."[21] This Beyond is, then, the fact that in this present time God keeps both the one and the other, Muslim and Christian, firmly attached to him.

This Beyond is the revelation of the communion of saints gathered now in the heart of God; it is the heavenly Jerusalem for all, "the mystery of this universal spiritual solidarity." Eschatology is thus the beyond-death in which everyone can live, the communion of saints already realized in God, and for all participants in authentic interreligious encounter the point of support on the One Rock.

A Mystery Crying for Incarnation

The eschatology of Christian de Chergé is not, we have seen, futurist; it is not an expectation of the last things, because it is now, today, that the parties in dialogue are seated together at the table of sinners. Yet neither is his eschatology presentist, despite the fact that it is lived in the present, for there is a tension between the present and the future. It is not, as it is in Moltmann's theology of hope, the present that strives after its realization, that hopes for it, and that lives in the tension of a promise of fulfillment. Rather, fulfillment strives to be incarnated, for "everything is fulfilled"— the last word of Jesus, which he utters unceasingly throughout history. The mystery of universal spiritual solidarity, this "beyond death," is "crying to be incarnated." This mystery, fully realized, calls forth its own incarnation or, again, its signification:

> It is at the table of sinners that I learn best of all to become a sign, to the extent I have attained it, of the promised mystery of the communion of saints. The multiplied loaves that we Christians and Muslims are given to break together are the bread of absolute trust in the mercy of God alone. When we accept to discover each other anew in this sharing, doubly

21. De Chergé, "L'échelle mystique," 17.

brothers, both prodigal and pardoned, there can be a celebration among us something of the feast ordained from all eternity to gather us together into his House. There is among us, already, a table spread, a mystery that is written yet always in need of deciphering.[22]

The table is already spread. Once again, the mystery of the incarnation is central.

Hope: A Summation

For de Chergé, hope was the virtue that allowed him to live the Beyond here and now. It was in hope that the mystery of the communion of saints was incarnated. Through and in hope, he lived out this mystery here and now in the context of a relationship with the believers of Islam, a relationship centered on and signified by the eucharistic table where pardoned sinners sit side by side. This mystery crying out for incarnation was for de Chergé the communion of saints lived out, signified, and incarnated in "the community of saints in birth pangs."[23] Hope was an attitude that enabled him to dwell here and now in "the beyond-death," to dwell in, and so incarnate, the communion of saints. Hope was what kept de Chergé and his brothers stable in their place, in the world but not of it. It made them hold fast

> amid the fear of tomorrow, conquered by the patience of each today. . . . Amid the fear of violent death, conquered by the presence of the Living One. . . . Amid the fear of civil war, conquered by the certainty that peace is not of this world. . . . Amid the fear of Islam and intolerance, conquered by the gift of the Spirit laboring to create the communion of saints.[24]

This list of what it meant for the monks of Atlas to live the Beyond in the present is not exhaustive. Everyone can add to it.

---

22. De Chergé, "L'échelle mystique," 24.
23. De Chergé, "L'échelle mystique," 16.
24. De Chergé, *L'invincible espérance*, 243.

Hope does not deny fear, but it helps us dwell beyond fear, beyond death. Hope is a "way of being in the world." "Both Muslims and Christians are marked by the call of the Beyond, but according to the logic of the Beyond, we must together make things better between us, here and now. . . . The judgment of this world has already begun."[25]

Hope incarnates the logic of the Beyond. Thus the Beyond is not something we are striving toward but something coming toward us. It is not so much a world to come but rather a coming world whose logic insists that we incarnate it here and now, that we live it "under the banner of time." "It is always from beyond the horizon of our reason that God comes to us, whatever our respective faiths, and we can truly expect something new each time we make the effort to decipher the signs of the Beyond at the horizons of worlds and of hearts."[26]

For de Chergé, hope turns community into an incarnation of the communion of saints. It is not a case of striving to live a communal life *in the hope* that the communion of saints will one day come to pass. Rather, the communion of saints is truly offered to us *in hope*, and the community is nothing other than the sign and the concrete fulfillment of this communion of saints that has been offered but remains hidden from view. We are, here and now together, gathered in the hand of God. The more we enter into this mystery, the more we recognize and live it. Community incarnates the communion of saints. How is it incarnated? Here Christian de Chergé is extremely concrete: through community life, through association in work, through prayer—a reference to the definition of the brothers of Tibhirine as "praying among others who pray"—through works of mercy, and, finally, through the simple everyday routine of a life lived together with neighbors. So community is accessible to everyone, across the diversity of vocations and states of life, in the ordinariness of the everyday.

25. De Chergé, "L'échelle mystique," 6.
26. De Chergé, *L'invincible espérance*, 183.

The Object of Eschatology

Christian de Chergé's eschatology is a realized eschatology. It is not a matter of continual expectation, of something to be awaited, as for a promise or a pledge. It is realized now, an eternal present. The eternal is present in the present time. The goods of the world that comes [*monde a-venir*] are in this world as it comes to us. The times are fulfilled: "Everything is accomplished." The last word of Jesus suddenly takes on an incalculable force. Through faith and hope we can give it incarnated form. Eschatology is God's coming [*l'a-venir de Dieu*], the future in the mode of the present or the present in the mode of the future. Eschatology is "the mystery of his will, according to his good pleasure . . . as a plan for the fullness of time, to gather up all things in [Christ]" (Eph 1:9-10). This mystery has been hidden since the foundation of the world, but it has been revealed in these times, which are the last days. Jews and Gentiles have access to one and the same mystery: "[T]he mystery that has been hidden throughout the ages and generations but has now been revealed to his saints. To them God chose to make known how great among the Gentiles are the riches of the glory of this mystery, which is Christ in you, the hope of glory" (Col 1:26-27).

The mystery is Christ: Christ present in our midst, Christ present in the works of creation, Christ without whom nothing exists, Christ offered to the Jews and the Gentiles. This mystery is not waiting until the end of time to be realized. It is already realized and revealed to us today. It is today that the Word has reconciled all people and gathers them at the table of the kingdom. It is today that everything is being recapitulated in Christ.

A Way of Being in the World

This faith in present eschatology is incarnated in a way of being in the world: "seek the things that are above, where Christ is, seated at the right hand of the Father" (Col 3:1). It is a particular way of regarding the world and events, a way of truly being in the world and not of the world, for "your life is hidden with Christ in God. When Christ who is your life is revealed, then you also will be revealed with him in glory" (Col 3:3-4). Many things remain hidden from sight, but signs are given to those with eyes to see.

Eschatology Grounds the Theology of Religions

Eschatology is the center of gravity of the theology of religious encounter. As long as eschatology remains the theology of the "last things" it has but little effect on our daily life. It is true that on "the last day" God will gather together around God's table all the children of God, but that hope needs to be translated into a way of being in the world now. Christian de Chergé insists on the present fulfillment of eschatology. In his view, the tension is not so much between the present and the future as it is between the God who comes and the present, in the Advent of God's incarnation. Therefore, the theology of religious encounter is a theology of hope, a sacramental, as it were, of the plan of God already realized and revealed in Christ. The plan of God is that all people should be gathered around the same table. Yet his work of reconciliation has been accomplished. The mystery of unity is deeper than all differences. Again, as John Paul II put it, unity is "radical, fundamental and determinative."[27] It is therefore necessary to anchor the theology of world religions in this mystery of accomplished hope, this mystery of unity as willed by the Father, accomplished in the Son, and signified in the Spirit. From this standpoint, interreligious dialogue and the theology of religious encounter participate in the sacramental mission of the Church. They are signs, not the only ones, to be sure, but privileged and indispensable signs, of this accomplished unity that today we are trying to do justice to and to incarnate in concrete ways as the signs of the times.

With its center of gravity in eschatology, the Christian theology of religious encounter is protected from the double deviation already mentioned—relativism and dogmatism. Relativism is

27. John Paul II, "To the Roman Curia at the Exchange of Christmas Wishes"; see chapter 9 above.

a deviation because, while it claims to seek for unity, it ends up relativizing the legitimate particularity of both Christianity and the other religions and often substitutes political necessity for a theological foundation. Dogmatism, for its part, while claiming to oppose all relativism, is so preoccupied with defending the uniqueness of Christianity that it forgets that Christianity is oriented toward a unity that is an ever-greater mystery that transcends it and is the very *raison d'être* of Christianity.

We can now better understand Pope John Paul II's speech of December 22, 1986. Unity is determinative of the sacramental mission of the Church, which is precisely to reveal this unity of all people and to set forth the signs that incarnate here and now this fundamental, radical, and determinative unity. Interreligious dialogue—the theology of religious encounter in practice—is one of the most manifest signs of how the Church is living out her vocation as a sacrament of unity.

The Sign of Monastic Life

If eschatology is the focal point or axis of a theology of religious encounter, then the monastic life (and the apostolic religious life too, when it is sufficiently compelling) is a necessary sign of interreligious encounter.

Monastic life has always played an important role in the Church, providing pioneers who have helped the Church advance along this path that is still to be cleared.[28] This is no accident. The magisterium of the Church has often encouraged monastics to be daring and creative with regard to interreligious monastic dialogue. In the world of Islam, the experience of Tibhirine and of Our Lady of Atlas in Midelt, Morocco, modest and precarious, are examples of the ways Christian monastics have responded to this challenge. The influence of Tibhirine, especially after the deaths of Christian and his brothers, has already made an exceptional

28. Christian Salenson, "De *Nostra aetate* à Assise, la vie monastique," *Chemins de dialogue* 28 (2006): 15–29.

contribution to the reflection on and sensitization to the need for dialogue among Christians and Muslims. Why does the monastic life play such a role? Precisely because, like the theology of world religions, monasticism is centered in eschatology. Monastic life is a sign to the whole Church of the need to anchor dialogue with other believers and the theology of world religions in eschatology, remembering the words of Raimundo Panikkar: "Inasmuch as we try to unify our lives around the center, all of us have something of the monk in us."[29] The theology of religious encounter needs this grounding in hope. Eschatology is the gravitational center of both the monastic life and the theology of religious encounter. Every monastic thus becomes the sign of this hope and a privileged actor in interreligious dialogue, even if he or she has no more contact with believers of other religions than Thérèse de Lisieux, "patroness of foreign missions," had with the missions.

29. Raimundo Panikkar, *Blessed Simplicity*, 15.

Transition

The time has come to review the road traveled thus far. It began when Christian de Chergé responded to a call. Sounding through Mohammed, this call was a vocation to live, as a member of a monastic community in Algeria, in dialogue with Islam. It was not a vocation simply to be a silent Christian presence among Muslims. To be sure, that silent witnessing to Christ was part, but only a part, of de Chergé's call. He received a vocation to live out an existential dialogue not only with Muslim friends but with Islam itself as a great religious tradition and to allow his monastic life, his thought, and his prayer to be formed within this relationship, willing to accept the shifts and conversions he might have to undergo.

De Chergé knew that he had been placed on this path, that it was his vocation, but he still did not know the exact place of Islam in the plan of God. His theology of world religions did not give him an a priori answer to the question of how the plurality of religions fits into the plan of God, an answer upon which he could then base his way of being in the world. He did not know, and he accepted not knowing. He consented to follow the path of encounter and dialogue with the other on the basis of this not-knowing.

This dialogue, termed "existential," consisted in encounter with Muslims, those whom life already put in his path, so all he had to do was draw near: ordinary Muslims, villagers, some guests passing through, members of a Sufi brotherhood. It consisted also in deepening his knowledge of Islam, including the Qurʾan, its theology, and its tradition, without boxing Islam into an a priori definition or even into the picture it presented of itself. Thus, existential dialogue became his road on a long quest. Essentially, what motivated de Chergé to dialogue was his not knowing the exact place of Islam, together with his faith that this great religious tradition, which fosters a taste for God in so many men and women, was no stranger to the plan of God, even though he could not say how, in what respect, or to what extent it fit into that divine plan.

We saw that de Chergé's insight was a unique contribution to the theology of religious encounter. We are not obliged to know a priori if and to what extent other religions are paths to salvation, nor what exact place they occupy in the plan of God. All that the theology of religions needs to do is leave the question open and have faith that the religions do have a place; this is the necessary and sufficient condition for entering into constructive dialogue both with believers in other religions and with the religious traditions themselves.

Often Christians who live in the Islamic world speak of their fraternal bonds with their Muslim friends. One can recognize from their accounts how much these Christians are men and women of dialogue, often having been profoundly influenced by the spirituality of Charles de Foucauld. Christian de Chergé takes us a bit further. With the support of the Second Vatican Council, he called for a positive consideration of Islam itself as a religion, not only esteem for Muslims. All the more so because Islam, in his view and that of many other theologians and experts on Islam, is not simply a "natural religion."[1]

This dialogical stance led Christian de Chergé to develop and deepen both his approach to Christ and his sense of the Church. Such a fundamental attitude obliged him, in fidelity to the faith of the Church, to go beyond a Christology that is sometimes no more than a "Jesus-ology." De Chergé revived that classical Christology of the Word of God, a Christology whose culmination, the mystery of the incarnation in Jesus of Nazareth, nourishes the whole history of humankind.

---

1. Robert Caspar, *Pour un regard chrétien sur l'islam* [*Toward a Christian View of Islam*] (Paris: Bayard, 2006), 28–29; *Traité de théologie musulmane*, vol. 1 (Rome: PISAI, 1987), 102–5. Claude Geffré, *De Babel à Pentecôte* [*From Babel to Pentecost*] Cogitatio Fidei Series 247 (Paris: Cerf, 2006), 168–72.

It is necessary and vital for someone thoroughly committed to the dialogical stance to have an understanding of Christ as an "ever greater Christ." This was the spiritual experience of Teilhard de Chardin in lively dialogue with the science of his day. It was also the experience of Christian de Chergé in existential dialogue with Islam. On a personal level, for myself, a constant study of the texts of de Chergé as well as my position in the Institute of Sciences and Theology of Religions have led me over time and through prayer to modify and enlarge in a remarkable manner my understanding of the faith of Christ. I believe that such an enlargement in Christology is indispensable for anyone directly interested in religious diversity. It is becoming necessary for today's men and women who are, after all, immersed in a context of multiculturalism and religious pluralism. A Christology of "the ever greater Christ" seems to me to be one of the greatest riches offered by the positive consideration of other religions.

The same shift must necessarily be brought about in regard to the Church. Interreligious dialogue immediately raises the question of the essence of the Church and its mission. It calls us to come face-to-face with the mystery of the Church and to stand before the Father's plan of unity. Only from this position can we fashion an ecclesiology.

The horizon of religious and cultural diversity takes us back to the questions of the origin and destiny of the human family and to the question of the manifestations of its unity in history. And then, what about difference? Why the difference among religions? What is the relationship between the Church and that without which the Church would have no meaning, namely, the mystery of unity? The very existence of the Church would have no meaning outside the mystery of unity and difference.

Forthrightly to face the mystery of the communion of saints, the People of God, the heavenly Jerusalem, both purifies much of the discourse about the Church as a sociohistorical reality and confronts it with its own identity, a mystery of the incarnation of the communion of saints, and its vocation, to signify that mystery.

We have been led to what seems to us to be the center in de Chergé's theology of religious encounter: eschatology. We have highlighted the fact that de Chergé benefited both from twentieth-century theological thought (though he belonged to no particular school) and from his rootedness in monasticism, for the monastic vocation is nothing if not eschatological. We have seen the precious and indispensable contribution monastic life has to make to dialogue and to the theology of religions, for monasticism too has its center of gravity in eschatology. Distortions in the theology of religions, whether through relativism or through dogmatism, arise from an ignorance of eschatology. The theology of religious encounter in turn can help restore to eschatology its rightful place in the theological reflection of the Churches, especially when they wish to promote and support a keener sense of evangelization.

After having set out the conditions of interreligious dialogue and having tried to show how interreligious dialogue brought Christian de Chergé to a richer understanding of the mystery of Christ, the mystery of the Church, and the mystery of time in God, we would like to draw out some consequences for the life of the Church. What did interreligious dialogue and the taking seriously of religious diversity as one of the "signs of the times," along with the christological and ecclesiological shifts we have noted in the thought of Christian de Chergé, lead de Chergé to think about the mission of the Church? Christian de Chergé was preoccupied with the Church's mission. The fact that his patron saint was Thérèse of the Child Jesus reminds us of that. Frequently, men and women who have a passion for interreligious dialogue are men and women with a passion for mission.

What did Christian de Chergé write about mission? We will pay particular attention to what he had to say about sacramentality. Then, given that traditionally the mission of the Church is expressed through three *munera* (gifts)—*leiturgia* (liturgy), *marturia* (witness), and *diakonia* (ministry)—we will examine him on these aspects of the Church's mission. We wish to acknowledge what de Chergé's theology of religious encounter contributes to the enrichment of the understanding of Christian faith. His message can help Christians better understand their faith and the apostolate.

Chapter 11

The Church of the Visitation

One's perception of the Church's mission differs according to the way one views other religions. Obviously, from an exclusivist point of view that interprets the dictum "outside the Church there is no salvation" in the sense of the Council of Florence, other religions are obstacles to salvation, and Christian mission takes on such importance that the administration of baptism becomes the primary imperative. This was the reasoning of Francis Xavier, whose zeal for and love of humanity was impressive but whose expression of it today gives pause.

At the other extreme, from a point of view that relativizes paths to salvation, mission is seen as nothing more than mutual emulation among the different religious traditions. In one sense, this was the position of Ernst Troeltsch. For Troeltsch, mission should allow for an encounter between religions and mutual fertilization without any ulterior motive of conversion. To be sure, mutual fertilization is not a negligible outcome. It is one of the fruits of dialogue and, in this sense, it is part of the meaning of mission. It does not, though, provide a complete definition of it.

For Ernst Troeltsch mission should not be understood as the extension of Christianity. In his view, the goal of mission is not the growth of Christianity but the fulfillment of the plan of God. The former is subject to the latter, so that the Church was born through the proclamation of the kingdom.

141

Karl Barth, in a famous lecture, called attention to the fact that it is only from the time of Ignatius of Loyola and the Counter-Reformation that the term "mission" in the sense of the Church's evangelizing outreach has been used in reference to the Church.[1] Traditionally, the term "mission" was reserved for the *missio Dei*, the mission(s) within the Trinity: the sending of the Son by the Father and the sending of the Spirit by the Father and the Son. There are risks involved in using a term traditionally associated with the trinitarian action of God to speak of the life of the Church. There is the risk of imagining that the mission of the Church can be substituted for the mission of the Son and the Spirit, or that the goal of the Church's mission and its justification are to be found in the increase of the Church.

A cursory glance through history shows that periods of great expansion of the Church are not the periods of its greatest evangelical vitality. The Church participated extensively in the genocide of the native peoples at the time of the conquest of the New World, for example. There is also the risk of the Church deciding what its mission is at a certain historical moment. History demonstrates that at various times, in completely good faith, the Church has invoked what it believed to be its mission in order actually to resist Gospel values supported by its "adversaries," only later to recognize them as such—human rights, for example.

This is why Barth's reminder deserves to be taken very seriously; it invites the Church to consider mission as essentially the mission of God in which the Church participates. The Church understands itself within the story of God-with-the-world, at the heart of this trinitarian history. "Taking part in mission is taking part in the movement of love of God for the world." Vatican II referred to this understanding of mission in *Ad Gentes*: "Missionary activity is nothing else, and nothing less, than the manifestation of God's plan, its epiphany and realization in the world and in history."[2] That is why "it is not through the Church that mission is to be understood

---

1. Karl Barth, "La Théologie et la mission à l'heure présente," *Cahiers du monde non chrétien* 4 (1932): 70–104.
2. *Ad Gentes* 9.

but through mission that the Church is to be understood." Paul Tillich said, "If mission takes as its starting point a particular way of salvation—Protestant Christianity, Orthodoxy, liberal Christianity, Catholic, Methodist—it may well be the extension of a religious community, but it does not proclaim the fullness of Revelation."[3] Likewise, the mission of the Church will be perceived differently according to one's conception of Christian revelation. What does the mission of the Church become if we say with Vatican II, "It pleased God . . . to reveal himself,"[4] and this self-communication of God throughout history is still active today? Defining revelation as the self-communication of God in the present to each person and in each culture is undoubtedly quite different from considering it essentially as a message to be transmitted, whose transmission is incumbent upon the Church, or, a fortiori, thinking of revelation as a compendium of truths to be believed. None of these three aspects ought to be neglected, let alone rejected, but depending on where the emphasis is placed—on the self-revelation of God, or the message to be transmitted, or the truths to be believed—very different missionary attitudes will result.

It goes without saying that there is still a great deal to be done concretely in order to integrate the perspective of the *missio Dei* into the Church's theology of mission. It is true that our elders in the faith in the First Testament already dreamed of being a religion like the others, like those around them, to the detriment of their own unique place in the plan of salvation. In the Church, a collective lack of faith could lead to the same ingratitude. Yet the Church and its development often continue to be in many ways the goal of mission in the Church's pastoral practice.

The Mission of Other Religions

The theology of religious encounter also raises the question of the mission of other religions. The Church cannot act as though

---

3. Paul Tillich, *Dogmatique*, ed. André Gounelle and Jean Richard (Paris: Éditions du Cerf, 1990), 55.

4. *Dei Verbum* 2.

it is the only one with a mission in the world. At the time of the meeting at Assisi, a meeting with the express purpose of praying for peace on the occasion of the International Year of Peace declared by the United Nations, it was made manifest that all religions have, together, a common vocation and a common mission: to open humanity to transcendence. It is a vocation on which depends the very life of humanity.

As for the mission of the Church, it is dependent on the mission of Israel. For God gave to the Chosen People a mission in the midst of the nations and "the gifts and the calling of God are irrevocable" [Rom 11:29]. The mission of Israel will continue to the end of time. The Church does not supersede the mission of Israel and must avoid speaking of fulfillment in order not to reintroduce surreptitiously another form of supersession. The mission of the Church is rooted in the mission of Israel, and the mission of Israel continuously calls the Church's mission to account. Both the common vocation of all the religions and the specific and foundational mission of Israel ought to make Christians more tactful in their manner of speaking about the mission of the Church.

Christian de Chergé accepted that he could not know the place of Islam in the plan of God, and he left this place wide open. We cannot eliminate a priori the idea that Islam has its own mission. As Henri de Lubac said in reference to Buddhism, "We do not resign ourselves to thinking that God has left himself without witnesses everywhere outside of Christianity. . . . And of all the signs that are offered to us, those that touch on the spiritual life are without doubt the most worth keeping."[5] Without denying any of the revelation to which it bears witness, "Christianity must leave open the question whether the essence of Christianity is realized in other places, thus, whether other religions play a role in the in-breaking [of the fullness of revelation] itself."[6] By doing this, Christianity fully becomes what it is: "Definitively, it is Christianity's freedom with respect to itself, that is to say, its capacity to deny itself in

---

5. Henri de Lubac, *Amida*, Œuvres complètes, vol. 22 (Paris: Éditions du Cerf), 306–7.

6. Tillich, *Dogmatique*, 58.

order to affirm the fullness of Revelation, that grounds its claim to possess a revelation of concern to all humankind."[7]

How did Christian de Chergé pose the question of mission? A response to that question must take into account the fact that he is not a party to theological debates; he is a monk in the land of Islam. From the position that he occupies, what does he have to say about the mission of the Church?

The Sacramental Mission[8]

Commenting on the statement on mission in the *Catechism of the Catholic Church* de Chergé said, "The mission of the disciples is here expressed in classical terms. This is a definition we cannot be totally satisfied with, for it leaves no place for the monastic vocation."[9] We cannot omit monastic life from talk of mission. What kind of mission would it be that failed to take the

---

7. Jean-Marc Aveline, *L'enjeu christologique en théologie de religions* [*What Is at Stake for Christology in the Theology of Religions*], Cogitatio Fidei Series 227 (Paris: Cerf, 2003), 411.

8. For what follows, see de Chergé, Chapter talk for August 2, 1994, in Christian de Chergé, *Dieu pour tout jour, chapitres du père Christian de Chergé à la communauté de Tibhirine (1985–1996)* [*God for Each Day: Chapter Talks of Fr. Christian de Chergé to the Community of Tibhirine*], 2nd ed., Les cahiers de Tibhirine (Montjoyer: Abbé d'Aiguebelle, 2006), 503.

9. [Following are paragraphs from the *Catechism of the Catholic Church* (CCC) referring to the Church's mission. – Ed.]

CCC 1122 Christ sent his apostles so that "repentance and forgiveness of sins should be preached in his name to all nations." "Go therefore and make disciples of all nations, baptizing them in the name of the Father and of the Son and of the Holy Spirit." The mission to baptize, and so the sacramental mission, is implied in the mission to evangelize, because the sacrament is prepared for by *the word of God and by the faith* which is assent to this word:

> The People of God is formed into one in the first place by the Word of the living God. . . . The preaching of the Word is required for the sacramental ministry itself, since the sacraments are sacraments of faith, drawing their origin and nourishment from the Word.

CCC 1123 "The purpose of the sacraments is to sanctify men, to build up the Body of Christ and, finally, to give worship to God. Because they are signs they also instruct. They not only presuppose faith, but by

contemplative dimension into account? "The mission of the contemplative in non-Christian lands that are not evangelized (in the active sense of the word) is 'to be urged on by the love of Christ to recognize and honor in the multitudes Christ's Presence as the leaven of history' to discover that Jesus has preceded us 'on the other side of the lake,' among 'the nations.' "[10]

Nevertheless, by describing mission as she does in the *Catechism*, the Church recognizes that the Word of God takes priority in mission. "It [the Word] is prior to the disciple's actual proclamation, which itself is of a sacramental nature. The *Verbum* is handed over to the multitude, and it is the work of the Spirit to watch over this seed at work in every heart. Thus the word of the disciple is anticipated [by the Word], and, if God wills, confessed in faith." Only a trinitarian approach to mission does justice to the contemplative dimension of mission. What is most lacking from mission work today is not so much an effective preaching of the faith, as we hear all too often, but the contemplation of the *Verbum* and of the Spirit's work.

The works of creation are themselves missionaries:[11]

> The heavens are telling the glory of God;
> and the firmament proclaims his handiwork.
> Day to day pours forth speech,
> and night to night declares knowledge.
> There is no speech, nor are there words;
> their voice is not heard;
> yet their voice goes out through all the earth,
> and their words to the end of the world. (Ps 19:1-4)

Francis of Assisi "did not seek to baptize the sun and moon. He welcomed the Gospel of inanimate beings. He welcomed them as

---

words and objects they also nourish, strengthen, and express it. That is why they are called 'sacraments *of faith.*' "

10. De Chergé, *Dieu pour tout jour*, 503, quoting Moubarac.

11. De Chergé, homily for August 8, 1983, in Christian de Chergé, *L'autre que nous attendons, homélies du père Christian de Chergé (1970–1996)* [*The Other Whom We Await: Homilies of Fr. Christian de Chergé*], Les cahiers de Tibhirine (Montjoyer: Abbé d'Aiguebelle, 2006), 110.

bearers and signs of the Gospel. . . . He thanked them for having contributed to his conversion." Like Francis, de Chergé took it for granted that we must welcome the Good News proclaimed by creation and recognize in it the testimony of the Spirit.

The Martyrdom of the Holy Spirit

In his commentary on 1 John 5:6 ("the Spirit is the one that bears witness [Greek: *to marturoun*]"), Christian de Chergé gave the Holy Spirit its full due when he spoke of the "martyrdom" of the Holy Spirit. The Holy Spirit is therefore a *martyr* in the etymological sense of the word. "When the Advocate comes . . . the Spirit of Truth . . . , He will bear witness [*marturêsei*] on my behalf. You also are to bear witness [*martureite*]" (John 15:26-27). The witness of the Christian agrees with the witness of the Holy Spirit because it is the Spirit that testifies. The Christian bears witness that It bears witness in him or her. Without the witness of the Spirit, apostolic witness is empty. The Spirit is "the Witness that never ceases to communicate Its own Self, from generation to generation, from language to language, from life to life, as in a relay race, carrying the flame of love to the very limits of the heart."

Since the true witness is the Spirit, those who come from other religious traditions can also be true witnesses through the Spirit. Witness is tied not only to those who recognize themselves as disciples of Christ but also to those who accept living in the domain of the Spirit. Christian de Chergé cites the case of Sheik Bouslimani, an Islamic militant and head of a kind of Muslim *Caritas*. Bouslimani, refusing to issue a *fatwa* authorizing violence in the name of Islam, was arrested, tortured, and put to death. De Chergé remarked, "[F]or us he is a witness, because he refused to sin 'against the Holy Spirit.' We testify that his 'martyrdom' comes from the Spirit, and we declare that this expert in Muslim law shared in the grace of simple people and of infants, which is to bear witness to the truth."[12]

12. De Chergé, *L'autre que nous attendons*, 431.

Islam includes among the ninety-nine names of God *Shahid*, "witness." In the Qur²an, *Shahid* means that God as Witness is sufficient unto himself. Undoubtedly, Islam converges here with Christian revelation. The Spirit's witness is the only testimony and in a certain way is sufficient unto itself, even if the Spirit gives us by pure grace the opportunity to participate in its mission and to be associated with the testimony it gives. On the other hand, in our talks about mission we sometimes give the impression that it is we who, by grace, associate the Spirit with what we believe mission to be.

Therefore *poverty* is what characterizes the apostles on the day of Pentecost:

> The frightened apostles whom we see praying behind closed doors have come to realize that they are resourceless in the face of a mission too big for them; they wait on God for everything, including the first word of their witness; they wait on God for God, for him to be the one who bears witness. And the miracle will be born from the encounter of two poverties, that of the apostles and that of the crowd that is there, also waiting. In this event, everyone seems to bear witness, everyone in his or her own language and in accordance with his or her own grace.[13]

Sending out the disciples, Jesus commanded that they take nothing for their journey. The Church—and each believer—is undoubtedly still much too weighed down by all the things it wants to bring along and to suggest, by everything it believes it knows, to "go forward in freedom and trust" to meet other cultures and persons. The Church simply has not sufficiently integrated the reciprocity that is implied by the proclamation and signified by dialogue.

From this perspective, the mission of the Church and the witness of the disciples constitute what is sacramental. They point to a mystery that precedes them and over which they have no

---

13. Christian de Chergé, *L'invincible espérance* [*Hope Unconquerable*], ed. Bruno Chenu (Paris: Bayard, 1996), 250.

control but which they learn to know and experience. Mission is a sacramental ministry of the Church.

Mission, or the Mystery of the Visitation[14]

There dwells within us a Good News that is not a kind of knowledge but rather a life, the Life of our life:

> It is entirely obvious that this mystery of the Visitation [Luke 1:39-56] should be given a privileged place in the Church which is ours [that is, the local monastic Church; the Church that is the monastic community of Atlas]. I can well imagine that we are in the position of Mary who is going to see her cousin Elizabeth and who is carrying inside her a living secret—the same one we carry ourselves—the living Good News. She received it from an angel. It is her secret and it is also God's secret.[15]

What can we say about this Life that dwells within us? There are many Christians who do not know how to speak of God, do not know how to approach the subject with those close to them even when they are truly living out of this Good News in an apostolic way. And Mary?

> It must be that she does not know how to go about communicating this secret. Is she going to say something to Elizabeth? Can she say it? How is she to say it? How to go about it? Should she hide it? And yet everything in her is full to overflowing, but she does not know. In the first instance it is God's secret.[16]

And what about the other whom we encounter—our friends, our neighbors, our companions on the journey—who often do

---

14. See Jean-Pierre Flachaire, "Notre-Dame de l'Atlas, une présence de visitation" ("Our Lady of Atlas: A Presence of Visitation"], *Chemins de dialogue* 26 (2005): 165–76.

15. From an unpublished retreat given by de Chergé to a group of Little Sisters of Jesus in Morocco, 1990.

16. De Chergé, see n. 15, above.

not know the Gospel and frequently reject the Church, seeing it as nothing but a pious musty society clinging desperately to what it believes and determined to impose its belief on everyone else? The Church cannot refuse to believe that these people too have been deeply damaged.

> And then something similar is happening inside Elizabeth. She, too, is bearing a child. What Mary does not really grasp is the bond, the connection, between the child she herself is bearing and the child Elizabeth is bearing. She only knows that there is a bond since this is the sign that she has been given: her cousin Elizabeth. It would make it easier for her to express herself if she knew about this bond. But on this very point she has had no revelation: on the mutual dependence of the two children.[17]

Christians sometimes forget that the sign given to us is that the other also is a bearer of a word, a sign given in confirmation of a revelation. I am able to go to meet the other because the life of the Spirit dwells within the other too. Still, however well I might know it notionally it is always disconcerting to realize, as apostles of every age must, that, as Peter said about Cornelius and his family, "God gave them the same Gift that he gave us" (Acts 11:14).

"We know," Christian de Chergé goes on, "that those whom we have come to meet are like Elizabeth: they are bearers of a message that comes from God. Our Church does not tell us and does not know what the exact bond is between the Good News we bear and the message that gives life to the other. In the end, my Church does not tell me what the bond between Christ and Islam is. I go out to Muslims without knowing what this bond is."[18] We may never know exactly what that bond is, but we do know that the other is also a bearer of a message that comes from God. What should we do? What does witness then consist in? What about mission? Again, we can consider the scene of the Visitation in Luke 1. Mary did not preach the faith:

17. De Chergé, see n. 15, above.
18. De Chergé, see n. 15, above.

And see, when Mary arrives, it is Elizabeth who speaks first. Or did she?—for Mary certainly said: *as salam alaikum!* And that is something that we can do! We say, Peace: Peace be with you! And this simple greeting made something vibrate, some-*one*, inside Elizabeth. And in this vibration, something was said. . . . Which was the Good News, not the whole of the Good News, but what could be glimpsed of it in the moment. And why has this happened to me that . . . the child who is inside me leapt? In all likelihood it was the child that was inside Mary that leapt first. In fact, whatever was happening was between the children.[19]

What the one is carrying has come to meet what the other is carrying. All things being equal, this is a common occurrence in the ordinary interactions of life, in the simple and authentic encounters where each person can say what they are carrying and bringing to the encounter. The word of the other finds an echo in one's own existence. This experience is rightly called "visitation." But who is visiting whom? Peter visits Cornelius but is also visited *by* him, and both together are visited by the Spirit.

Artists of every period have painted the Visitation. They have sensed in it the mystery of encounter, of every true encounter. The Visitation as encounter is the heart of the apostolic life.

And Elizabeth released the *Magnificat* of Mary. In the end, if we are attentive, if we situate our encounter with the other in the attention and the desire to meet the other, and in our need for the other and what he has to say to us, it is likely that the other is going to say something to us that will connect with what we are carrying, something that will reveal complicity with us . . . , allowing us to broaden our Eucharist, for in the end, it is the *Magnificat* which we are given to sing that is the Eucharist. The Church's first Eucharist was Mary's *Magnificat*. What this points to is our need of the other in order to do Eucharist: "for you and for the many."[20]

19. De Chergé, see n. 15, above.
20. De Chergé, see n. 15, above.

All too often the apostolic life, the mission of the Church, imitates the law of supply and demand. The Church's missionary schemes are tainted by the ideologies of the times. In her desire to promote the faith she sometimes has recourse to marketing methods. It is as if the Good News were something the Church possessed and would like to give to others.

Such a position reflects the worldliness of the Church. As long as Christians think in this way they barely scratch the surface of the mystery of encounter that is the Church's true mission. Mission is the trinitarian life to which by grace the Church is associated. Mission is not born out of a surplus that Christians might have to communicate to others; it is born out of a lack of the other, and without the other, without my meeting him, I will never be able to release my own *Magnificat*. Without the encounter with Islam, the Church will never completely sing its *Magnificat*. Without the encounter with other religions, the Church will not be able fully to celebrate the Eucharist "for you and for the many."

The road to the Visitation is long.

Chapter 12

Witness, or The Question of Martyrdom

Under the emblematic rubric of *mission* understood in terms of Visitation can be situated the functions of the Church's mission that correspond to the threefold office of Christ, namely, the prophetic, the kingly, and the priestly functions. Christian de Chergé takes up these functions of mission; renames them witness, brotherhood, and prayer; and deepens their implications.

The world values witness. It has been said that our world prefers witnesses to teachers. No doubt this is linked to the primacy of the individual and of subjective personal experience so valued by today's culture, especially in the West. Contributing to the creation of this "witnessing" style has been a kind of Pentecostalism, both Protestant and Catholic, in harmony with society and firmly "in the world" with its values of efficiency, marketing, and personal well-being. Moreover, the Church's emphasis on the explicit proclamation and presentation of the faith contributes to favoring that particular feature of the *prophetic* vocation of each Christian over a spirituality of the hidden witness of Nazareth, a spirituality considered in many quarters of the Church to be a thing of the past. The emphasis on witness understood in this way is not infrequently accompanied by the desire to convince the other, to convert the other, to form the other in one's own religious tradition and even in one's own Christian denomination. Religious diversity and interreligious dialogue call this concept of witness into question. Like every dialogue, interreligious dialogue, inasmuch as it presumes that all participants should be themselves and not be silent about their choices and convictions, must also reject the desire—of any party—to convert the other. Interreligious dialogue obliges us to distinguish between conversion to God and change of religion. Although conversion remains the heart of dialogue, this conversion of all participants does not mean a change in religious affiliation but a turn to God.

It is no surprise that Christian de Chergé wrote substantial pages on the subject of conversion.[1] It would have been useless if not impossible for the monks of Tibhirine to have wished to privilege an explicit declaration of Christian faith. Christian de Chergé spoke out strongly against any wish to convert the other to one's own religion.[2] Interreligious dialogue excludes all opportunity for proselytism. Rather, de Chergé applied what Vatican II said about ecumenism to interreligious dialogue: "There can be no ecumenism worthy of the name without interior conversion."[3]

Nevertheless, it is impossible for the Christian to reject witnessing. It is essential to the Christian faith: "you will be my witnesses in Jerusalem, in all Judea and Samaria, and to the ends of the earth" (Acts 1:8). The document Dialogue and Proclamation says:

> All Christians are called to be personally involved in these
> two ways of carrying out the one mission of the Church,

1. Chapter talks from May 21, 1986 to June 6, 1987, in Christian de Chergé, *Dieu pour tout jour, chapitres du père Christian de Chergé à la communauté de Tibhirine (1985–1996)* [*God for Each Day: Chapter Talks of Fr. Christian de Chergé to the Community of Tibhirine*], 2nd ed., Les cahiers de Tibhirine (Montjoyer: Abbé d'Aiguebelle, 2006), 121–90. These texts are analyzed by Christophe Purgu, "Processus de conversion," *Chemins de dialogue* 24 (2004): 155–72.

2. [Tr. note: See Christian de Chergé, "Prier en Église à l'écoute de l'islam" ["Praying with the Church While Listening to Islam"], *Chemins de dialogue* 27 (2006): 17–24; also published in the journal *Tychique* 34 (November 1981): 48–55.]

3. *Unitatis Redintegratio* (Decree on Ecumenism) 7.

> namely proclamation and dialogue. . . . They must never-
> theless always bear in mind that dialogue . . . does not con-
> stitute the whole mission of the Church, that it cannot simply
> replace proclamation, but remains oriented toward proclama-
> tion. . . . In order to be able to do this, Christians should
> deepen their faith, purify their attitudes, clarify their language
> and render their worship more and more authentic.[4]

Once more we note that the fact of religious diversity, on the one hand, purifies witness of all wish to convert others, of all latent proselytism that would disfigure the apostolic life, and, on the other, calls believers to understand their faith more deeply. By acknowledging the fact of religious diversity, believers put themselves on a more authentic evangelical path, a path configuring them to Christ, whose witness was in the total gift of his life.

The monks of Tibhirine can be our companions on this path. Their *witness* is incontestable. These simple men, lost and hidden in a Trappist monastery deep in the Atlas Mountains of Algeria, never stopped bearing witness; neither did they yield for an instant to any drift to proselytism, which, in any case, was forbidden to them. Under the conditions to which they were subject, there was little place or rationale for explicit testimony. There was no need to talk; it was enough for them simply to remain faithful to their vocation as monks.

Their example leads us to the very heart of the prophetic office of every Christian, an office that can be understood in terms of witness as long as we take witness to its conclusion: *martyrdom*. To put it another way, to witness is not to preach the faith, much less one's own experience. There is only One witness to the Father, and he died on the cross. For every Christian, witness means the total gift of life. The Greek word for "witness" or "testimony," it

---

4. "Dialogue and Proclamation," *Chemins de dialogue* 20 (2002): 82. This 1991 document was produced by the Pontifical Council for Interreligious Dialogue and the Congregation for the Evangelization of Peoples. [Tr. note: An official English version is available online on the Vatican web site: http://www.vatican.va/roman_curia/pontifical_councils/interelg/documents/rc_pc_interelg_doc_19051991_dialogue-and-proclamatio_en.html.]

should be recalled, is *marturion*. All who engage in interreligious dialogue, in the positive consideration of other religions, discover very quickly that they are brought to this level of depth in what it means to witness to the faith. Such was the experience of the monks of Tibhirine.

Apostolic witness cannot be limited to presenting the faith; it is a matter of the total gift of one's life. At the same time, witness in this sense is not reserved for Christians alone. Every person is called to this total gift. Demonstration of these two propositions is given by a consideration of the experience of the monks, of their martyrdom, in which the very idea of martyrdom is transformed in the light of a theology of religious encounter. From their experience and example, conclusions can be drawn for others who are trying to live their lives and their faith with a similar openness.

Were the Monks of Tibhirine Martyrs?

It is legitimate to ask whether the monks were martyrs or innocent victims of a political conflict.[5] The *sensus fidelium* had no hesitation in recognizing them immediately as the former.[6] All Christians unanimously recognized in the life and tragic end of these men the witness of martyrdom. John Paul II was able to discern the sense of the faith of the Christian people and confirmed his brothers in this faith. Dom Bernardo Olivera, abbot general of the Cistercian Order of the Strict Observance at the time, reported a discussion he had with John Paul II in November 1997 during a private meal:

> Father Stanislas Dziwisz, the Pope's private secretary, asked me: "When are you going to beatify the monks of Atlas?" I

5. This line of thought has been developed further in Christian Salenson, "Le martyre selon Christian de Chergé" ["Martyrdom according to Christian de Chergé"], *Chemins de dialogue* 27 (2006): 25–38.
   6. This expression, "the sense of the faithful," refers to the capacity possessed by the Christian people as a whole to recognize doctrinal truth; it was reaffirmed by the Second Vatican Council in its documents. See especially *Lumen Gentium* 12, 35.

replied: "There is no hurry, these things take time." He shot back: "You have to start right away, because they are martyrs." Then he turned toward John Paul II and said to him: "Holy Father, is it not certain that they are martyrs?" The Pope looked straight at me, in that way that only he could, and said, emphasizing each word: "They are martyrs!"[7]

Three years later, in May 2000, during the celebrations for the third millennium, when the Twentieth-Century Witnesses to the Faith were honored in the Coliseum in Rome, the monks of Atlas were mentioned in the long list of those who had given their lives in witness to their faith.[8]

May We Speak of Martyrdom in Reference to the Christian Tradition?

But are they martyrs in the strict sense of the word? According to classical theology, "Martyrdom consists in the voluntary acceptance of death[9] for faith in Christ, or for any other act of virtue for God's sake."[10] The goal of martyrdom, to use the language of Saint Thomas Aquinas, is the faith. The martyr is someone who bears witness to faith in Christ through the violent death that he or she endures.[11] (In Islam, too, martyrdom is witness to the faith. Christian de Chergé points out, as we saw in the last chapter, that in Arabic the word for "martyrs" is *shuhada*, plural

---

7. "Tibhirine Today" (Circular Letter to the Members of the Order on the Tenth Anniversary of the Passing of our Brothers of Our Lady of Atlas), May 21, 2006. Available on the OCSO web site: http://www.ocso.org/index .php?option=com_docman&task=doc_download&gid=279&Itemid=147& lang=en.

8. "Tibhirine Today."

9. One can hardly speak of voluntary acceptance by the Holy Innocents, who are nevertheless considered martyrs.

10. *Dictionnaire de Théologie Catholique*, vol. 10 (Paris: Letouzey et Ané, 1928), s.v. "Martyre," col. 226. Hereafter *DTC*. [Tr. note: English-speaking readers are referred to the *Catholic Encyclopedia*, vol. 9 (New York: Appleton, 1910), 735ff., s.v. "Martyr."]

11. As opposed to the confessor of the faith, who may well be the victim of tortures or agonies but who does not suffer violent death.

of *shahid*, which is from the same root as *shahâda*, the word for the Muslim profession of faith.[12]) Were the monks asked to deny their faith? That question cannot be answered. It is only possible to affirm that the monks were faithful to their faith in Christ and that it is this faith that makes sense of their fidelity to a people, a land, their Church, and their monastic community.[13]

Christian de Chergé distanced himself from martyrdom for the faith, whose excesses and possible deviations he criticized on at least three counts. We can be surprised or even shocked, he wrote, at the arrogance of certain martyrs toward their judges and persecutors, astonished, as well, at their "awareness of their own purity," of their assumption of complete innocence, and surprised at their conceited claim to know the judgment awaiting their persecutors in the afterlife. Finally, he said, martyrdom for the faith can be tainted by a certain fundamentalism.[14]

This critique of martyrdom for the faith is traditional. It is not permitted to provoke the persecutor, wrote Thomas Aquinas.[15] The Christian tradition has always denounced provocation and

12. De Chergé, Homily for Holy Thursday, 1995, in Christian de Chergé, *L'autre que nous attendons, homélies du père Christian de Chergé (1970–1996)* [*The Other Whom We Await: Homilies of Fr. Christian de Chergé*], Les cahiers de Tibhirine (Montjoyer: Abbé d'Aiguebelle, 2006), 455.

13. Other arguments could be adduced, as, for instance, the fact that the religious motive was emphasized by the members of the GIA in the communiqué addressed to the French government on April 18. The communiqué begins with two quotations from the Qurʾan, one concerning the People of the Book and the other all polytheists, and the GIA was explicit that it was "relying on these teachings" that it acted. See also Dom Armand Veilleux, "Une opinion islamique extrême, à propos des sept frères de Tibhirine" ["An Extreme Islamic Opinion, with Reference to the Seven Brothers of Tibhirine"], *Collectanea cisterciensia* 62 (2000): 72–80.

14. Perhaps he had in mind the Franciscans of Marrakesh, contemporaries of Saint Francis, who insulted the Prophet in the main square until they finally brought down violence upon themselves and were executed.

15. [Tr. note: This assertion does not actually occur in Saint Thomas's treatment of martyrdom in *Summa Theologiae*, 2a 2ae, q. 123–40. The closest statement is this: "[P]eople ought not to provide each other with opportunity for unjust action" (Q. 124 a.1, r.3, in vol. 42 of the Blackfriars edition, trans. and ed. Anthony Ross and P. G. Walsh [New York: McGraw-Hill, 1966]), 430.]

pride. "We do not commend those who volunteer to come forward [and thus risking martyrdom], since this is not the teaching of the Gospel."[16] Everyone should be ready to confess his faith, but no one should run toward martyrdom, said Saint Cyprian.[17] Likewise, it is wrong to irritate or provoke the unbelievers. It is not permitted to insult or strike the statues of the gods;[18] or again, in the words of the Council of Elvira, "If someone has broken idols and on that account was put to death . . . he shall not be included in the ranks of the martyrs."[19] The Christian tradition has fought against the possible excesses of martyrdom for the faith, namely, pride, arrogance, and conceit.[20]

What Did the Monks' Martyrdom Consist In?

The monks had a lively awareness of the risk of death from the time of the events of Tamesguida and even more clearly after the visit of the emir Sayah Attiyah.[21] The question arose as to what they should do next and, in particular, whether they should go away, at least temporarily, from Our Lady of Atlas. The abbot general of the Cistercians of the Strict Observance at the time, Dom Bernardo Olivera, had told Christian de Chergé, "The Order needs monks more than martyrs. So you must do all that you can to avoid a dramatic end that would serve no one."[22] Monsignor

16. Martyrdom of Polycarp, 4; *Ancient Christian Writers* 6, ed. Johannes Quasten and Joseph C. Plumpe (Westminster, MD: Newman Press, 1948), 42.
17. [Tr. note: See the *Acta Cypriani*, the account of his life and martyrdom.]
18. See Origen, *Against Celsus*, 8.38.
19. Council of Elvira (309 CE), canon 60. The list of canons is reproduced in English in Samuel Laeuchli, *Power and Sexuality: The Emergence of Canon Law at the Synod of Elvira* (Philadelphia: Temple University Press, 1972), 126–35.
20. [Tr. note: For a balanced and highly readable account of early Christian attitudes to martyrdom, see Paul Middleton, *Martyrdom: A Guide for the Perplexed* (London: T & T Clark, 2011), esp. 46–56.]
21. The Croats were assassinated at Tamesguida on December 14, 1993, and the "visit" of the emir Sayah Attiyah took place ten days later, on December 24.
22. During a meeting at the Abbey of Timadeuc in France in February 1994. [Tr. note: The exchange is also recounted in Dom Bernardo Olivera, "Tibhirine Today."]

Teissier, the archbishop of Algiers, on a visit to Tibhirine a few days after the visit of the emir Sayah Attiyah, had told them, "The worst thing for everyone would be for you to meet the same end as the Croats. We cannot take that risk."[23] And in one of his chapter talks, Christian spoke of the reaction of the aged Cardinal Duval: "I still hear the reply of the cardinal after Christmas of '93. To the question: 'What do you advise?' he replied, 'Constancy.' " Christian's comment is absolutely direct: "constancy" comes from the Latin *cum-stare*, "to stand with." "So the answer is to stand firm and to stand together."[24]

The authorities in Medea offered the monks various forms of protection but the monks refused them.[25] They took time for reflection; each one made a personal decision to stay in the monastery and eventually to accept the total and brutal giving of his life. There is no doubt that the brothers prepared themselves personally and collectively for the gift of their life in martyrdom.[26] The personal journal of Brother Christophe is highly revealing of the fears the brothers had to overcome and the difficulties they faced in living out this total gift.[27] Those who visited the community spoke of how much the community had changed in appearance over the three final years, had drawn closer together, and had been transformed.

What Were the Reasons for Their Choice?

As Cistercian monks following the Rule of Saint Benedict, the brothers of Atlas had made a vow of stability binding them per-

23. De Chergé, Chapter talk for November 7, 1995, in de Chergé, *Dieu pour tout jour*, 532.

24. De Chergé, Chapter talk for December 14, 1995, in de Chergé, *Dieu pour tout jour*, 536.

25. The options were to leave the monastery, to spend the nights at Medea, or to accept the protection of a military guard.

26. The final series of chapter talks given by Christian de Chergé was titled "The Charism of Martyrdom"; de Chergé, *Dieu pour tout jour*, 531–49.

27. Christophe Lebreton, *Le souffle du don, journal de frère Christophe* [*The Breath of the Spirit: The Journal of Brother Christophe*] (Paris: Bayard/Centurion, 1999).

manently to their chosen community. For them, this monastic vow now took on a peculiar dimension: it included fidelity to a people, to neighbors, to acquaintances, to Muslim friends, and to the Algerian Church. The brothers of Atlas found it morally impossible to leave their monastery, Algeria, their neighbors, or the local Church.[28] For some of the monks, the choice of Algeria was bound up with their initial calling, and so the idea of leaving the monastery or Algeria, even temporarily, without denying their vocation was impossible. Their writings testify to this, and the *Testament* of Christian de Chergé sums it up forcefully: "I would like my community, my Church, and my family to remember that my life was given to God and to this country." They made the choice to stay:

> To the quip of our Abbot General to the effect that our Order needs monks more than martyrs, our answer has to be that we are truly being monks by continuing to live here the mystery of Christmas itself, of God living with human beings . . . and being exposed in this way, from the cradle on, to the massacre of the innocents.[29]

When Interreligious Dialogue Deepens the Meaning of Martyrdom

Interreligious dialogue led the monks of Atlas to confirm and deepen the Christian theology of martyrdom. Those who live in the spirit of Vatican II have a positive regard for other religions and other believers. Martyrdom for the faith cannot be reduced to a peremptory and even provocative or haughty affirmation of faith in Christ. Believers of other religions are brothers and sisters; even if they are radical Islamists, they are the "brothers of the mountain." The spirit of Assisi desired by the Church cannot

---

28. Thomas Georgeon, "Donner sa vie pour la gloire de T'aimer: Tibhirine ou un chemin communautaire vers le martyre" ["Giving One's Life for the Glory of Loving You: Tibhirine, or a Communal Path toward Martyrdom"], *Collectanea cisterciensia* 68 (2006): 76–104.

29. Chapter talk for January 4, 1996, in de Chergé, *Dieu pour tout jour*, 539.

coexist with a witness that makes faith in Christ a truth excluding every other path and in opposition to other believers.

Thus, Christian de Chergé privileges what he calls "the martyrdom of love." In the Holy Thursday homily already cited he emphasized that it was not until Maximilian Kolbe that the Church recognized the validity of "the title of martyrdom for a witness less to faith than to supreme charity."[30] He got the expression "martyrdom for love" from Jeanne de Chantal.[31] We recognize in Maximilian Kolbe the same martyrdom as that of Jesus, which was essentially a martyrdom for love: "Having loved his own who were in the world, he loved them to the end" (John 13:1). Jesus gave a sign of this during the Last Supper when, in a gesture of love, he washed the feet of the disciples and thereby gave meaning to his passion and death on the cross. Again, traditionally "martyrdom consists in the voluntary acceptance of death for faith in Christ or for any other virtuous act for God's sake."[32] Without getting caught up in the arguments of canon law,[33] we can nevertheless speak legitimately within the tradition of martyrdom about acts that are not directly or explicitly concerned with the mere confession of faith in Christ before one's persecutors, a confession that would entail violent death.

While the tradition makes this approach to martyrdom legitimate, the situation after Vatican II makes it desirable. Indeed, in a dialogical context witnessing to Christ is expressed essentially

---

30. Homily for Holy Thursday 1994, in de Chergé, *L'Autre que nous attendons*, 419. [Tr. note: Also in de Chergé, *L'invincible espérance*, 226.]

31. "Neither Saint Basil nor the majority of our Holy Fathers and pillars of the Church were martyred. Why? I believe it is because there is a martyrdom of love in which God sustains the life of his servants in order that they may work for his glory, making them martyrs and confessors at one and the same time." Saint Jeanne Chantal speaking to her daughters in religion, quoted in de Chergé's chapter talk for December 12, 1995, in de Chergé, *Dieu pour tout jour*, 535–36.

32. See n. 10, above.

33. The criteria of martyrdom have been elaborated at length in the course of the tradition, in particular, by Pope Benedict XIV, *DTC*, col. 223. [Tr. note: The *DTC* here summarizes the relevant portion of Benedict's 1737 treatise: "On the Beatification and Canonization of the Servants of God."]

in the gift of one's life out of love for one's own, out of love for other believers, a witness that is a sign of fidelity manifested to a point that includes the forgiveness of enemies. For the monks of Atlas, this love took the form of faithfulness to a people, to their neighbors, to their friends, and to their Church and led them to the total gift of their lives. Thus, their martyrdom is one with that of Jesus, "a martyrdom of love, of love for humankind, for all people, even for thieves, for assassins and torturers, and those who act in darkness, ready to treat you like an animal destined for slaughter (Ps 49)."[34] According to the Church's positive understanding of its relation to the believers of other religious traditions, martyrdom too must include this positive approach to others and their religious traditions. This approach disposes martyrdom, which always continues to be martyrdom for faith in Christ, a witnessing to Christ, to become essentially a martyrdom for love.

The Renewal of the Concept of Witness

The spirit of Assisi leads to a deepening of the Christian theology of martyrdom and, consequently, to a renewal of the concept of witness.

Christians Are Not the Only Ones Who Witness to Christ

If Christian martyrdom is essentially a martyrdom for love, and if to be Christian is rightly understood as consisting in "having loved his own who were in the world, he loved them to the end" (John 13:1) and therefore in the free gift of one's life—"No one takes it from me, but I lay it down of my own accord" (John 10:18)— then, paradoxical as it seems, we are obliged to admit that Christian martyrdom is not lived out only by Christians: "From experience, we know that the martyrdom for love is not the exclusive preserve of Christians."[35] Christian de Chergé knows

---

34. [De Chergé, *L'invincible espérance*, 227. – Tr.]
35. [De Chergé, *L'invincible espérance*, 230. – Tr.]

whereof he speaks: "Mohammed gave his life like Christ." The martyrdom of love, Christian martyrdom par excellence because it is Christ's own act, is so much a Christian martyrdom that it can be lived out by many others who are, in this way, made partners in the paschal mystery.[36] Every person, Christian or not, who lives a life given in love bears witness to Christ.

Witnessing Is the Gift of One's Life out of Love

If, as always in the Christian tradition, the term "martyrdom" is restricted to cases of violent death, then ordinary witness will be the life lived out of love in the banality of the everyday. But this witnessing by the daily gift of self in love is not any easier to live. Christian de Chergé is right to point out that "we have given our heart 'wholesale' to God, and it costs us dear to have him take it from us piece by piece!"[37] (This is probably our invitation to "the martyrdom of the everyday.") Christian de Chergé's prayer during his last three years was, we recall, "Disarm me, disarm them!"[38] Perhaps it is in the everyday that one learns to let himself be disarmed enough to consent to the gift. The everyday is the long apprenticeship during which we learn to lower our guard, let fall our armor, even if it consists of being "disarmed" of our most cherished convictions, in order to move forward on the path of self-giving. But how could one do this without the mediation of the other, without the many faces of the other, including the other believer, that mysterious other on the journey of faith?

The Freedom of the Gift

Witnessing through the gift of one's life presumes that the gift is lived out in real freedom. "No one takes [my life] from me, but I lay it down of my own accord," says Jesus at the moment when his life was about to be taken from him. The martyrdom of the

36. See *Gaudium et Spes* 22.
37. De Chergé, *L'invincible espérance*, 228.
38. De Chergé, *L'invincible espérance*, 314.

monks of Tibhirine can only be recognized *as* martyrdom because these men, fully aware of the danger, out of love chose to remain. By this decision they gave their lives freely.

It is the same for those who are called to give their lives in the everyday and who commit themselves to the gift of their lives to their loved ones: to a spouse, to children, to friends, to neighbors, to fellow travelers, in the banality of the everyday, as banal and ordinary as was the daily rhythm of monastery for the monks. Freedom is a necessary condition of authentic witness, of a true gift of one's life. Not a life taken, not a life lent, but a life freely given.

The Initiative of God

Finally, there is one point that merits particular attention. The human gift of self, in Christian revelation, is never primary. It is secondary. The initiative of love comes not from humankind but from God. Was it not God who loved us first?[39] The initiative in every life belongs to God, in the twenty-first century as much as in the first. Christian de Chergé provides a striking illustration. The gift he made of his life was in response to the initiative of God. It was given to him to recognize this fact through the gift that Mohammed, the village policeman, made of his own life. As we have seen, this is not an insignificant detail of de Chergé's vocation. It involves the very idea one has of sacrifice in the framework of Christianity. What characterizes Christian sacrifice (and the Eucharist allows us to celebrate daily) is precisely this reversal of sacrifice.[40] Whereas in human history sacrifice was always a human initiative in relation to God or the gods to obtain benefits, pardon, or protection, the Christian reversal consists in the fact that from now on it is God who gives himself in sacrifice, the one and only sacrifice. It is God who, through the Son, kneels before

39. [Tr. note: See 1 John 4:19.]
40. Christian Salenson, *Catéchèses mystagogiques pour aujourd'hui, Habiter l'Eucharistie* [*Mystagogical Catechetics for Today: Inhabiting the Eucharist*] (Paris: Bayard, 2008).

human beings and washes their feet. Human beings may, if they wish and in full freedom, respond to this gift of God, in love, by giving their own life to the Father out of love for their brothers and sisters, turning it into a sacrifice of praise.

We are here at the heart of witness. Here is where witness reveals its deepest nature. Witness has its source in God. God unceasingly bears self-witness in the initiative that he takes in every life through the Holy Spirit. God's testimony is true. Thus when people bear true witness, what is it they witness to? Certainly they do not witness to a religion, nor to themselves; rather, they witness to the antecedent love of God. And they witness to it truly, not by self-referential speech, but by the gift of their life.

The Prophetic Function of the Church

The mission of the Church is sacramental. The Church signifies in a sacramental sense the gift that God made of himself through God's own Son. This gift continues to be given in every life, and there are many who respond to this initiative of love through the total gift of their life in the everyday and occasionally through the violent extinction of a life given in love.

The Church is the sign that every total gift, whether in the ordinariness of the everyday or in the extraordinariness of bloody martyrdom, configures the giver to Christ himself, who gave himself out of love for humankind.

> [A]s one who has been made a partner in the paschal mystery, and as one who has been configured to the death of Christ, [the Christian] will go forward, strengthened by hope, to the resurrection.
>
> [T]his holds true not for Christians only but also for all people of good will in whose hearts grace is active invisibly. For since Christ died for all, and since all are in fact called to one and the same destiny, which is divine, we must hold that the Holy Spirit offers to all the possibility of being made partners, in a way known to God, in the paschal mystery.[41]

41. *Gaudium et Spes* 22.

The theology of religious encounter helps us deepen the meaning of witness. Witness is not restricted exclusively to Christians. Everyone is called by the Spirit to bear witness to Christ, whether or not they are even aware of the existence of Jesus of Nazareth. And the Church has as its sacramental office to signify Christ. The Church celebrates him in particular in the Eucharist, the sacrament of gift, the covenantal mystery of life received and life given, "for you" but also "for many." A sound theology of religious encounter purifies the Church's witness of deviations.

Chapter 13

My Brother's Keeper

Christian de Chergé gave particular attention to *fraternity*, a component of the Church's royal office. He often asked, within his local context of extreme violence, about the right attitude Christians should have in relation to their Muslim brothers and sisters. It goes without saying that the right attitude would include *tolerance* and *respect*. Vatican II goes further and speaks of *esteem*.

De Chergé often talked to his community about fraternal life.[1] Betraying the profound influence upon him of Charles de Foucauld, de Chergé reflected long on what it meant to enter into universal fraternity. For de Chergé, "the theme of *brother* is not something appended, not an accessory, not even something of the natural order; it is as essential to the faith as the dogma of universal salvation which is expressed in the mystery of the communion of saints."[2] The point is not simply to invent a way of living together serenely according to a devoutly-to-be-wished universal world ethic—the dream of Hans Küng[3]—but rather to enter into the

---

1. Especially in his chapter talks from July 1, 1985, to November 29, 1985, in Christian de Chergé, *Dieu pour tout jour, chapitres du père Christian de Chergé à la communauté de Tibhirine (1985–1996)* [*God for Each Day: Chapter Talks of Fr. Christian de Chergé to the Community of Tibhirine*], 2nd ed., Les cahiers de Tibhirine (Montjoyer: Abbé d'Aiguebelle, 2006), 35–75.

2. Chapter talk for September 11, 1985, in de Chergé, *Dieu pour tout jour*, 47.

3. [Salenson does not reference this remark. – Tr.]

mystery of universal fraternity, for "we cannot truly pray to God, the Father of all, if we treat any people in less than brotherly fashion, for all are created in God's image."[4] At the end of the Vatican II declaration *Nostra Aetate*, the Church invites all the faithful "as far as depends on them, to be at peace with all men . . . and in that way to be true sons of the Father who is in heaven." [5]

Christian de Chergé found additional solid support for his stance in the visit of Pope John Paul II to Morocco and his speech in Casablanca:

> [A]ll men . . . should live in harmony and serve the universal brotherhood. . . . [T]he human person, man or woman, should never be sacrificed. *Each person is unique* in God's eyes. Each one ought to be appreciated for what he is, and, consequently, respected as such. No one should use his fellow man; no one should exploit his equal; no one should condemn his brother. It is in these conditions that a more human, more just, and more fraternal world will be able to be born, a world where each one can find his place in dignity and freedom.[6]

The Entry into Fraternity

Am I my brother's keeper? How do we enter into fraternity? Without forgetting the fraternal relations within his own family, let us recall de Chergé's experience being looked after by his "brother," Mohammed, the "elder brother" with whom he developed a genuine friendship. This elder brother, a married man with children, attended to him while de Chergé was still a young officer stationed in Algeria. He also in a sense watched over his Christian faith as a young seminarian, and Christian was grateful to him for this. Did he not say that this brother helped "liberate his faith"?

---

4. *Nostra Aetate* 5, quoted in chapter talk for September 16, 1985, in De Chergé, *Dieu pour tout jour*, 53.

5. *Nostra Aetate* 5.

6. Quoted in the chapter talk for September 18, 1985, in De Chergé, *Dieu pour tout jour*, 54. Official English version available at Vatican web site, http://www.vatican.va/holy_father/john_paul_ii/speeches/1985/august/documents/hf_jp-ii_spe_19850819_giovani-stadio-casablanca_en.html.

Finally, this brother looked after him when his life was in danger, protecting him and coming to his defense at the cost of his own life. Christian's entry into fraternity was brutal, yet similar to every experience of fraternity it meant sooner or later being joined by a brother or sister, by brothers and sisters. Fraternity is the taste of a love that comes from elsewhere, that has a flavor of the beyond. These others who join us make it possible for us to set out again on the road of fraternity with all those brothers and sisters we have not chosen and who are all so different and thus to enter into the mystery of this fraternity; for the mystery of the "brother" is the mystery of the Word who was made brother, in and through a multitude of brothers.

The Test of Fraternity

Christian de Chergé long meditated on God's entry into fraternity, on the fraternity experienced by Christ, the firstborn of this multitude of brothers and sisters. "The Word was made brother, the brother of Abel and also of Cain, the brother of Isaac but also of Ishmael, the brother of Joseph and of the eleven others who sold him into slavery, the brother of the plain and the brother of the mountain, the brother of Peter, of Judas, and of the Peter and the Judas within me."[7] The entry into fraternity of the Word of God, rejected by his own people, was painful: "The hour came for God to learn what it costs to enter into fraternity. An only son, he came from God. A brother to the infinity of humankind, he returns to God, bringing the multitude all the way to the One."[8] De Chergé knew that this was his path too and his community's. Referring to Jesus' washing his disciples' feet in John 13, de Chergé said,

---

7. De Chergé, Homily for Holy Thursday 1995, in Christian de Chergé, *L'autre que nous attendons, homélies du père Christian de Chergé (1970–1996)* [*The Other Whom We Await: Homilies of Fr. Christian de Chergé*], Les cahiers de Tibhirine (Montjoyer: Abbé d'Aiguebelle, 2006), 455. [Also in Christian de Chergé, *L'invincible espérance* [*Hope Unconquerable*], ed. Bruno Chenu (Paris: Bayard, 1996), 254. – Tr.]

8. De Chergé, Homily for Holy Thursday 1995, in de Chergé, *L'autre que nous attendons*, 455.

"The Master's Book is this gesture of a slave, both heart and body handed over in that very act—from foot to foot, from brother to brother—to engrave it in their memory."[9]

In the difficult context of Algeria, this fraternity with family, neighbors, and fellow workers was lived with respect for all the brothers of Algeria, even those who spread violence, whether Islamists or the military. Even the way de Chergé talked about these latter "brothers" was respectful: "[I]n community we refer to the mountain dwellers, those who are called terrorists, as 'the brothers of the mountain,' and the armed forces we call 'the brothers of the plain.' It is way of remaining in fraternity."[10]

Fraternity under the Challenge of Violence

The encounter with Sayah Attiyah, on December 24, 1993, a few days after the assassination of the Croats of Tamesguida, brought this *fraternity* face to face with the challenge of fear and violence— a double violence: that of the "brothers of the mountain," but also its own interior violence. In the day of recollection for the laity that he preached a few days before the monks' abduction, de Chergé went over the facts:

> We went outside. . . . [A]s far as I could see, he was weaponless. We were there face to face. He set out his three demands, and three times I was able to say: "No," or "Not like that." He said: "You have no choice"; I said, "No, I do have a choice." Not just because I was my brothers' keeper, but also because I was the keeper of this brother who was there, face to face with me, and who needed to be able to discover something within himself other than what he had become. And that was what was revealed a little inasmuch as he yielded and made an effort to understand.[11]

---

9. De Chergé, Homily for Holy Thursday 1995, in de Chergé, *L'autre que nous attendons*, 455.

10. De Chergé, Lenten retreat for March 8, 1995, in de Chergé, *L'invincible espérance*, 316.

11. De Chergé, *L'invincible espérance*, 309.

It was after this "visit," de Chergé would say, that there began for him the long interior work in which he asked God both to disarm the brothers of the mountain and to disarm him himself: "Disarm me, disarm them!"[12] On December 28 he wrote a letter to Sayah Attiyah "man to man, believer to believer."[13]

This way of being in the world is applicable to everyone. Entering into fraternity means learning to lay down arms, to lower the guard, and to purify oneself of the violence within. Words can be weapons, and ways of speaking can betray violence:

> We hear people say that [the brothers of the mountain] are filthy beasts, that they are not human, that you can't have dealings with them. As for me, I say: if we talk like that, there will never be peace. I know that he has slit the throats of one hundred forty-five people. . . . But I try to imagine his [that is, Sayah Attiyah's] arrival in paradise after he died. It seems to me that beneath the gaze of our dear Lord I have the right to present three attenuating facts. First: as a matter of fact, he did not slit our throats; secondly: he left when I asked him to; and thirdly: after our conversation in the night, I told him, "We are in the midst of preparations to celebrate Christmas, for us that is the birth of the Prince of Peace, and here you come in with weapons!" He replied, "I'm sorry, I didn't know."[14]

Becoming Our Brother's Keeper

Was Christian de Chergé his brother's keeper during the years in Algeria when people were turning into killers and violence was being unleashed? Was he later the keeper of this brother, Sayah Attiyah? The answer is yes. He believed that he had a share of the responsibility to protect the man from his own violence.

> We cannot wish for death, not only because we fear it, but because we cannot wish for a glory that we can acquire only

---

12. [Tr. note: De Chergé, *L'invincible espérance*, 314.]

13. [Tr. note: The letter can be found in full in Dom Bernardo Olivera, *How Far to Follow: The Martyrs of Atlas* (Petersham, MA: St. Bede's, 1997), 17.]

14. De Chergé, *L'invincible espérance*, 310.

at the expense of a murder, and which would make the person
to whom I owed the glory a murderer. God cannot permit that:
the commandment, "Thou shalt not kill," falls also on my
brother, and I must do all that I can to love him enough to
divert him from what he might be tempted to do.[15]

De Chergé also takes on a responsibility to see that the other's
religion is not damaged or disfigured, not even by another Muslim. It is not enough to respect the other's religion from a distance.
One must also help others to respect their own religion and their
own country. "I love them, all these Algerians, enough not to want
a single one of them to be a Cain to his brother,"[16] said de Chergé,
and in his *Testament*, he wrote, "It would be too high a price to
pay for what will perhaps be called the 'grace of martyrdom' to
owe it to an Algerian, whoever he might be, especially if he says
he is acting in fidelity to what he believes to be Islam."[17] Christians owe it to themselves to defend the culture and religion of
others. "For me, Algeria and Islam are . . . a body and a soul."[18]

Reciprocal Conversion: The Heart of Fraternity

The other matters. The other's life of faith and also conversion to the One God matter because it is by conversion, both the
other's conversion and mine, that we will enter together into the
communion of saints.

> Our readiness to recognize and welcome the portion of truth
> lodged in the heart of a brother will express, better than any
> words, our thirst and love for the Truth that exists only within
> God. Those who make an effort to grow in this way in mutual
> love cannot fail to progress together toward the Truth that
> surpasses them and unites them in infinity.[19]

15. De Chergé, *L'invincible espérance*, 313.
16. De Chergé, *L'invincible espérance*, 313.
17. De Chergé, *L'invincible espérance*, 222. See Appendix below, 200.
18. De Chergé, *L'invincible espérance*, 222.
19. Christian de Chergé, "Prier en Église à l'écoute de l'Islam" ["Praying as Church While Listening to Islam"], *Chemins de dialogue* 27 (2006): 23.

That is why it matters to me that the other fulfills his vocation and grows, in his own way, in response to the One God.

The preceding reflection leads to another way of speaking and thinking about believers of other religious traditions, that is, speaking and thinking not only with an attitude of respect but also with an esteem of their own path. I cannot become indifferent to the path of the other, his or her vocation, or, in the present context, of the Muslim community. Entering into fraternity will always lead me further than simple respect will, or an agreement mutually to defend values held in common and to respect each other's faith. In point of fact, "The Word was made brother"[20] and has left on the table for us the loaf and cup of universal fraternity.

This universal fraternity goes beyond mere relations with other believers. Each needs the other; each needs what the other carries within himself, what he believes and what does not believe, what makes him set out on his journey, and what gives him life. Each learns over time to let himself be disarmed in order to enter into a fraternity that makes both wish that everyone, on his own path, would respond to his vocation as a human being and believer.

The Royal Office of the Church

Interreligious dialogue clarifies the sacramental mission of the Church in service of the kingdom of God. The Church is the sacrament of universal fraternity. The Church, the Body of Christ, participates in Christ himself who became the brother of all, of Jew and pagan, of the centurion and the Samaritan woman, and even of the thief on the cross. Given that the Word has become the brother of all people, can the Church, which is his Body, neglect being part of universal fraternity? "The Church of Christ subsists in the Catholic Church," affirmed Vatican II.[21] In the truth of that

---

20. [Tr. note: There is an elegant rhyme in French between "The Word was made flesh (*chair*)" and "The Word was made brother (*frère*)."]

21. [Tr. note: Perhaps the most famous line from *Lumen Gentium* 8, a revision of the traditional assertion that the Church of Christ *is* the Catholic Church. See chap. 8, n. 14, above.]

affirmation, the Church has a magnificent opportunity to give universal brotherhood to the world.

The Church, and thus every Christian, best signifies universal fraternity and helps bring it about through relations with other believers in the initiatives of encounter and dialogue with other religions. The interreligious gatherings at Assisi and the spirit of Assisi remain the symbols of this sacramental mission of the Church.

But fraternity does not depend only on harmonious reciprocity, however desirable this is. The Church cannot live out fraternity simply by talking about it, or in simple initiatives of hospitality and friendly understanding. As the brothers of Tibhirine demonstrated, fraternity includes forgiveness too.

The Church is its brother's keeper, whether the brother is a Muslim, a Hindu, or anyone else, for the Church's desire is that all should be faithful to their vocations as human beings and believers. By living out this sacramental mission, by signifying and serving universal fraternity, the Church does its best to purify itself of the temptation to be in rivalry with other religions. Rivalry is the mortal illness of fraternity, of every fraternity, including the fraternity among believers. The Church is not in competition. It is not a religion like other religions. It has a different mission in the world: to signify fraternity among all human beings because its face is turned toward the Father and because Christ is "the firstborn among many brothers" (Rom 8:29). The Church is not an end unto itself but the humble servant of a divine plan that transcends it.

Chapter 14

Praying among Others Who Pray

A consideration of the sacramental mission of the Church leads us to conceive of each of the Church's functions as sacramental functions. The one that occupied the most prominent position in the thought of de Chergé was the *priestly* function as manifested in the act of prayer. A theology of religious encounter should give a place of honor to the priestly function; it should remind the Church of this primary priestly responsibility and help the Church live it out within the horizons of the Father's desire that all people are to be saved, of the Son's prayer for humankind, and of the power of the Spirit who inspires all true prayer.

Prayer is a fundamental, necessary, and indispensable dimension of interreligious dialogue. Prayer has taken the form of partners in dialogue praying *for* each other. For Christians, the Liturgy of the Hours may include petitions for members of other religions, and in the great prayer of intercession of Good Friday Christians pray for the Jews, for other believers, and for people who do not believe. The meeting at Assisi offers another example of interreligious prayer. Without praying *together*, religious leaders *came together to pray*, to use the expression chosen to describe the prayer that day. Finally, prayer can be done *with* the others even when they are not present and outside the framework of an encounter. (Historically, prayer has sometimes taken the form of a prayer of one side *against* the other, each party invoking God to annihilate the other. This can still be the case today. This use of prayer has the advantage of acknowledging the existence of the other, but it can readily be agreed that it is not the most evangelical form of dialogue.)

Through and in prayer interreligious dialogue surpasses by far the mere visible coming together of other believers. Being together to pray is somewhat analogous to doing theology in the horizon of different cultures and religions. One's way of thinking changes. In addition, when prayer takes place in communion with other believers, prayer itself is no longer the same. *Lex orandi, lex credendi*—the way believers pray and how they understand their prayer reveal something about the way they believe. What place do Christians give to the prayer of others? How is it present to their own prayer? As Church, we have much to learn, for we have only a limited regard for the prayer of others, and, as Christians, we do not spontaneously think of ourselves as being in the midst of praying humanity.

Monks are not specialists in prayer, but they have a ministry of prayer in the world and in the Church. The Cistercian monks of Tibhirine, like those of Midelt today, live out their ministry of prayer in the land of Islam. Thus, their witness is unique. A monastic community completely embedded in an Islamic land in order to pursue, explore, and thus signify the Church's relations in faith and prayer with Muslims is a precious treasure of the Church.

Reaction to a "Missionary Priest"

Reading an article published in the journal *Tychique*,[1] a journal of spiritual formation intended for prayer groups, de Chergé was stopped by the sentence, "Today we would like to invite you to

---

1. "À propos de l'islam" [Concerning Islam], *Tychique* 34 (November 1981). Christian de Chergé's reply, "Prier en Église à l'écoute de l'islam" [Praying as Church While Listening to Islam], was published in *Chemins de dialogue* 27 (2006): 17–24. [Tr. note : The journal *Tychique* is subtitled "La revue de formation au service des groupes de prière et communautés du renouveau charismatique " (The educational magazine for prayer groups and charismatic renewal communities); it is published in Lyon, France.]

pray that all our Churches receive in one and the same vision the work of evangelization in the Muslim world." In a written response to the article, Christian de Chergé expressed his shock that such a journal could include something so contrary to the teachings of Vatican II and to the pastoral letter of the bishops of North Africa.[2] In the context of the article, "the work of evangelization" meant proselytism. De Chergé found that position intolerable. In his response to the article de Chergé began by appealing to what John Paul II said in Nigeria in 1982:

> All of us, Christians and Muslims, live under the sun of the one merciful God. We both believe in one God who is the Creator of Man. . . . We adore God and profess total submission to him. Thus, in a true sense, we can call one another brothers and sisters in faith in the one God.[3]

Next he gave his own testimony, beginning with his experience as a youth in Algeria:

> I saw some men praying differently from my elders. I was five years old, and I was discovering Algeria during a first stay of three years. I remain profoundly grateful to my mother who taught us, my brothers and me, respect for the uprightness and attitudes of this Muslim prayer: "They are praying to God," my mother would say. And so I always knew that the God of Islam and the God of Jesus Christ are not two.[4]

De Chergé encountered the prayer of Islam at a very young age and respected it from the start.

---

2. Conference of North African Bishops of May 4, 1979, "Chrétiens au Maghreb: le sens de nos rencontres" ["Christians in the Maghreb: The Meaning of our Encounters"], 10.3; *Se Comprendre* 79, no. 11 (15 novembre 1979), and on the web at http://www.le-sri.com/CERNA_79.htm.

3. Address of John Paul II to the Muslim Religious Leaders, Kaduna, Nigeria (February 14, 1982), 2. Official English version available on the Vatican web site, http://www.vatican.va/holy_father/john_paul_ii/speeches/1982/february/documents/hf_jp-ii_spe_19820214_musulmani-nigeria_en.html.

4. De Chergé, "Prier en Église à l'écoute de l'islam," 18.

The House of Prayer[5]

In the course of a retreat at Constantine, de Chergé was given the task of introducing a sharing session among priests. Pointing out that he was not a specialist in prayer, de Chergé then stated three principles. The first was to recognize oneself and every person as "a house of prayer" (Isa 56:7), a house built "to the open sky." Second, this house of prayer is "for all peoples":

> [In Algeria] when we tune in faithfully to another people in prayer, we discover that the simplest attitudes and words of spiritual expression know no religious boundaries. That discovery translates into a deep bond in prayer with other people and other believers. There I come to know a communion which transcends boundaries.

Prayer is a privileged form of opening toward other believers and other people.

Finally, there is such a thing as "a house of prayer which is also a den of thieves" (Luke 19:46). I am the thief, so is the other, and it is this thievery that perverts the whole. At its core, theft comes from fear: fear of the Wholly Other and fear of other people.

A Personal Appeal

Mohammed called de Chergé to prayer, not least when he said, "As you see, Christians do not know how to pray!" De Chergé confirmed this vocation from Mohammed when on the day of his monastic profession he said, "On this road of praise and intercession, I would like most especially to meet other men of prayer among whom I have accepted to hide away my life, simply because one among them addressed to me this 'call to prayer' by noting that the Christians of this country had not been able to be an example in this sphere."[6]

---

5. De Chergé, "Une maison de prière" ["A House of Prayer"], talk given December 8, 1978, in Christian de Chergé, *L'invincible espérance* [*Hope Unconquerable*], ed. Bruno Chenu (Paris: Bayard, 1996), 44–57.

6. De Chergé, "Prier en Église," 18.

In chapter 3 we described de Chergé's encounter in prayer with his "brother of one night" in the chapel after Compline.[7] That encounter, it is worth repeating, was another confirmation of de Chergé's unique vocation to be, in a Muslim context, one who prays among others who pray.

Those Who Pray Among Others Who Pray

It was in 1975 that the monks of Tibhirine came up with a definition of their monastic life in the specific context of the Atlas mountains: "Those who pray among others who pray."[8] It is with these words that de Chergé began his talk at the *Journées romaines* [Days in Rome].[9] This expression takes on its full meaning if we remember that Christian de Chergé was replying to the question, "Christians and Muslims: What Common Vision of Society?" He emphasized that the monks had come up with this definition in 1975 when they had been given only a week to abandon their location.[10] The slogan speaks to both the heart of their monastic vocation and their exact position in relation to Algeria. It contains the recognition of the prayer of others, without which this monastic prayer would not be what it is. But how would it be lived out?

Every Call to Prayer Comes from God

There is always a call to prayer. Prayer is the response to a call, signified for Christians by a bell, for Muslims by a muezzin.

Calls to prayer cannot leave me indifferent. On the contrary, they provoke me to engage in prayer. . . . No one but God

---

7. De Chergé, "Nuit de feu" ["Night of Fire"], Sunday, September 21, 1975, in de Chergé, *L'invincible espérance*, 33–38.

8. "Priants parmi d'autres priants." Christian de Chergé, "L'échelle mystique du dialogue" ["The Mystical Ladder of Dialogue"], *Islamochristiana* 23 (1997): 1.

9. September 1989.

10. On October 17, 1975, the monks were ordered by the local police to leave their premises. Tibhirine was saved by the intervention of Cardinal Duval.

can call to prayer. Here (in Algeria) I am better able to understand that all are called, that human beings were created for this praise and this adoration.[11]

Hearing the Muslim call to prayer helped de Chergé to understand that "all are called" and that in the end, the very nature of prayer is "convocation."[12] The reply of Y, recently baptized, to Christian's inquiry about how he would henceforth hear the muezzin's call to prayer comforted him and set him on this path: "He answered me simply: 'I try to unite myself to Christ who is going to offer that prayer to his Father.'"[13] The prayer of the one calls forth the prayer of the other so they can converge beyond anything that can be said about prayer: "whether they come from our bell or the muezzin, the calls to prayer establish between us [Muslims and Christian monks] a healthy reciprocal emulation."[14] "Bell and muezzin, whose calls to prayer rise from the same enclosure, make common cause to invite us together to praise, beyond what words can tell."[15]

Opus Dei and Salât

Christian compares the monastic *opus Dei* and the Muslim *Salât*, listing their common points.[16] Saint Benedict in his Rule describes prayer as *opus Dei*.

> The Work of God, *opus Dei*, means both that it comes from God—it is He who works—and that it brings us back to God—

---

11. De Chergé, "Une maison de prière," 48.
12. De Chergé, "Une maison de prière," 49.
13. De Chergé, "L'échelle mystique du dialogue," 23.
14. "Questionnaire en préparation du synode 1994 sur la vie consacrée, 1 janvier 1993," in Christian de Chergé, *Sept vies pour Dieu et l'Algérie* [*Seven Lives for God and Algeria*], ed. Bruno Chenu (Paris: Bayard, 1996), 83.
15. De Chergé, *Sept vies*, 83.
16. De Chergé, chapter talk for Thursday, December 16, 1993, in Christian de Chergé, *Dieu pour tout jour, chapitres du père Christian de Chergé à la communauté de Tibhirine (1985–1996)* [*God for Each Day: Chapter Talks of Fr. Christian de Chergé to the Community of Tibhirine*], 2nd ed., Les cahiers de Tibhirine (Montjoyer: Abbé d'Aiguebelle, 2006), 460.

this work is for Him and it is we who do it. Likewise, liturgy is work *of* the people, but also work *for* the people, which is to say that it is God's work. We recall, too, Jacob's ladder (or Nathanael's) with its liturgy of angels "ascending and descending." We recall also to the Son of Man: "No one has ascended into heaven except the one who descended from heaven" (John 3:13). We have here a work of "coming and going" between God and humankind, between humankind and God, which is the specific "service" of the Holy Spirit.

What about the *Salât*?

We can affirm that there is something identical that happens in the *Salât*, the Muslim ritual prayer whose vocation it is to be oral and public. There is a "call of God" to this prayer. The answer comes from human beings: it consists in ablutions and preparations, a formulation of intention. . . . And then, there is the ritual psalmody. . . . And the Qurʾan is to be received and interpreted within this framework, exactly as the Word of God is the kernel of our *opus dei* in our liturgies.

The common point, then, between the *opus dei* and *Salât* is that in both cases it is God who invites and humans who respond.

De Chergé wished to highlight not only the common points but also the common goal: through and in prayer to join with those of Islam who pray and, further, eventually, to be recognized by them [as ones who pray]. "As monks we are fortunate in the dialogue with Islam to be able to join in the experience of Muslims who pray and also to let ourselves be recognized by them [as ones who pray]."[17]

Invited by Others: The Alawites

The experience with the Alawiyya, a Sufi confraternity,[18] confirmed for de Chergé that prayer in communion with the other who prays is both the privileged place and privileged method of encounter. Some had sought out the monks and said:

17. De Chergé, "L'échelle mystique du dialogue," 15.
18. [Tr. note: Not to be confused with the Syrian Shiite sect of the same name, to which the Assad family belongs.]

We do not want to get involved in a theological dialogue with you, because this has often erected barriers which are of human handiwork. But we feel called by God to unity. So we must allow God to invent something new between us. This can only be done in prayer. There is doubtless only a small number of Muslims who could understand this, and doubtless also a very small number of Christians who will believe in it. But this is what we feel called to do with you.[19]

De Chergé commented on this invitation several years later:

The instinct of the Alawites invites us to prayer and to dialogue concerning the faith: "God wants to invent something new between us: let us give him the chance. This can only be done in prayer." Then, we go back down the mountain, but our mutual relations have changed, we can no longer call each other strangers, nor, a fortiori, excommunicate each other. We will have to take into account what has happened between us in order to "enlarge the space of faith."[20]

Prayer opens a space in which God can invent something new. We have here a tremendous intuition of what interreligious dialogue is about. It is not fundamentally a human creation, the result of a human will for unity; dialogue is a space made for God so God can work and create something new. That is why prayer, which is common to all religions, is a privileged path of interreligious dialogue.

Praying Together

This was the experience of the monks' encounter with the Alawites on November 22, 1989. The Alawites prayed with the monks; the two groups prayed together. They were not "together in order to pray," as in the formula adopted at the meeting at Assisi, but

19. A talk given by Christian de Chergé to the General Chapter of the Cistercians (OCSO), 1993, in de Chergé, *Sept vies*, 91.
20. De Chergé, chapter talk for Thursday, August 11, 1994, in de Chergé, *Dieu pour tout jour*, 505.

they prayed together. Christian de Chergé made this point in a chapter talk the following week. Speaking for himself and for his brothers, de Chergé said that the monks were moved to this common prayer by the encounter itself. He recognized that the experience was a novel one for both them and for the Church, and he was fully conscious that it would raise questions; nevertheless, for him it was an essential aspect of his vocation:

> It is important for us to allow ourselves to be caught up, as deeply as possible, in the prayer of the other, if I want to be more than a Christian presence among Muslims. I have a vocation to unite myself to Christ through the one who lifts up every prayer and who offers to the Father, mysteriously, this prayer of Islam along with the prayer of every upright heart.[21]

If at Assisi the arrangement was made so that the prayer of one participant followed the prayer of another, de Chergé judged that this, quite apart from the different context, would not be a good solution with the Alawites.

> I do not think it right to speak of successive or juxtaposed prayers. . . . If this were to be the case it would obviously be necessary to monitor the allocation of time and words, to make sure that each party had as much say as the other. There would be a kind of one-upmanship which would make the scene resemble the assembly at Carmel and the duel between the prophets of Baal and the prophet Elijah.[22]

What happened in the encounter? After their ritual prayer the Alawites offered the monks one by one a sign of peace. Then, following forty-five minutes of silence, the monks contributed some elements of the office of Vespers to the prayer, including the *Magnificat*. Christian commented on the old adage, *lex orandi, lex credendi* ["the law of prayer is the law of belief"], interpreting it, though, in a different way: "There must be a few guiding ideas

21. De Chergé, *Dieu pour tout jour*, 304.
22. De Chergé, *Dieu pour tout jour*, 304.

that guarantee a solid coherence between faith and prayer: *lex orandi, lex credendi!* This is what I believe I can say (and what helps me pray freely with the other)." Recognition of the other's *faith* helped de Chergé to *pray* with him.

The expression "praying among others who pray" thus receives a whole new meaning. It is not simply a juxtaposition, but a case of being "in the prayer of the other." De Chergé takes this intuition further: it is a means of union with Christ, since Christ presents every prayer to the Father. As John Paul II would write, "Every true prayer is prompted by the Holy Spirit, who is mysteriously present in every human heart."[23]

The Prayer of the Pope

Did the pope pray with young Muslims during the meeting in Casablanca?[24] What did the pope do? "At the side of the 'commander of the faithful'[25] the Pope became the Imam of the faithful: the one who prays in front."[26] It is a daring formulation. De Chergé was referring to "the communion of the Beyond already realized in Christ," for "this prayer of the Pope is significant: it is a visible sign of the unceasing intercession of Christ to the Father." With his prayer, the pope manifests "the unique priesthood of the Word taking up human words and making of them his own quasi-sacramental substance, constituted by the young people present and the words that bind them together for God." Christian de Chergé goes even further, affirming that this prayer made concrete

> the exercise of [the pope's] apostolic office, which is to summon to an encounter with God all people who are strengthened and to strengthen his brothers in the living faith by

23. Encyclical of John Paul II, *Redemptoris Missio* (1990), 29. Official English version available at the Vatican web site, http://www.vatican.va/edocs/ENG0219/_P5.HTM.

24. See *Chemins de dialogue 20* (2002).

25. [Tr. note: *Amir al-Mu'minim*, a title given to the early Caliphs and, according to the Moroccan Constitution, the King of Morocco.]

26. De Chergé, *Dieu pour tout jour*, 54.

leading them to drink at the spring of the Spirit that prays and groans in the heart of every person. It is a *Eucharistic ministry in action*, to the extent that the pastor gathers together all the scattered children of God, his brothers, in order to make of them the members of a living Body entering into a sacrifice of praise, at the evening hour, to the greater glory of God.[27]

The pope truly was a *pope*. He exercised his ministry to strengthen his brothers in the faith. He lived out a *"Eucharistic ministry in action"* (de Chergé underlined the phrase in his hand-written text). This meeting did more than go beyond the question of whether we should "pray with" or simply "be together to pray." The pope's attitude signified to the highest degree the priestly sacramental ministry of the Church: in communion with the Beyond, together with the believers of the different world religions.

Prayer with Other Believers and the Liturgy

The liturgical commission of the diocese of Algiers organized a consultation on this subject in 1972. Tibhirine had requested the inclusion in the Proper of Saints the holy figures of the Old Testament: those whom Christ associated with himself in his transfiguration, those whom the Qurʾan mentioned and Islam venerated, and those to whom the Eastern Church had been long devoted—Saint Abraham, patriarch of believers (October 9 in the martyrology); Saint Moses, witness of the covenant (September 4); and Saint Elijah, father and master of prophets (July 20). Christian went further and submitted concrete proposals for implementing his desire for a Christian celebration of Muslim feasts, for instance, a Mass of Saint Abraham the day of the *Eid al-Adha*.[28] He repeated his requests during the *Journées romaines* [Days at Rome] in 1989: "For the moment Abraham has won his case. But what about

27. De Chergé, *Dieu pour tout jour*, 54.
28. "Festival of Sacrifice" (of Isaac); in North Africa, it is known as the "Greater Feast" (as opposed to the "Lesser Feast" celebrating the end of Ramadan) and is transliterated into French as *Aïd el Kébir*. This feast has now been recognized in the Christian liturgy.

Moses, Elijah, Melchizedek, Zechariah, and Elizabeth? Could not these great witnesses help us enter, in our own way, into the outstanding celebrations of the Muslim calendar?"[29]

The Eucharist and Ramadan

De Chergé wished to welcome as a Christian the month of Ramadan. "Experience proves that consecrating our present time as the Presence of God can help deepen the sense of the Eucharist as a feast of the Word and a substantial sharing in the Bread of Life."[30] He reacted against the official prohibition against mentioning departed Muslim friends and neighbors in the Eucharist and suggested some concrete changes that would allow them to be mentioned in the *Memento* of the eucharistic prayer. Finally, de Chergé suggested that it would be a good idea to have a Mass, similar to the Mass of Christian Unity, "for spiritual understanding and sharing among all believers."

The Prayer of Islam

Christian de Chergé affirmed the prayer of Muslims. For de Chergé, Muslim prayer was not in the first place the prayer of human beings to God; it was, rather, the prayer of God toward human beings, and only in a second moment the response of humans to God—a response to a call, for God is the only one who can call. The prayer of Islam, then, for de Chergé, was a response to a summons from God or, as we saw above, the prayer of Islam—the *Salât*—is *opus Dei*, at once an act of the God who calls and a response to God's call. As an authentic response to the Father, Islamic prayer, for de Chergé, was thoroughly in accord with Christian theology. Islam is the place where God reaches out to Muslims and the place of their response to this summons from God.

29. De Chergé, "L'échelle mystique du dialogue," 24.
30. De Chergé, "Suggestions pour une celebration chrétienne du calendrier musulman" [Suggestions for the Christian Celebration of the Muslim Calendar], 1982.

Not only did de Chergé affirm the prayer of Islam; he knew that he himself, through Mohammed, had been called to it. It was from the people of the prayer of Islam that he had received his vocation to be a man of prayer. Thus, through Islam, God speaks to and calls all people to prayer. It is Christ who presents the prayer of Muslims and the prayer of Christians alike before the Father. In the prayer of Islam Christ is present as saving mediator. We recall again the "brother of a single night" and Christian's request at that moment: "Teach us to pray together." This request is, of course, the request the apostles addressed to Christ, "teach us to pray," but with the addition, "but to pray together." This desired common prayer is possible in virtue of the communion of saints, which includes the children of Islam. The point of learning to pray together is to enter into and incarnate the communion of saints. This is a reversal of perspective after centuries of ignorance and conflict.

In the Alawites' similar request for prayer together, de Chergé understood once again that in the sphere of interreligious relationships it is of fundamental importance to leave the initiative to God, to leave a space where God can do something new, and prayer with the other and for the other constitutes that space. It is intriguing to imagine that the practice of effective prayer in this sense could supplant the need for "encounters among believers of different religions" as such encounters have been understood and experienced up to now.

Christian Prayer, Interreligious Prayer

The distinction between "praying together" and "being together in order to pray" is valid, but it should not obscure the horizon. The real question is how in prayer one constantly can be open to the other, and how to link one's prayer to the prayer of all who pray, especially those who have faith in the One God. What place do those believers have in my prayer? Are we in communion with one another?

The fact of religious diversity challenges the Church regarding its prayer. At its deepest essence the Church's prayer is sacramental; it is for the whole of humanity. But can the Church authentically live out the sacramental truth of her prayer while remaining ignorant of the prayer of the different religions? Positive regard for other believers and other religious traditions invites the Church to exercise its sacerdotal office in this domain. For my own part, I see here one of the most important contributions for the Church, called as it is to live out its ministry of intercession and praise in communion with all believers throughout the earth whose life is prayer. This ministry of prayer is a way for every Christian to engage in interreligious dialogue, even for those who will never have the opportunity for encounters and exchanges with the believers of other religious traditions. In fact, this ministry of prayer is the most useful and effective means of dialogue there is. "I know a communion which transcends boundaries." Christians today can claim for themselves the monks' self-designation: Christians can all consider themselves as "those who pray among others who pray."

As the Rite of Christian Baptism makes clear, Christians are not only prophets and kings; they are also priests. They receive from Christ himself a mission to intercede for the world, first and foremost by raising up a prayer of praise and by offering themselves in the gift of their life as a "sacrifice of praise." This priestly office defines them and characterizes their apostolate; it makes them people of prayer. Often Christians are moved to say, as did the apostles, "Teach me to pray, because I do not know how to pray." Christians, in their prayer, are in no way superior to other believers who pray.

Any idea of superiority is rendered impossible by Jesus' warning to his disciples that the only prayer that is not received is that of the Pharisee in the temple who compares himself against the publican and judges himself superior (Luke 18:10). The prayer of the publican is accepted; that of the Pharisee is rejected. So it is impossible for a Christian to discredit the prayer of a Muslim or to judge it with condescension. Christians at prayer are in communion with all the believers throughout the world who pray. Pope John Paul II explained to the cardinals and members of the Curia, after the meeting at Assisi, that the vocation of the Church was to reach out a hand to all its Christian brothers and sisters from the other churches and, with them, to all believers. Prayer forms a human chain of believers. It is part of the common vocation of the religions whose mission it is to open humanity to transcendence.

When the disciples of Jesus saw the followers of the Baptist praying, they asked Jesus to teach them to pray. We note that Jesus does not give them a particular method but shows them where [*la tournure*] the Christian should direct his prayer: "When you pray, say: 'Our Father.' " He gives them, strictly speaking, an orientation, a "conversion." Thus, Christian prayer orients us to, turns us toward, the Father. Jesus invites the disciples to say "Our," and he does not limit this "Our" solely to those who will become his disciples. This "Our" encompasses the totality of those who have God for their Father, which is to say, all of humankind.

Thus, when Christians are praying people in the midst of other praying people they cannot set themselves apart, let alone consider their prayer superior to that of any other believer. Prayer grounds us in a great solidarity with all other believers and with all people, in a communion that transcends all boundaries. Christians receive from Christ a unique role: "When *you* pray, say: 'Our Father.' " That is where the uniqueness of Christian prayer is to be found: to hold hands in prayer with our brothers and sisters and to turn toward the Father. In this communion of prayer, which in no way denies differences, unity in God is already realized. The communion of saints incarnates itself in prayer.

The Church should hear today this invitation to live out its sacramental mission of unity by emphasizing a prayer that is in relation to the prayer of all people, including those who say they do not know whether God exists but from whose very depths a desire arises.

The Church demonstrates that it takes religious diversity seriously and that it is dedicated to interreligious dialogue when, turning toward the Father in prayer, she lives out the priestly role bequeathed her uniquely by Christian revelation. The Church exercises her ministry of prayer daily in the Liturgy of the Hours as well as in the celebration of the sacraments. But this turning toward the Father implies the recognition of an increasingly effective solidarity with others in prayer. It would be highly desirable to make this solidarity in prayer with others more clearly evident in the Church's liturgy. The Church's prayer is essentially Jewish. The prayer of Jesus was the prayer of a Jew. Thus, it is no accident that in its origin and in its very being the prayer of the Church is, one might say, interreligious.

The Church's liturgy is inscribed in the heart of creation. It is inscribed in the heart of humanity. By living out its prayer in solidarity with all believers, the Church has the means of exercising in the highest degree its sacramental mission of unity among all people and the unity of all people with God.

Conclusion

It is time to conclude this modest essay. While it has aimed at a certain logical coherence, it does not pretend to offer a comprehensive account of the thought of Christian de Chergé. Anyone familiar with de Chergé knows that his thought reveals itself only slowly and that entry into it cannot be achieved solely by rational analysis. There are features of his thought that can be approached only by someone who has had a spiritual experience similar to his. Thus, I hope that this modest work will inspire others to clarify, correct, and bring to light many elements I have left obscure. A more thorough acquaintance with the archives will undoubtedly contribute new insights.

At the end of this journey, with the benefit of some distance, what answer can I give to the question: what, essentially, is Christian de Chergé's original contribution to a theology of religious encounter that is still in a stage of gestation?

There is, first of all, the originality of his context, an originality owing to his life in a monastic community situated in a Muslim environment and his rootedness in a sustained liturgical life. De Chergé was positioned to be in *existential dialogue* with Muslim neighbors and also with "the brothers of the mountain." In addition, de Chergé's particular vocation came to him through a Muslim. All of this has helped define a unique theological posture that I would characterize in the following manner.

Though de Chergé was aware of and influenced by the current trends in the theology of religions and of interreligious dialogue, he did not take these as his starting point. Neither did he start from admonitions from the magisterium. Rather, de Chergé started from an eschatological stance, one strongly influenced by monastic life: "The monk is the witness of hope's 'last things.'"

His thought was anchored in an eschatology realized in the death and resurrection of Christ. It seems to me that this is his fundamental contribution. It has often been said that christological questions are the decisive ones in the theology of world religions. It has also been held that ecclesiological questions are the most delicate. While all this remains true, perhaps Christian de Chergé's point was that the real center of gravity of a theology of religious encounter is eschatology and that the contours of any theology depend on how this eschatology is conceived.

His second decisive contribution, in my view, was precisely his own theology of eschatology. For de Chergé, influenced as he was by monastic literature, eschatology was not projected into a distant future that we need to prepare for and make happen. Eschatology was, rather, a future in the present, the Beyond right here. This understanding of eschatology inspires a theology of religious encounter that calls for an unremitting faith in eschatology's fulfillment. Whoever engages in such theology is invited to believe in God's plan of salvation and unity of the human race here and now.

One of the most practical consequences of this eschatological approach is the refusal to decide in advance, based on a priori theological understandings, what a theology of religious encounter might be called to become. At its core, de Chergé's theology of world religions is an evolving theology; its very nature is to be in evolution. It is a theology ever on the watch for the signs of the times and for those that emerge from an existential dialogue that is at once conceived, sustained, constructed, and carried out under God's gaze, for such a dialogue is the place where the Holy Spirit makes all things new.

On the other hand, lack of faith in what the Spirit can inspire would be the ruin of a theology of religious encounter. This lack of faith would be manifested in one of two ways: either by immobilizing this theology in the shackles of theories or else by limiting it through fear-based dogmatism or through the easy answers of relativism.

If it is true that right now we are seated together at the Father's table, the table that Christ has prepared and to which all people are called, the table of sinners, then, strong in this unity realized in God, we can make progress on the path of diversity. The Spirit uses diversity to establish communion and to make similarities emerge more clearly. De Chergé did not know where this approach would lead. He did not know what God willed at the present moment to do with religious diversity:

> To wish to see or imagine the future is to make a fiction out of hope, and this seems to me to be doing violence to hope. . . . Obviously, since we do not have God's imagination, when we think of the future, we think of it in terms of the past. . . . When we are in a tunnel, we see nothing, but it is absurd to want the landscape when we come out to be the same as when we went in. . . . Let us let the Holy Spirit do its work. . . . It is the Spirit's business; this is what I call poverty.[1]

Christian de Chergé's theology of world religions is from beginning to end a theology of hope.

Christian de Chergé did not write a book about his theology of hope. Instead, he wrote it in his life, with his brother monks and his brother Muslims. He wrote it not because he wished to produce an original work or out of intellectual interest. He wrote it because one day, through Mohammed, the Spirit called him to map out this route. He signed this work with the gift of his life given to the very end. One and the same gift unites Mohammed and Christian in one and the same death. Together they sealed a single communion in Christ, a communion to which all, Christians and Muslims, are called.

The sequel is up to us.

---

1. Christian de Chergé, Retreat for March 8, 1996, *L'invincible espérance*, ed. Bruno Chenu (Paris: Bayard, 1996).

Appendix

Testament de Père Christian de Chergé
(ouvert le dimanche de Pentecôte, 26 mai 1996)

Quand un A-DIEU s'envisage . . . .

S'il m'arrivait un jour—et ça pourrait être aujourd'hui—
d'être victime du terrorisme qui semble vouloir englober maintenant
tous les étrangers vivant en Algérie,
j'aimerais que ma communauté, mon Église, ma famille,
se souviennent que ma vie était DONNÉE à Dieu et à ce pays.
Qu'ils acceptent que le Maître Unique de toute vie
ne saurait être étranger à ce départ brutal.
Qu'ils prient pour moi :
comment serais-je trouvé digne d'une telle offrande ?
Qu'ils sachent associer cette mort à tant d'autres aussi violentes
laissées dans l'indifférence de l'anonymat.
Ma vie n'a pas plus de prix qu'une autre.
Elle n'en a pas moins non plus.
En tout cas, elle n'a pas l'innocence de l'enfance.
J'ai suffisamment vécu pour me savoir complice du mal
qui semble, hélas, prévaloir dans le monde,
et même de celui-là qui me frapperait aveuglément.
J'aimerais, le moment venu, avoir ce laps de lucidité
qui me permettrait de solliciter le pardon de Dieu
et celui de mes frères en humanité,
en même temps que de pardonner de tout coeur à qui m'aurait atteint.

Je ne saurais souhaiter une telle mort.
Il me paraît important de le professer.
Je ne vois pas, en effet, comment je pourrais me réjouir
que ce peuple que j'aime soit indistinctement accusé de mon meurtre.
C'est trop cher payé ce qu'on appellera, peut-être, la "grâce du martyre"
que de la devoir à un Algérien, quel qu'il soit,
surtout s'il dit agir en fidélité à ce qu'il croit être l'Islam.
Je sais le mépris dont on a pu entourer les Algériens pris globalement.
Je sais aussi les caricatures de l'Islam qu'encourage un certain
*   islamisme.*
Il est trop facile de se donner bonne conscience
en identifiant cette voie religieuse avec les intégrismes de ses extrémistes.
L'Algérie et l'Islam, pour moi, c'est autre chose, c'est un corps et une
*   âme.*
Je l'ai assez proclamé, je crois, au vu et au su de ce que j'en ai reçu,
y retrouvant si souvent ce droit fil conducteur de l'Évangile
appris aux genoux de ma mère, ma toute première Église,
précisément en Algérie, et déjà, dans le respect des croyants
*   musulmans.*
Ma mort, évidemment, paraîtra donner raison
à ceux qui m'ont rapidement traité de naïf, ou d'idéaliste :
"qu'Il dise maintenant ce qu'Il en pense !".
Mais ceux-là doivent savoir que sera enfin libérée ma plus lancinante
*   curiosité.*
Voici que je pourrai, s'il plaît à Dieu,
plonger mon regard dans celui du Père
pour contempler avec lui Ses enfants de l'Islam
tels qu'Il les voit, tout illuminés de la gloire du Christ,
fruits de Sa Passion, investis par le Don de l'Esprit
dont la joie secrète sera toujours d'établir la communion
et de rétablir la ressemblance, en jouant avec les différences.
Cette vie perdue, totalement mienne, et totalement leur,
je rends grâce à Dieu qui semble l'avoir voulue tout entière
pour cette JOIE-là, envers et malgré tout.
Dans ce MERCI où tout est dit, désormais, de ma vie,
je vous inclus bien sûr, amis d'hier et d'aujourd'hui,
et vous, ô amis d'ici, aux côtés de ma mère et de mon père,

de mes soeurs et de mes frères et des leurs,
centuple accordé comme il était promis !
Et toi aussi, l'ami de la dernière minute, qui n'aura pas su ce que tu
    faisais.
Oui, pour toi aussi je le veux ce MERCI, et cet "A-DIEU" en-visagé
    de toi.
Et qu'il nous soit donné de nous retrouver, larrons heureux,
en paradis, s'il plaît à Dieu, notre Père à tous deux.

AMEN !   INCH'ALLAH !
Alger, 1er décembre 1993
Tibhirine, 1er janvier 1994

Christian.+

Testament of Dom Christian de Chergé
(opened on Pentecost Sunday, May 26, 1996)

Facing a GOODBYE . . . .

If it should happen one day—and it could be today—
that I become a victim of the terrorism which now seems ready
    to engulf
all the foreigners living in Algeria,
I would like my community, my Church and my family
to remember that my life was GIVEN to God and to this country.
I ask them to accept the fact that the One Master of all life
was not a stranger to this brutal departure.
I would ask them to pray for me:
for how could I be found worthy of such an offering?
I ask them to associate this death with so many other equally
    violent ones
which are forgotten through indifference or anonymity.
My life has no more value than any other.
Nor any less value.
In any case, it has not the innocence of childhood.

I have lived long enough to know that I am an accomplice in
    the evil
which seems to prevail so terribly in the world,
even in the evil which might blindly strike me down.
I should like, when the time comes, to have a moment of
    spiritual clarity
which would allow me to beg forgiveness of God
and of my fellow human beings,
and at the same time forgive with all my heart the one who
    would strike me down.
I could not desire such a death.
It seems to me important to state this.
I do not see, in fact, how I could rejoice
if the people I love were indiscriminately accused of my murder.
It would be too high a price to pay
for what will perhaps be called, the "grace of martyrdom"
to owe it to an Algerian, whoever he might be,
especially if he says he is acting in fidelity to what he believes
    to be Islam.
I am aware of the scorn which can be heaped on the Algerians
    indiscriminately.
I am also aware of the caricatures of Islam which a certain
    Islamism fosters.
It is too easy to soothe one's conscience
by identifying this religious way with the fundamentalist
    ideology of its extremists.
For me, Algeria and Islam are something different: it is a body
    and a soul.
I have proclaimed this often enough, I think, in the light of
    what I have received from it.
I so often find there that true strand of the Gospel
which I learned at my mother's knee, my very first Church,
precisely in Algeria, and already inspired with respect for
    Muslim believers.
Obviously, my death will appear to confirm
those who hastily judged me naïve or idealistic:
"Let him tell us now what he thinks of his ideals!"

But these persons should know that finally my most avid
   curiosity will be set free.
This is what I shall be able to do, God willing:
immerse my gaze in that of the Father
to contemplate with him His children of Islam
just as He sees them, all shining with the glory of Christ,
the fruit of His Passion, filled with the Gift of the Spirit
whose secret joy will always be to establish communion
and restore the likeness, playing with the differences.
For this life lost, totally mine and totally theirs,
I thank God, who seems to have willed it entirely
for the sake of that JOY in everything and in spite of everything.
In this THANK YOU, which is said for everything in my life
   from now on,
I certainly include you, friends of yesterday and today,
and you, my friends of this place,
along with my mother and father, my sisters and brothers and
   their families,
You are the hundredfold granted as was promised!
And also you, my last-minute friend, who will not have known
   what you were doing:
Yes, I want this THANK YOU and this GOODBYE to be a
   "GOD-BLESS" for you, too,
because in God's face I see yours.
May we meet again as happy thieves in Paradise, if it please
   God, the Father of us both.

> AMEN ! INCHALLAH !
> Algiers, 1st December 1993
> Tibhirine, 1st January 1994
>
> *Christian +*

Bibliography

Works by Christian de Chergé

L'invincible espérance [*Hope Unconquerable*]. Edited by Bruno Chenu. Paris: Bayard/Centurion, 1996.[1] Paris: Bayard, 2010.[2]

Sept vies pour Dieu et l'Algérie [*Seven Lives for God and Algeria*]. Edited by Bruno Chenu. Paris: Bayard/Centurion, 1996.

Dieu pour tout jour, chapitres du père Christian de Chergé à la communauté de Tibhirine (1985–1996) [*God for Each Day: Chapter Talks of Fr. Christian de Chergé to the Community of Tibhirine*]. Revised and enlarged edition. Les cahiers de Tibhirine. Montjoyer: Abbé d'Aiguebelle, 2006.

L'autre que nous attendons, homélies du père Christian de Chergé (1970–1996) [*The Other Whom We Await: Homilies of Fr. Christian de Chergé*]. Les cahiers de Tibhirine. Montjoyer: Abbé d'Aiguebelle, 2006.

"Prier en Église à l'écoute de l'islam" ["Praying as Church While Listening to Islam"]. *Chemins de dialogue* no. 27 (2006): 17–24.

"L'échelle mystique du dialogue" ["The Mystical Ladder of Dialogue"]. *Islamochristiana* 23 (1997): 1–26.[3]

Works about Christian de Chergé

Ray, Marie-Christine. *Christian de Chergé, prieur de Tibhirine* [*Christian de Chergé: Prior of Tibhirine*]. Paris: Bayard, 1996.

---

1. The edition Salenson used.

2. The edition used in this translation.

3. This is the text of a lecture given at the seventeenth "Journées romaines" organized by PISAI, from August 31 to September 7, 1989. A somewhat abridged and revised version appears in *L'invincible espérance*, 167–204, under the title "Chrétiens et musulmans: pour un projet commun de société" ["Christians and Muslims: For a Common Vision of Society"]. The first two parts appeared in *Sept vies pour Dieu et l'Algérie*, 30–48, and the third part in *Lettre de Ligugé* 256 (1991–92): 18–28.

Ray, Marie-Christine. *Christian de Chergé, une biographie spirituelle du prieur de Tibhirine* [*Christian de Chergé: A Spiritual Biography of the Prior of Tibhirine*]. New pocketbook edition. Paris: Albin Michel, 2010.

Salenson, Christian. *Prier 15 jours avec Christian de Chergé, prieur des moines de Tibhirine.* Praying 15 Days Series. Paris: Nouvelle Cité, 2006.

Articles

Clément, Anne-Noëlle. "La croix de Tibhirine" ["The Cross of Tibhirine"]. *Chemins de dialogue* no. 24 (2004): 133–45.

Desprez, Vincent. "Père Christian de Chergé, lettres à un ami moine" ["Father Christian de Chergé: Letters to a Monk Friend"]. *Collectanea cisterciensia* 60 (1998): 93–215.

Durand, Françoise. "Notes de lecture" ["Reading Notes"]. *Chemins de dialogue* no. 24 (2004): 147–54.

Flachaire, Jean-Pierre. "Notre Dame de l'Atlas, une présence de visitation" ["Our Lady of Atlas: A Presence of Visitation"]. *Chemins de dialogue* no. 26 (2005): 165–76.

Michel, Roger. "Le thème de l'échelle sainte en islam et en christianisme" ["The Theme of the Holy Ladder in Islam and in Christianity"]. *Chemins de dialogue* no. 24 (2004): 129–33.

Olivera, Dom Bernardo. "Moine, martyr et mystique: Christian de Chergé (1937–1996)" ["Monk, Martyr, and Mystic"]. *Collectanea cisterciensia* 60 (1998): 279–94.

Purgu, Christophe. "Le martyre selon Christian de Chergé" ["Martyrdom According Christian de Chergé"]. *Chemins de dialogue* no. 27 (2006): 25–38.

———. "Processus de conversion" ["Processes of Conversion"]. *Chemins de dialogue* no. 24 (2004): 155–72.

Writings of the Brothers

Lebreton, Christophe. *Le souffle du don, journal de frère Christophe* [*The Breath of the Gift: The Journal of Brother Christopher*]. Paris: Centurion-Bayard, 1999.

———. *Aime jusqu'au bout du feu: cent poems de vérité et de vie* [*Love to the Fire's Edge: A Hundred Poems of Truth and Life*]. Annecy: Monte-Cristo, 1997.

———. *Adorateurs dans le souffle: Homélies du frère Christophe Lebreton pour fêtes et solennités (1989–1996)* [*Worshippers in the Breath of God: Homilies of Brother Christopher Lebreton for Feasts and Solemnities (1989–1996)*]. Montjoyer: Abbé de Bellefontaine, 2009.

"Extraits des lettres de frère Luc." *Chemins de dialogue* no. 27 (2006): 41–65.

Writings about the Brothers

Baudry, Dom Étienne. "Itinéraire spirituel de Fr. Michel Fleury, moine de Tibhirine" ["Spiritual Itinerary of Br. Michel Fleury, Monk of Tibhirine"]. *Collectanea cisterciensia* 63 (2001): 264–83.

Georgeon, Thomas. "Donner sa vie pour la gloire de T'aimer. Tibhirine ou un chemin communautaire vers le martyre" ["Giving One's Life for the Glory of Loving You: Tibhirine, or a Communal Path Toward Martyrdom"]. *Collectanea cisterciensia* 68 (2006): 76–104.

Minassian, Marie-Dominique. "Frère Christophe, priant parmi les priants" ["Brother Christophe: Praying among Those Who Pray"]. *Chemins de dialogue* no. 27 (2006): 67–80.

———. "L'acte d'écriture chez frère Christophe. Mouvement d'incarnation" ["The Act of Writing for Brother Christopher: A Movement of Incarnation"]. *Collectanea cisterciensia* 68 (2006): 133–46.

Olivera, Dom Bernardo. "Voici ta mère. L'expérience d'un martyr contemporain: Christophe Lebreton" ["Here Is Your Mother: The Experience of a Contemporary Martyr"]. *Collectanea cisterciensia* 68 (2006): 117–32.

Publications about Tibhirine

Ferchiche, Abdelkader. *L'innocence fertile* [*Fertile Innocence*]. Avignon: self-published, 1998.

Guitton, René. *Les veilleurs de l'Atlas* [*The Watchmen of the Atlas Mountains*]. Paris: Cerf, 1998.

———. *Si nous nous taisons, le martyre des moines de Tibhirine* [*If We Keep Silent: The Martyrdom of the Monks of Tibhirine*]. Paris: Calmann-Lévy, 2001.

Henning, Christophe. *Petite vie des moines de Tibhirine* [*A Brief Life of the Monks of Tibhirine*]. Paris: Desclée de Brouwer, 2006.

Kiser, John. *The Monks of Tibhirine: Faith, Love and Terror in Algeria*. New York: St. Martin's Griffin, 2002. French translation: *Passion pour l'Algérie, les moines de Tibhirine*. Translated by Henri Quinson. Paris: Nouvelle Cité, 2006.

Louvencourt, Jean-François. *Les sept martyrs de Tibhirine* [*The Seven Martyrs of Tibhirine*]. Saint-Benoît-du-Sault: Éditions Bénédictines, 2006.

Masson, Robert. *Jusqu'au bout de la nuit, l'Église d'Algérie* [*Till the Night's End: The Algerian Church*]. Paris: Cerf/Saint Augustin, 1998.

Olivera, Dom Bernardo. *How Far to Follow? The Martyrs of Atlas*. Petersham, MA: Saint Bede's Publications, 1997. French translation: *Jusqu'où suivre? Les martyrs de l'Atlas*. Paris: Cerf, 1997.

Wehbé, Louis, and Armand Veilleux. "Une opinion islamique extrême. À propos des sept frères de Tibhirine" ["An Extreme Islamic Opinion: Concerning the Seven Brothers of Tibhirine"]. *Collectanea cisterciensia* 62 (2000): 72–80.

On the Theology of Religious Encounter
Church Documents

Nostra Aetate (Declaration on the Relation of the Church to Non-Christian Religions), published October 28, 1965. In *Vatican Council II: The Conciliar and Post Conciliar Documents*, edited by Austin Flannery, 738–42. Collegeville, MN: Liturgical Press, 1975.

International Theological Commission. "Christianity and the World Religions." In *International Theological Commission*. Vol. 2, *Texts and Documents 1986–2007*, edited by Rev. Michael Sharkey and Fr. Thomas Weinandy, 145–86. San Francisco: Ignatius Press, 2009.

Paul VI, *Ecclesiam Suam* (encyclical), promulgated on August 6, 1964. Official English text on Vatican web site, http://www.vatican.va/holy_father/paul_vi/encyclicals/documents/hf_p-vi_enc_06081964_ecclesiam_en.html.

John Paul II. *Redemptoris Missio* (encyclical), promulgated December 7, 1990. Official English text on Vatican web site, http://www.vatican.va/holy_father/john_paul_ii/encyclicals/documents/hf_jp-ii_enc_07121990_redemptoris-missio_en.html.

———. "To the Roman Curia at the Exchange of Christmas Wishes," December 22, 1986. English text in *L'Osservatore Romano*, January 5, 1987, pp. 6-7. Official Italian version on Vatican web site, http://www.vatican.va/holy_father/john_paul_ii/speeches/1986/december/index.htm.

Pontifical Council for Interreligious Dialogue and the Congregation for the Evangelization of Peoples. "Dialogue and Proclamation," 1991. Official English text on Vatican web site: http://www.vatican.va/roman_curia/pontifical_councils/interelg/documents/rc_pc_interelg_doc_19051991_dialogue-and-proclamatio_en.html.

Congregation for the Doctrine of the Faith. "Declaration '*Dominus Iesus*' on the Unicity and Salvific Universality of Jesus Christ and the Church," 2000. Official English version on the Vatican web site, http://www.vatican.va/roman_curia/congregations/cfaith/documents/rc_con_cfaith_doc_20000806_dominus-iesus_en.html.

Books

Aebischer-Crettol, Monique. *Vers un oecuménisme interreligieux: jalons pour une théologie chrétiennes du pluralism religieux* [*Toward an Interreligious Ecumenism: Signposts for a Christian Theology of Religious Pluralism*]. Cogitatio Fidei Series 221. Paris: Cerf, 2001.

Aveline, Jean-Marc. *L'enjeu christologique en théologie de religions* [*What Is at Stake for Christology in the Theology of Religions*]. Cogitatio Fidei Series 227. Paris: Cerf, 2003.

Basset, Jean-Claude. *Le dialogue interreligieux*. Cogitatio Fidei Series 197. Paris: Cerf, 1996.

Caspar, Robert. *Pour un regard chrétien sur l'islam* [*Toward a Christian View of Islam*]. 1990; rpt. Paris: Bayard, 2006.

———. *Traité de théologie musulmane*. Vols. 1 and 2. Rome: PISAI, 1987, 1989.

Le dialogue des Écritures [*The Dialogue of the Scriptures*]. Edited by Isabelle Chareire and Christian Salenson. Brussels: Lessius, 2008.

Dupuis, Jacques. *Toward a Christian Theology of Religious Pluralism*. Maryknoll: Orbis, 1997. Translated as *Vers une théologie chrétienne du pluralism religieux*. Cogitatio Fidei Series 200. Paris: Cerf, 1997.

Fédou, Michel. *La voie du Christ: genèses de la christologie dans le contexte religieux de l'antiquité au début du IVᵉ siècle* [*The Way of Christ: Origins of Christology in the Religious Context of Antiquity to the Beginning of the Fourth Century*]. Cogitatio Fidei Series 253. Paris: Cerf, 2006.

Geffré, Claude. *De Babel à Pentecôte* [*From Babel to Pentecost*]. Cogitatio Fidei Series 247. Paris: Cerf, 2006.

GRIC (Groupe de Recherches Islamo-chrétien) [Muslim-Christian Research Group]. *Ces Écritures qui nous questionnent* [*These Scriptures Which Interrogate Us*]. Paris, Bayard/Centurion, 1987.

Thils, Gustave. *Propos et problèmes de la théologie des religions non-chrétiennes* [*Topics and Problems in the Theology of Non-Christian Religions*]. Paris: Castermann, 1966.

Articles

We recommend to the reader the journal *Chemins de dialogue* in its entirety, but in particular:

Aveline, Jean-Marc. "L'engagement de Dieu et la mission de l'Église" ["The Involvement of God and the Mission of the Church"]. *Chemins de dialogue* no. 16 (2000): 37–58.

Doré, Joseph. "La présence du Christ dans les religions non-chrétiennes" ["The Presence of Christ in Non-Christian Religions"]. *Chemins de dialogue* no. 9 (1997): 13–50.

On Monastic Life and Interreligious Dialogue

Flachaire, Jean-Pierre. "Le monastère Notre Dame de l'Atlas au Maroc" ["The Monastery of Our Lady of Atlas in Morocco"]. *Collectanea Cisterciensia* 68 (2006): 147–66.

Leclercq, Jean. *Nouvelle page d'histoire monastique, histoire de l'AIM, 1960– 1985 [A New Page of Monastic History: The History of the AIM]*. Belmont-Tramonet: Publications de l'A. I. M., 1986.

Salenson, Christian. "De *Nostra Aetate* à Assise, contribution de la vie monastique" ["From *Nostra Aetate* to Assisi, the Contribution of Monastic Life"]. *Chemins de dialogue* 28 (2006): 15–29.

———. "Vie monastique et dialogue interreligieux sous le signe de l'eschatologie" ["Monastic Life and Interreligious Dialogue under the Sign of Eschatology"]. *Collectanea cisterciensia* 68 (2006): 105–16.